A MAN OF SUBSTANCES

Keep On Rollin' to
the
Core.

A Man of Substances

*The Misdeeds and Growing Pains
of a Pot Pioneer*

by
Gerald McCarthy
with
David Partridge

iUniverse, Inc.
New York   Bloomington

A Man of Substances
The Misdeeds and Growing Pains of a Pot Pioneer

iUniverse books may be ordered through booksellers or by contacting:

iUniverse
1663 Liberty Drive
Bloomington, IN 47403
www.iuniverse.com
1-800-Authors (1-800-288-4677)

ISBN: 978-1-4502-2468-0 (sc)
ISBN: 978-1-4502-2470-3 (ebook)
ISBN: 978-1-4502-2469-7 (dj)

Library of Congress Control Number: 2010905162

Printed in the United States of America

iUniverse rev. date: 5/24/2010

Cover photograph of Gerald J. McCarthy by Kim Bouchard.

Literary matchmaker, compass,
benefactor, and all too often,
referee—
for Donald F. McCarthy,
the tirelessly patient man
in the striped shirt
with the silver whistle.

—Gerald McCarthy and David Partridge

CONTENTS

Preface
If You Light Up the Occasional
Candle, You're Allowed
the Occasional Curse

Gerry McCarthy is certainly not the only small-community lad to hit the big-city counterculture with a resounding wallop. He wasn't the first, nor will he be the last. He isn't even the most recent. But the circumstances of his interaction with the counterculture, or more accurately, the underculture, are no less remarkable because his story begins at a well-worn crossroads.

He was raised, as were many, with a good, Catholic core—a basically honest soul whose sense of moral obligation became a mitigating factor in the predicament in which he found himself.

So how does a properly reared kid, pursuing peace and love, end up trapped by loan sharks, abusing serious drugs, and cultivating the devil's weed?

He came to the big city in the throes of adolescence, in need of a purpose, a lifestyle, and a way to make a buck. At a time when the tumble toward adulthood shoved all of us toward something—anything—to define ourselves, Gerry embraced the pulsating pop culture of the sixties. He did so on an idealistic basis—at first. But, like all of us, Gerry soon found that it takes more than ideals to make ends meet. He tried the traditional business paths, but he found himself in the kind of debt that emerges from the smoking remnants of youthful dreams crossed with commerce.

This is the point where Gerry's path and that of most others diverges. Most find a job, ride the bus until a car is affordable, and save their money until they can afford a place called home with a cozy chair. There, they curl up with a lover or a laptop or a television or even this book. The details vary slightly; maybe the bus they're riding is a train, and they read the book there. But there's a job and a boss and a spot—however modest—in the great, admirable mosaic we call law-abiding society.

Gerry never got on that bus. He got a motorcycle; he got a flashy car; and he got a stretch limousine. And he got them by selling drugs. Not the bad, dead-in-an-alley-in-vomit-with-a-spike-in-your-arm kind, rather the fun, recreational kind that give you the giggles at the convenience store at midnight. Gerry sold the kind of drugs that make contemporary comedy movies bearable.

This is neither a cop-out nor an apology. As you will soon see, Gerry's not big on apologies. And even if he were, he'd be making a large number of them to himself. So if an apology is what this isn't, here's what it is: it's a plea for a sense of context. Gerry bought, resold, and eventually cultivated weed in a world very different from the one in which we live. This tale of drug dealing has no three thousand-dollar suits, no killers with slicked-back braids, and no organized crime. Disorganized crime is closer to the mark.

Sure, there's suspense, intrigue, and more than a few close calls, but Gerry's milieu is not the ugly—some would say evil—world of the twenty-first-century drug lord. And make no mistake, that's where the marijuana business is now. The murderous gangs of Mexico and South America that regularly bloody our newscasts still get their core revenue from a drug that elicits snickers from most of the enlightened public.

Weed is funny. Its contemporary journey into our culture is not. But Gerry's story is not a contemporary one. His is a leafy, crazy journey from his personal crossroads: the place where the grow-your-own marijuana business began.

CHAPTER ONE
CAN'T YOU HEAR ME KNOCKIN'?

Nothing in the movies—no matter how big the screen or mighty the soundtrack—can prepare you for the singular crack of your front door being shredded by a battering ram. It resonates in your internal organs, shaking you through to the very core.

As the police fly up the stairs of your family home, all gun metal and Kevlar, barking like dogs charging upright, the disorientation from the top of the stairs is palpable.

Particularly if you're stark naked and still slightly high from the night before.

When the cops demand to know whether there are others, or weapons, or dogs in the house, it's hard to focus on anything but the questions at hand. I can tell you from experience that a man with a nine-millimetre Glock pressed to his temple tends not to muse on the location of anything; even something as pressing as one's pants. When the arresting officer, having assessed the true nature of the situation, gives his dozen comrades the order to stand down, it is not a time conducive to reflection. You're occupied with the mortification of your physical situation, the discomfort of the handcuffs, and the splinters protruding from the door.

But be assured that I've had the opportunity and the inclination for plenty of reflection since—in the passing months and years since my arrest, I've logged many hours on the simple, seminal question: How in heaven's name did it come to this?

How did I, the son of a yawning Ontario town, become the alleged kingpin of a multimillion-dollar, multilocation, multipartner marijuana cultivation enterprise? How did a struggling family man become the target of a massive, multiforce police initiative? How did the supposed mastermind of a lucrative and tax-free, illicit endeavour become the proud owner of hundreds of thousands of dollars worth of compound interest debt?

Well, there's an answer to that, and therein lies our journey. Let's begin by going back—all the way back to where my naked encounter with the body armour boys first took root.

Chapter Two
Bright Lights, Big City

Call me G. My full name is Gerald Joseph McCarthy, but just G will do. It's the moniker my close friends know me by. I'm not a ball player or a rock star or an actor or one of those people who's well known without having done anything of note except being famous. I've had my name in the paper, but not in a way I'm proud of and, likely, not in a way that you'd remember. I live in a lovely, little town with a wonderful wife and a lovely daughter—all of which is remarkable to me but of no consequence to you. What I do have that you may not is a past. And with the dark and light of a past comes a story. My story is not inspirational; my actions are not praiseworthy; and my path is certainly not to be emulated. But this story is mine, and as true stories often do, it compels its owner to tell it.

I come from farming stock, but we were city kids. My maternal grandparents' farm was a nearby outing on weekends, but when my parents took the brood to visit the world of livestock, crops, and the tyranny of weather, we were not in our element. We overfed and practically poisoned the pigs with their own medicated food. We shattered discarded bottles with target practice and subsequently rendered the cattle lame with the broken glass. We encouraged the chickens to fly, pitching them into the air and inadvertently cracking their skulls on the rafters of the barn. We had too much energy and too little comprehension of the rural circumstance before us. We were

3

locusts out for a Sunday drive. In very short order, we went from unsuited to the farm to unwelcome at the farm.

But we were also unconcerned. I was, as I say, a city kid of a sort. Our city was Peterborough, a modest Southern Ontario metropolis. Peterborough boasted not only a General Electric plant, the community's largest employer, but the Canadian headquarters of Quaker Oats. There was also work to be had in the business of play– it was also home to a thriving leisure boat industry and a tourist industry to complement it. Peterborough would evolve into a college town with the establishment of Trent, a picturesque university on the banks of the Trent-Severn river system. That busy waterway ran through our community with the assistance of a hydraulic lift lock, welcoming boats to its currents and motor travellers to its banks. Both sets of visitors gawked and marvelled at the giant wonder of turn-of-the-century engineering that was able to raise a boat—water and all—from one level of the canal to another and back again.

Peterborough was a thriving town but not wholly a rich one. If there was a prosperous part of town, it was *not* where my family resided. Born in 1950, I was the second of seven profoundly Catholic offspring of an Irish-descended father and a French-Canadian mother. My father could trace his lineage through a substantial immigration to the Peterborough area from the fabled County of Cork in the 1800s. If my mother could trace hers back beyond the family farm in nearby Marmora, she certainly didn't mention it. Her parents spoke French at the farm, but they were sufficiently pragmatic about the future of their culture in Anglo Ontario that they did not pass the language on to their daughter. Hers became a world of English, church, and an Irishman—*her* Irishman, possessed of the fierce pride that flourishes so far from the ancestral home. She managed much and many on little and was her husband's unwavering ally.

Our life and community revolved around the church. My parents served dutifully and contributed weekly or, perhaps more accurately, weakly, given their modest means. Even so, I wouldn't call us a God-fearing family—the Pope was about as far up the ladder as my parents' allegiance seemed to go. I myself began more along the line of God-tolerating, although as each passing year brought more faces to our table and not much more *on* it, my tolerance for the Pope and his edicts grew as frayed as the sweater I wore to school every day.

But we were not destitute by African or, for that matter, Canadian Aboriginal standards. When I was born, my parents were the proud owners of a small bungalow, but it grew progressively smaller with each subsequent "gift from God." When I was six, we moved to a two-storey brick house; it was still modest but bigger and closer to the river. I was closest with two of my brothers, one older and the other younger than me by the smallest of biologically feasible margins. All things considered, it was a happy childhood. We had bikes and clothes as the spoils of Christmas and birthdays. Being the second son, I was reasonably well served in the hand-me-down chain. But we didn't play organized sports, because we couldn't afford the equipment; and the concept of an allowance was abandoned, as I recall, after a one-week trial, when the obvious repercussions of that many outstretched, upturned hands hit home for my father. But crucially, we were neither better nor worse off than our church and schoolmates.

The old man made his living as a pest control operator, expert at both the gritty intricacies of the job and the personal charm that spawned loyal customers. He was a solid, hard-working man, who spent the best part of his soul putting food on our well-attended table. My father was of the strongly held opinion that his hours toiling to rid the world of pestilence comprised the sum total of his duties to the household. And the house that his toil provided was his to rule. The comfy chair was his throne, and the television was his jester. He graced our table with the modest harvest of his substantial labours. But beyond subsistence, seven children left little time for any individual child. Attention and nurturing were luxuries in a household with little of those to offer, and as it turned out, I was the sort of soul who had a substantial need for both.

One day, six children on and no great distance into my adolescence, my father announced that he was being given a promotion to manager and that we would be moving to Toronto. A better job, a bigger town—the concept seemed tantalizing to an aspiring "city kid." No pigs to poison, no cows to cripple, and our lives were about to take flight as those chickens could not. What could possibly go wrong?

So there we were—two adults and six kids, my second sister a babe in arms—jammed into the station wagon, which was the old man's service vehicle, on the highway to what my father insisted on calling the Big Smoke. With General Electric, Outboard Marine, and the country's premiere canoe factories within the city limits, Peterborough may not have been called the Little Smoke, but it certainly qualified. When we arrived in Toronto in July during the illusory summer vacation months, the Big Smoke seemed not far removed from the little one.

We landed in suburban Scarborough, which was not as leafy as Peterborough but every bit as bland and far removed from the downtown towers of Canada's biggest city. The neighbourhood was a cracker box maze ten years into its existence but as yet devoid of distinguishing characteristics. The street that hosted our two-storey, green-roofed house was long and curved out of sight at either end as if someone had paved an Olympic track and dropped it into suburbia as a prank. This is not as fanciful an idea as it seems, because, for me, those streets would be rife with hurdles.

First, you should recall, it was the sixties. Everything was in upheaval—music, fashion, and the social fabric in its entirety. None of that stuff had been evident in sleepy, square-dancing Peterborough, but Toronto was determined to reflect the best innovations of London just as it rejected the worst shames of Birmingham. Suddenly, *we* were the hicks, and no amount of city kid disregard for livestock counted for anything. As diverse as our old town may have been overall, our Peterborough neighbourhood was homogeneous. Everybody wore the same clothes to school every day, had baloney sandwiches for lunch, and fished in the river on weekends. I was to discover that this new area had well-heeled, driven-to-school kids with snow crab sandwiches, Twinkies, and folded napkins in their lunch bags. In contrast, there were also plaza-haunting, auto shop toughs with narrowed glances and clothes and coifs that Elvis would have envied. Then there were the jocks, who were rabid disciples of athletics, all spotlessly attired and expensively equipped. And get this: these exotic, foreign locals and my family of rural immigrants were all jammed, sprinkler to sprinkler, into the same damned subdivision!

Every adolescent struggles to discover who he or she is. However, I was about to get a crash course in who I was not.

The local denizens were not the only culture crunch. In my former town, I had spent my grade school years, as had all my siblings, in the Catholic school system. Starting with my first school year in Toronto, I was in high school. Catholic high school cost money. The modest McCarthy fortune was all in that green-roofed house and not at liberty to be spent on us "gifts from God," regardless of the papal edicts that had some part in our conception. Suddenly, I was at high school's door as both a small-town hick and a kid who'd never been taught by a teacher not toting a rosary. And it got worse.

Believe me, these hurdles are not ranked by suffering caused, and unlike the field sport variety, they were not of uniform height. Chief among my burdens was the irrefutable fact that I was in the throes of puberty. My brothers were of sufficient age to suffer similarly, but my particular form of agony was my own. More than any other encumbrance of the coming-of-age process, I was driven by the excruciating importance that adolescents put on the opinion and approval—no matter how spotty or ill informed—of their peers. Believe me, we will return to that later.

But for those first two holiday months, I was blissfully ignorant of the perils of our newfound home. I had a used bike in a brand new world, and I naïvely pedalled those maze-like streets, hoping to discover what I did not yet know. I was exploring and meeting new kids. Among them was a guy who was giving up his paper route and offered it to me. That seemed like impossibly good fortune. He had an income, and he was casting it off! Was the guy nuts?

Then school started. Everybody wore different clothes every day and bought their lunches in the cafeteria. Half of the grade nine class smoked for God's sake! The auto shop guys would spill your books or your blood depending on their moods when you walked by. Nobody went fishing. The sad little creek that ran near the school was the principal habitat of upturned supermarket buggies and upturned public school kids who had gotten in a bully's way. Every activity but TV cost money, and my old man's cartoon and sitcom regimen scratched that off the list. It was a contrary, expensive world to infiltrate, and we were the most ragged family in the 'burb.

That circumstance was not about to improve. The manager job that was the beacon for our pilgrimage to the big city disappeared. That was after the mortgage had been signed. A combination of French grit and Irish obstinacy kept us from slinking back to the shores of the Trent-Severn. My father took a pest control route in Toronto and set out with his proven skills to build what he had left in Peterborough, possibly glad to be relieved of a desk to pilot and reports to write. We had a company car and a company phone. Mother handled the paperwork and the division of a can of tuna into seven sandwiches. A bigger mortgage, a higher standard of living, and another mouth on the way left me to find myself (adolescence, remember?) without much in the way of parental attention or financial support. Something had to be done.

The paper route was helping me save and get an appreciation for money—two skills I've subsequently lost—but it was becoming a problem. I knew what my friend had known when he had passed it on: a paper route was really uncool, and its primary tool, the bicycle, was just as embarrassing. In prepubescent Peterborough, a bike had been a crucial, life-enhancing joy. In teenage sixties Scarborough, it was a millstone, as likely to sink you into the creek of uncool as that ubiquitous shopping cart. In Toronto, an offer of a ride on the handlebars to a pretty girl with a long walk ahead of her was greeted with derision and a head quickly turned in the opposite direction, even if she was in grade eight and you were in the ninth. Scarborough may have been bland, but it was also cruel. The bike and the paper route had to go.

But before they went, they did some good. I had saved just enough money for an electric guitar. I had an old acoustic that the parents had bought me when I was ten as intended parity for the hockey team my older brother had been allowed to join as goalie because the team supplied the equipment. But I was not a New Christy Minstrel. I was a Rolling Stone. I loved music, yes, but more to the point, I saw an inroad into cool culture—the electric guitar was an investment, and the hair could be grown for nothing. The guitar was a Zenon—dirt cheap but crassly flashy. I was already intimate with the former and aspired desperately to the latter.

Now, I had an electric guitar but no case, so I slung it over my back as I walked the streets. I shunned the vagaries of the weather in the hope of being mistaken for someone interesting or possibly important. If I couldn't afford a case, I was nowhere near the league of those who had an amplifier, but I could plug in to the second input of someone else's at a jam or a practice or, dream of dreams, a gig. Besides, no one on earth, male or female, ever managed to look cool hauling an amp. So my priorities were sorted, and my plan was in motion. I was a rocker, man.

One amazing thing about the post–British Invasion sixties is that, were you to walk the byways of any town in North America with a guitar on your back, you would soon be invited to join a band. The Beatles and Stones spawned bands the way the English kings before them had spawned illegitimate offspring—frequently and with little regard for the quality of result. It was not long before my shoulder-numbing strategy bore fruit. I met a drummer, a bass player, and another guitarist. We met, as all bands do, in a restaurant that served French fries and bore the greasy evidence on all of its fixtures. We discussed a name, our repertoire, and other pressing issues. This dispatched, we turned to lesser topics along the lines of who we were and where we came from. I vividly remember one of my bandmates asking what my father did. When I replied that he was an exterminator, my bandmates snickered. Snickered!

I was stricken. Had I grown that hair, hauled that guitar, and abandoned my paper route only to be derided for what my father did? I didn't care about their bank manager parents or what they drove to work. But in that adolescent Toronto world, what it said on the side of my father's station wagon was going to reflect on *me*. It wasn't enough that we were struggling financially; my father's toil itself was not cool. I wish I could tell you that I was bigger than that and rose above my bandmates' insensitivity, but I was crushed.

As time went on, I became more and more dissatisfied with my lot, and I blamed those who, I believed, had visited the pestilence upon me. Now, you might wonder why I never sought the counsel or comfort of my parents on these issues, but I felt the distance of one seventh of their attention and the competition of my father's affair with the TV to be insurmountable. Besides, I was an adolescent. As shallow as it seems now, I sought self-affirmation elsewhere.

Let's talk for a minute about my chosen vehicle of deliverance: rock and roll. I love music. I loved it then, and I love it now. I flatter myself that I'm musical. I believe that, with proper application, I could have developed musically. To this day, my older brother is an active and able musician, and his son is developing in his footsteps. Believe me—the genes are there, so I'm convinced that I could have been a good player. Then again, I consider myself a writer, philosopher, and world-class lover as well, so factor that into the argument. But potential aside, there were impediments beyond the crappy equipment, the daunting prospect of practice, and my shredded fingertips.

As much as I loved the music, I loved the lifestyle more. At some point, the culture of music and the music itself changed places in the crossed hairs of my aspiration. I coveted the clothes, aspired to the hours, and craved the resultant esteem of my peers. I was building an image and praying that no one would see past it. And it was working. I actually began to draw the attention of girls, who appeared to buy into the idea that I was cool. I loved the freedom and the opportunity for emotional expression that playing offered, but songs eventually end. I felt the need to express myself outside of the short-term confines of band practices and infrequent performances. For a time, though, the persona of hungry bohemian and driven musician had to do.

But at that point, I had not entirely abandoned the idea of actually playing music. As is the pattern of all aspiring musicians, I kept my ears open for opportunities, and it was not very long before I traded up. I befriended a new rhythm section that was better, tighter, and more sophisticated than my restaurant comrades. Given the chance, as the impatiently ambitious are wont to do, I jumped. And I will admit that their derision regarding my father's employment was not far from my mind when I kissed off my initial bandmates.

We named the new band the Berserks. The new guys were substantially more developed; they were better players; and I enjoyed their musicianship and craved their camaraderie. But, puberty holding sway, they were not the only form of companionship I sought. For the very first time, I was in love. It was the gut-wrenching, stomach-turning, cold sweat kind of love that feels so good. As hard as that is to believe, she was the very same girl who had graciously declined my handlebar invitation early in our relationship. But where my trusty bicycle had failed me, my shiny guitar did not. She became the first of the three great loves of my life. So this became my circle: my band, my girl, and me.

I was making progress. In the summer of '65, my financial status had not improved, but I was *in*. I maintained my relationship with my girl and my band for the duration of '65 until the next uneven hurdle: I turned sixteen.

I'm painting a picture of more innocent times, but in its narrow way, suburban sixties culture was as guilty of consumer gluttony as our current one. There was music to buy, girls to impress, and clothes to parade. The clothes were as crucial to the time as the zoot suit before and the leg warmer after. The pressure to stay ahead of the curve was enormous.

The pressure led my best friend and bandmate to the changeroom of The Bay with a magnificent pair of black corduroy bell-bottoms. It also led him out of said changeroom with the bell-bottoms. However, they were hidden under the pants that he had worn on the way in. That simple ruse to leave the store without troubling the cashier had worked before for my friend, so imagine his surprise when a large, store detective followed him out into the car park. Of course, my friend ran. I say "of course," because the shop cop was big, and because I had broken into a run mere moments before, inspiring my friend to do the same. I think my exact advice was, "RUN!"

You've got it; I was there. I wasn't in the changeroom, and I certainly wasn't in the stolen pants, but to my chagrin, I was in the sights of the store detective. Did I mention that he was big?

What happened next was that, despite my Beatle boots, I outran the store detective. My friend did not. He was detained. When the police arrived, an officer convinced him that it would serve him well to give the name and address of his swifter companion in order that the police could enlighten me as to the perils of contravening the law. Reasoning that it was not my legs in the stolen pants but his own, my friend gave up my name and the address of the two-storey house with the green roof.

So for the first time, the authorities arrived at the door of my residence. We were in the midst of a typically crowded but modest family dinner. In our tiny living room in the presence of my father and a police officer, I got my lecture. And I got arrested. I was charged with being an accessory to a theft.

Let me underline this: I was not in the changeroom. I was not in the pants. I was in the parking lot when the store detective pursued my friend. If there was a law against running on asphalt in Cuban heels, I was guilty as sin. But, otherwise, it was bullshit. For the first time—but believe me, not the last—I had evidence that the police have both the capacity and the will to lie.

My court date was set. My family could not afford a lawyer. In a naïve attempt to muster a defence, my father, certain that a lawyer was a lawyer, convinced in-house counsel from the pest control company to show up at court with me. Perhaps if this guy was negotiating an ant service contract, I'd have been fine. If I'd been accused of burning a customer's lawn with DDT, he could have pled my case. But as it transpired, I was given nine months of probation and a police record for running away slightly faster than a pair of stolen pants. I was a month over sixteen and, by the law of the day, an adult. What of my overtrousered friend? He was fifteen and underage. He had a proper lawyer. He got off.

I'll admit to bitterness—toward my friend for turning me in and toward my father for inadequately protecting me. Add to my list the cop who tricked an underage thief into fingering his companion and, finally, the judge without compassion or the understanding that saddling a sixteen-year-old with a criminal record might narrow his future. I was sixteen, and I'd learned my lesson. Unfortunately, it was the wrong one.

Chapter Three
I Fight the Law, Part One

The future repercussions of the shoplifting conviction aside, there were immediate consequences from the incident. I have not yet mentioned that my best friend, the bellbottom bandit, was also the rhythm guitarist in The Berserks. In the wake of his cop-inspired rollover, he moved from soul mate to sellout in my estimation. Not surprisingly, this cast our friendship into the abyss, and it cast a long shadow over the future of the band as well.

Truth be told, our musical future had been in peril already. In the summer of my sixteenth year, a new school had been completed closer to my house, and the school district boundaries had been redrawn. The new line snaked down the centre of my subdivision, leaving me on one side and my bass player and drummer on the other. This was surmountable for the first year at my new school, but inconvenience turned intolerable once my guitarist/best friend delivered me to the constabulary. The combination left my band unravelling faster than the hem on those cheap department store corduroys.

The final blow hit even closer. I've said that my girl and my band comprised the core of my world. At some point around that time, my girl and my drummer became a couple. Now, it's hard to get too wrung out about that—they stayed a couple and remain one to this day. I'm very fond of them both, and I wish them well. But even if I did not, it's a foolish soul who blocks the outbound tracks when true love leaves the station.

In hindsight, my drummer friend left the station with the whole package. Always a genuine talent, he went on to become a successful, celebrated musician and married my handlebar-averse sweetheart. As I said, while I was not struck down by that turn of events, it made little sense to be a proximate witness to the development of their love story. Dissolution was complete. My relationships were cinders, and my band was toast.

But resilience is a prime attribute of adolescence, particularly in seekers like me. My drive to find my place resembled the flow of water—block its path, and it finds another. I was going to a new school, new in the literal sense that I was among the first students to attend it. The building's absence of history appealed to me. My own history had little more value to me than it does to most adolescents. But I was particularly anxious to put mine behind me. The fallout of suburban culture shock had contributed to me flunking my first year at the old high school; I had entered the new one, once again, as a ninth grader. Perversely, having failed a grade brought me a certain rebel profile. That and my tireless image-building efforts put me streets ahead of classmates, who were struggling with secondary school for the first time. As the year unfolded, I embraced it as a new opportunity; a fresh start is all the more appealing when it's a head start as well. My best friend had betrayed me; I had no band; and I had no girl; but I was as determined as ever to find my niche in the big 'burb.

At about that point, I started hanging out with a crowd from a part of the neighbourhood that was closer to home. Those guys had all gone to Maryvale, the local public school only a few streets from my house. Although it's hard to argue in the broad picture that anyone in grade school has *cool* of any real consequence, these guys had a *reputation*.

Let's pause for a moment to reflect further on sixties culture. Although it's convenient now to see the era's divergence from the monochrome fifties through the clunky specs of *Austin Powers*, there were several alternative subcultures thriving beyond the "England Swings" clichés of the time.

There was the final chorus of the folk movement. Much, and justly, maligned in its most commercial incarnations, it did produce Bob Dylan. For that alone, it cannot be dismissed with the banjos and button-down shirts of Zimmy's genre kin. My first acoustic guitar was a by-product of that particular cultural spark. But folk music was more likely to be influential on those just slightly older than me. The folkie aesthetic, though a real influence on the decade, was off the table as far as my friends and I were concerned.

Then there was surf culture. I love much of the Beach Boys' work to this day, but Peterborough was a river town, and although Lake Ontario's sheer size makes it resemble an ocean, there isn't much surfing off the Scarborough Bluffs. Still, the influence was felt. My older brother's first band had formed around a couple of Beach Boys enthusiasts, one of whom regularly walked to a store miles from home, because it stocked surfing magazines. The sight of an overbundled kid trudging through subdivision snow, clutching a magazine with a bright blue wave on the cover, indicates the degree to which we coveted the culture of others.

As an offshoot of the beach and board fad, there was car culture. Unlike the surf phenomenon, hotrod chic was not particular to California or to ocean, so it was strongly felt across the United States and in Canada as well. It was also better established, existing as a tolerated vehicle of identity and rebellion even in the fifties. A sturdy offshoot of car worship saw the motorcycle rise as an icon of freedom beyond its attributes as economical transportation. The legendary biker gangs grew and caught the public eye in that period. Biker movies like *Wild Angels, Born Losers,* and *Hells Angels on Wheels* were regular date movie fare in the sixties, which was rooted in *The Wild One* but churned out by the B-movie giants who, in attempting to reflect the youth culture of California, helped to feed that very culture in regions substantially removed from its epicentre. Yes, I'm talking Maryvale Public School, from whence sprung my brand new friends.

Like me, my new friends were looking for their niche. They were attracted to the tough guys, the bikers who were making an impression on the society of the time. Bear in mind that the sixties perception of biker culture had more to do with rebellion than with organized crime. Bikers also represented freedom and, as such, were seen as kindred souls by the hippie culture to come.

My friends loved the outlaw idea of the gangs, so they formed one—in public school! Today, the idea of gang culture in grade school is chilling, because it's a brutal reality in virtually every urban centre. But in sixties Scarborough, these aspiring rebels were more about image than any real threat. There were no driver's licenses, much less motorcycle licenses. There were few classic rivalries, because there was only one gang. Their colours were not the striking stitched crests of biker culture. They made do with magic marker letters on the backs of jackets their parents had purchased to insure their offspring's warmth. This was a gang whose primary activities consisted of sneering, talking loudly, and loitering at the local plaza. They were twelve-year-old tough guys, feared by eleven-year-olds and ten-year-olds alike.

But unless you were a few years their junior, their grade school age did little to lengthen their shadow nor did their name. They called themselves the Imperial Hodads. For those unfamiliar with the jargon of surf culture, a *hodad* is someone who aspires to the culture but does not, or cannot, surf. They had, in essence, named themselves the Wannabes. It may have been keen self-awareness that inspired the name but I doubt it. There is very little documented evidence of sly irony as an attribute of the prematurely pubescent. More likely, it was an exotic word that jumped from the screen of the local drive-in and caught some admiring moviegoer's ear. The *imperial* part is somewhat less puzzling. Canada is nominally a monarchy, and in that era, the queen's picture was present in every classroom in the land. Each school day started with a little ditty invoking the deity's vigilance regarding her safety. But beyond our local comfort with the concept of royalty, there is a long tradition of wishful aristocracy in names chosen to distinguish some over others—from Count Basie and Duke Ellington right through to Queen Latifah and the King of Pop. So choosing *imperial* is understandable but pairing it with *hodad* is, you must admit, perplexing. Even so, it speaks to the innocence of the enterprise—a triumph of aspiration over clarity.

In the year that I moved to my new high school, so did the Hodads. I've said that I saw myself as somewhat more worldly than first-time ninth graders, so I was drawn to these tough boys because they, too, came with a reputation. I became fast friends with, and something of an acolyte to, the head of the Hodads, King Ferd.

Alas, another aside: King Ferd is not his real name. One of the more durable attributes of outlaw culture is the nickname—a factor it has in common with adolescence. The bestowed moniker has been celebrated and amplified throughout popular culture and has produced alternative handles as diverse as The Lion of Judah and Big Pussy. As you will see, I plan to honour this tradition as we meet many remarkable folk who have lit or clouded my journey. Some are dead, and some are living, as the song says, and I don't intend the imperfections of my perspective to do any of them disservice.

But back to the King. He was a charismatic and energetic guy, one of those souls blessed with the accelerated development coveted by all adolescents. To be specific, he had facial hair. He was a born rebel and always seemed on top of the cultural moves or fads of the time. He was fun, he was funny and he was a drummer—a genuine rebel. He shunned his parents' advice and restrictions, unless of course he needed the car. His contrary stance in the face of parents, school, and society as a whole was innate. As a result, he took to the spoils and trials of leadership, and I, as a second son, bathed in the ancillary benefits of the loyal adviser. I was inside and under no pressure to lead. For me, it was the best of both worlds. With my new friends, I took on a role where adolescence and the sixties archetype intersect.

We were explorers. King Ferd had abandoned the formal elements of the Hodads but not the principle of rebellion or the determination to splash some colour into our Borough of Beige. We grew our hair. We liked our music loud. We laughed and spouted unspeakable nonsense and laughed again in turn. In short, we were determined to be free to have some fun.

One free but aimless night, hanging out in the schoolyard long after its rightful denizens were home and wrapped in milk-and-cookie sleep, we happened upon a guy known in our circles as JD. JD's house was around the corner, but he called another dimension home. He was a working musician, and he played jazz. Although he was roughly our age, he was a musical prodigy and had been gigging in his father's band for years. He led a band of his own when he was seventeen. He was the ultimate in *cool*. We admired him immensely. And we were not alone—the jazzers, too, would gather to marvel at the boy wonder, and in appreciation, they brought gifts. One of those gifts was in an envelope that JD offered to Ferd and me that night by the empty swings. I don't remember who rolled it or what JD had to say about its properties, but after a few coughs, our lungs were full, and we were on our way.

If you weren't there, it may be hard to grasp how fast things moved in the sixties. The stretch of time that produced "Love Me Do" through "Day in the Life" to "Come Together" was seven years—the entire breadth of the Beatles recording career as a band and, not coincidentally, the lifespan of the sixties themselves. As has been often said, the years 1960 through 1962 were more akin to the fifties. Regardless of the actual year of individual awakening, everyone awake and attuned to those times crossed the chasm from *was* to *am* at some point. My personal illustration of the rift and the speed of the leap across it is this: I went to my first rock concert not held at a school auditorium in a mohair sweater. I went to my second on acid. The first was Country Joe and the Fish, and the second was Iron Butterfly. They were not far apart. I note this to illustrate the accelerated transformation of the audience; the performers were already there.

It should not surprise you that, although my own band was gone, the music scene was a very big part of my life. I followed it with an almost religious zeal. I consumed the songs, absorbed the record jackets and was a regular in the audience at the Rockpile, Toronto's version of the Roundhouse, the Avalon, or the Fillmores East and West. Part of the attraction of the great sixties music is its message, from "My Generation" to "All You Need Is Love." When I heard the Beatles sing the latter, I was committed enough to the culture to truly hope, and at times believe, that it was so.

So with Ferd and my friends, I leapt headlong into what came to be called the counterculture. We were musicians at heart. But in the absence of hard-earned musical skill, that emotional expression found its outlet in drugs. For my part, when straight and sober, I was guarded and quiet, still afraid to show the inner me, to be caught out and found wanting. When I was high, I let it all out, and my peers didn't care. Sometimes, they were too stoned to judge. When they were not, being judgmental was considered hypocritical, and hypocrisy was not cool. The release from judgement was as intoxicating as the drugs themselves.

To slake our thirst for this newfound release, we would make the trek each week from the sameness of the subdivision into the big, bad city. Our destination was a part of Toronto known as Yorkville. Today, it's a snobby shopping district, but in the late sixties it was nirvana. It was Haight-Ashbury without tourists, Greenwich Village without litter, Soho without hookers. It was home to music as diverse as Joni Mitchell and Steppenwolf precursors the Sparrow. We called this nirvana—our nirvana—the Village.

The Village had one other notable attribute: drug dealers; more per block than any other part of town. King Ferd and I had many occasions to make their acquaintance, and we became trusted customers. Such was our zeal that soon our role as the passive congregation was not enough. We decided to be missionaries. We could deliver the Good Word of the Village to a village of our own. We were no longer wannabes. We had a calling.

Understand that, for me, drugs addressed an age-old problem. You could sell them for money. They brought the same clothes, camaraderie, and outlaw cache that being a musician did. And they beat the shit out of a rainy morning on the paper route. Yes, I was still my father's son, but no matter what my old man did for a living or could not provide to just one of seven because of it, I had cash in my pocket. "God bless the child that's got his own."

Chapter Four
And the Beat Goes On

So King Ferd and I had a calling. It was a modest calling, but a calling nonetheless. We'd borrow his mom's car and head for the Village, where we'd score an ounce of weed before returning to the suburbs. There, we'd repackage it as nickel-and-dime bags and sell it to our closely guarded circle of friends, financing our own indulgence and clearing a whopping ten bucks profit in the process. I'm making light of it now, but that was the first that I remember having any discretionary money in my pocket. No paper route savings plan there; this was for spending.

Yes, we were in business. And a business it was—we bought, we sold, the music culture wrote our ads, and the media did our marketing. There was a time in the sixties when you couldn't open a newspaper without a photo of a dishevelled rock star being led out of his luxury home or a more dapper version at the courtroom steps on his way in. On the days when no one was being arrested or tried, someone's song, past or current, was being scrutinized and banned. When combing the charts for hints of drugs, it never occurred to the guardians of morality that the audience took what authorities called a reference to be an artist's recommendation. In feeding our shaggy idols to the slaughter, the police, courts, and politicians were alerting us, the fans, to vices that had hitherto escaped our attention. Marijuana was on the radar, and a market was born.

Why did so many suburban sixties kids embrace drug culture? As late as the mid sixties, the suburban perception of illegal drugs was downtown and suspect, an artifact of the demimonde inhabited by the seedy and the desperate. The press was playing up the habits of our pop idols in a way that was unprecedented in the reporting of decades past, and there's no doubt that it brought the recreational use of drugs into our field of vision. To even the thickest of teenagers, the tacit endorsement of your idols may grab your attention; it might even get you right up to the door and desirous of entry. But a rock lyric wink won't move you to inhabit a lifestyle that offers nothing more than the prospect of emulating Brian Jones. You can't cite the consumer's personal circumstances as a universal inspiration to take drugs; Ferd and my new customers were from both good homes and bad, with comforts and hardships equally experienced. Our clientele had few specifics in common other than boredom and homework.

The truth is that I can't give you a profound sociological answer regarding the appeal of drugs to the middle class. I can only speak for Ferd and me. From where we stood, JD had given us more than our first joint; he had given us our pass into a secret society. Today, marijuana use is relatively commonplace and, though still illegal, is easily observed in every strata of our culture. But in the sixties, dope use was a potentially reckless step into a clandestine club that was, by its perversions of the law and of social convention, dramatically cloistered from the normal world. The jazzers opened the door for JD, and he, in turn, ushered us in. We initiated our friends and acquaintances. Without fully realizing it, Ferd and I were part of a wave of souls bringing pouches and papers to a broader and younger consumer. For better or worse, we were putting the *high* into high school.

But we didn't have much, and we didn't sell much. Our inventory and our cash flow limited our activities as much as our concern for discretion. In market terms, demand was outstripping supply. This seems like an ideal time for divine intervention, and although forces did, in fact, intervene, the exact portion of divinity involved is open to interpretation. Amongst our crew of former Hodads was a guy whose brother was a senior member of a bona fide motorcycle gang. Those guys were the real deal.

The biker clubs that sprang from California car culture inspired a motorcycle club in Oshawa, a small city just east of Toronto that was best known for its automotive assembly lines. As the denizens of small cities often do, the Oshawa bikers looked to the Big Smoke for their next foothold. It was not long before a new chapter sprang up in our neck of town, Scarborough. Our former Hodad suggested to Ferd that our relatively modest enterprise might benefit from some— ahem—muscle on the supply side. Forget the twiggy ounces we were securing COD in the Village. We were being offered a pound at a time, fronted—not paid for in advance—from a well-stocked source. At last, supply could meet demand. We were sorely tempted. Not surprisingly, we succumbed with equal appetites for the adventure and the cash. I had just finished grade eleven. I was not yet eighteen, and I had my first cartel.

The setup was pretty simple. There were four of us: King Ferd, myself, and two others. The duties were quite clear. Ferd was the mastermind, and as both of his parents worked and he enjoyed a pretty free reign, he kept the inventory. Can you imagine me in that role in a three-bedroom house with two parents and five brothers and sisters? I could barely keep track of my socks. Our pal with the biker brother was, quite logically, in charge of the supply side. As a relative of a member, the bikers considered him to be trustworthy and relatively immune to intimidation from rival forces. The remaining two, of which I was one, were in sales. We divided the territory that we believed our inventory could satisfy along lines befitting student entrepreneurs: he got his high school, and I got mine.

Each week, we would get our pound in what was known as a Mexican mini-brick. The weed, due to its packaged shape and red or green cellophane wrapping, bore a striking resemblance to a popular Lego-like construction toy of the era, hence the name. In fact, the brick terminology was quite legitimate; in order to compact and package the product efficiently, the Mexican originators of the weed had purchased a device originally designed for pressing adobe bricks. Now, instead of pressurizing and shaping clay and straw, it produced more economically transportable and concealable marijuana.

So two became four, ounces became pounds, and ten dollars profit became a hundred bucks between four partners. And, in foregoing our downtown source, we were saving Ferd's mom the gas as well as wear and tear on her car, not that we took the opportunity to advise her of her good fortune.

I should pause to warn you that as my story progresses, there will be math. It's been easy going thus far, but as we go, the numbers become a crucial part of my tale—to say nothing of their contribution to my downfall. But for the moment, please understand this simple truth: we were not getting rich. Supply had increased, and demand was being met, but the profit was going four ways in the place of two, and our benefactors are just as determined to profit. For anyone wondering if we were inclined to shave their end, let me be blunt and sacrilegious: They were bikers, for Christ's sake.

Because we were playing straight with them, however, our suppliers offered more opportunity than intimidation. They also offered acid—that would be LSD to the layperson. We had access to Orange and Blue Barrels, so named because of their shape and sought after because they were easily split—a real plus for the uninitiated. We also had the chance to proffer Orange Owsley, named after Owsley Stanley, one of LSD's earliest proponents/manufacturers. To top it off, we sold Purple Microdot, named for its tiny size but not its efficiency. At that point, LSD was the latest buzz and—thanks to Leary, Lennon, and the like—much in demand. We could sell a tab for ten bucks, and they cost us five. That's a 100 percent profit. We jumped at the chance. Our student business was beginning to diversify.

So in the summer of 1968, having completed grade eleven, I had another small epiphany. As much as I loved music, I was not a musician. Although I enjoyed learning, I was no fan of school. I had been enamoured of the outlaw life for as long as I could remember, fascinated with characters as far back as Al Capone and the old movie gangsters. Now, our benefactors, the guys responsible for the first significant coin in my pockets, were bikers. You can likely guess what I aspired to next.

Although it may shock you that any suburban kid who had experienced interaction with actual bikers would consider becoming one, consider the context of the times. At that point in the sixties, bikers were still considered part of the Brotherhood of Freaks with hippies and musicians. They were regulars at concerts and rock festivals and were a visible presence in the Village—the most likely candidates to be holding the substances that we so often sought. They were not yet considered a form of organized crime, but they were symbols of freedom within pop culture and were often the invited enforcers at the outdoor music events in North America and the United Kingdom. I saw the bikers as tough hippies, which was in line with the flattering media portrayal of bikers in the movies that had influenced the Hodads. They were outlaws; they had freedom; and they had respect.

They also had awesome wheels. I did not. In the summer of 1968 I was working full-time for the first time at the warehouse of a toy company. That supplemented my still-modest contraband revenues, and provided a reasonable cover to my parents and others as to where the money originated. I quit to go back to school, but I lasted in grade twelve for one day. The memory of money in my pocket and the lure of the teardrop gas tank haunted me. I decided to quit school for a year to earn enough money to buy a motorcycle with the general long-term intention of pledging for the gang that was supplying the cartel.

To my surprise, my parents seemed ambivalent. It was not thoroughly discussed, of course, because at that point, I rarely talked to my parents about anything. But they threw no roadblocks up to impede my plan. I was eighteen after all. I think, too, that their focus was more on the means than the end; the job was tangible; the motorcycle was nebulous; and the gang pledging went unmentioned.

Besides, they may have envisioned another end entirely. In an overcrowded household, the idea that I was approaching independence and possibly leaving home may have outweighed the prospect of frivolous transportation in the garage. If that seems an unfair characterization of their parenting, understand that my older brother was already gone. He had joined the navy and, when he was not sampling the ales of faraway lands, was stationed on Canada's east coast. Although he was missed, it would be hard to deny that the strain on the household was eased by his departure.

My reaction to his leaving was to swiftly gather up my things and stake a claim on his space. When my father got home that night, he was upset by the speed at which I had moved into the vacant bed. He didn't seem to understand my dissatisfaction with having to sleep in a double bed with one of my younger brothers since moving into our Scarborough home. It wasn't as if I had annexed the entire room. I still had to share with my other younger brother. But, proper and due respect to my older brother aside, I was anxious to have a bed to myself. Mother, ever practical, explained the sense of it all to the old man, who eventually came to terms with my right of succession as the household's newly minted eldest son.

So, with my parents' implicit approval, I embarked on my quest for chrome. After my single day of twelfth grade education, I went back to the toy warehouse and got my old job back. I worked there for $1.40 per hour, saving my pay for a bike. I was not saving it all, however. I had a taste—if that's the right word—for the sartorial concoctions from the great counterculture retailers of the downtown Toronto: ruffled shirts from the House of Lords or the Brick Shirt House, custom leather boots with snake or dragon appliqué from Master John, belts by Joe Mendelson. Oh, yes, one of my first purchases was a brown suede jacket with Wild West fringe. Man, I looked cool. Think of Buffalo Bill crossed with Lord Byron if they aspired to a life in the circus.

I wasn't alone in that extraordinary look, of course. My heroes dressed like that. My cartel friends dressed like that. They also managed to acquire motorcycles. But they didn't have to go out to work to do it. Between the cartel revenue and the support of their parents, my friends had the threads and the treads without dropping out of school. But I stuck to my job and focused on my goal. By November, I had enough to buy my bike: a striking, metal flake blue, 1967 Triumph Bonneville. It had high handlebars. It had a white, high-back seat with white fringe. It had chrome exhaust stacks that sailed up each side like folded wings. It had no baffles and was prone to spitting fire after dramatic deceleration, but it was beautiful and totally illegal. To top it all, my Bonny had a teardrop tank. To celebrate, after a few dramatic tears up and down my suburban street, I pushed my Bonny into the garage, where it remained for the duration of the Canadian winter, waiting for spring when I could roll it out and join the club. I might have paraded it more frequently if I had acquired it before November. A driver's license might have facilitated matters as well.

My pal King Ferd had also purchased a motorcycle with the similar intention of joining a club, but his commitment to two-wheeled freedom was more short-lived. On what seemed like his maiden voyage, he pulled out of his street, turned left, and was smacked by an oncoming car.

But in the absence of our motorcycles, we found other ways to facilitate our journey. Our generation was, to my mind, the first to enter the coming-of-age process with recreational drugs as a tool of passage. Our drug consumption combined with popular culture to bring entertainment, yes, but we also believed that it offered enlightenment. My friends and I were devotees of artists like Jefferson Airplane, Procol Harum, and the Moody Blues, not just because of the music they played or the clothes they wore but also because of the lifestyle espoused. We were drawn to what we saw as the profound concepts and cryptic messages in these records. We knew from experience that they were on the right track—one pill *does* make you larger, just as one pill makes you small. We believed that these musicians were speaking not just *to* us but *for* us, leading the way. And in the jingle-jangle morning, we went following.

But it was not music alone that inspired and informed our explorations. Another tremendous influence on me from that time was Stanley Kubrick's *2001: A Space Odyssey*. It was hard to miss in Toronto. *A Space Odyssey* played in one theatre, the Glendale, for years—literally. The cinema was oddly located, substantially north of the city's downtown but not quite in the suburban boonies that I called home. It was a specialty theatre and had been fitted years before to showcase the seventy-millimetre and widescreen Cinerama films that had been the vogue and purported future of film exhibition in the early sixties. To accommodate the increased real estate required by the film format, the Glendale's screen stretched not only from wall to wall but also from the ceiling almost to the floor. It was also laterally curved, its outer vertical edges extending farther into the theatre than its centre.

This unusual physical layout resulted in an odd feature at the base of the screen. In the place of the sort-of stage that fronted the bottom of most movie screens of the time, the Glendale sported a curved skirt that angled gently upward from the floor. I would estimate that skirt to have been a little more than six feet from floor to screen. Why, you ask, am I so sure of that arcane detail? Because, during the film's psychedelic final section, my friends and I would leave our seats and lie on our stomachs on this skirt, our upturned faces mere feet from the gargantuan images on the screen. During our execution of this odd cinematic viewing practice, we were, I can confirm, high on LSD. That trippy sequence begins with a black screen and the superimposed words "Jupiter and Beyond the Infinite." Exactly.

We performed that ritual not once but many times over the film's long run. We regarded the film in the same vein as our music: as an experience to be savoured over and over and as a comforting reaffirmation of our view of the world. I realize now that that was the beginning of our determination to stretch the boundaries of the institutions we had inherited. We were not content to stay in the seats provided but craved a proximity to the art forms we were experiencing. Around that time, I heard about a guy who, in his effort to better absorb a beloved song, held the edges of a speaker in both hands and pulled it down over his head, destroying the speaker cone and bringing the music to an abrupt halt. I was not that misguided, but I understood the sentiment that had inspired him. I can't confirm it, but I'd be surprised if that guy with the torn speaker cone on his head wasn't more than a little high. There's no getting around the fact that unchecked drug use can take you to some undesirable places; some simply embarrassing, and others much, much darker in nature.

At that time, I was regularly sampling our cartel's wares—not just marijuana but also hashish, LSD, and MDA, the forerunner of ecstasy. I was, for the most part, in control or at least manageably out of control. I indulged, but I did not overdose. I sought enlightenment but not oblivion. I felt I was learning not losing. But there was worse to come.

In the closing hours of 1968, had I taken a personal inventory, I would have been pleased at the distance between my '68 self and the Peterborough innocent that I had been in 1966. I had the look, I had the bike, and I had the keys to the culture. I followed the right bands, did all the right drugs, and hung with the hippest of the day.

All that was missing was all that you need: love. In February of 1969, that changed.

A party at our old friend JD's was where we met, but it was not the first place that I had seen Dawn. I had noticed her and her best friend at school, and although they were undeniably cute, they were two grades behind me—somewhat outside of my imagined social circle. But I was out of school then, and they were catching up. Fast. So on that chilly evening, when JD's door flew open and two girls wearing Salvation Army furs floated in, I did not note the age gap nor feel the cold. I did notice the change in Dawn's look and the difference in the way she carried herself since I had seen her last. The fur-wrapped creature in the drafty doorway blew my previous impression to bits. I went out of my way to make her acquaintance on that evening, and soon we were inseparable.

Dawn became the first fully consummated romantic relationship in my life, pulling me past the old longing and heartbreak into a vibrant partnership of discovery and shared experiences. Our relationship was like a party—full of music, noise, and overheated sexual energy. It was a great time to be alive and a great way to be living.

CHAPTER FIVE
WHEELS ON FIRE

The end of the sixties was brimming with the best of pop culture, and I continued to be an avid consumer. I remember heading downtown with Dawn at my side to see that monolith among biker flicks, the incomparable *Easy Rider*. The film may have had its roots in exploitation films, but it's earned its historic stature by breaking new ground. Its themes defined the era; its score married rock music to cinema; and it gave us two of the period's most enduring heroes.

Easy Rider's two principal characters are named Wyatt and Billy, after Wyatt Earp and Billy the Kid—the old soul and the impulsive youth of Old West yarns. Billy's 1969 getup would not be out of place in a film set one hundred years earlier, but to my eye, he more closely resembled rock superstar David Crosby. Wyatt's nickname was Captain America, and his leather jacket, his seldom-worn helmet, and his teardrop gas tank were adorned with the stars and stripes. His leather pants, however, were pure Jim Morrison.

In the film, these deliberately iconic characters finance their journey across America by selling coke to a rich Angeleno, played by legendary producer Phil Spector. They are portrayed as free, nonviolent souls, equally at home with a multiracial farm family, a commune of hippies, a drunken ACLU lawyer, and two New Orleans prostitutes. They are an alluring cross between symbolic American heroes and pure rock and roll. Their freedom and existential allure are eventually extinguished by hatred and small-minded intolerance. The film was pop culture philosophy wrapped in a killer soundtrack.

Whew. That film had me dialled in. Defining an era be damned, it had me pegged as well. I looked at the screen and saw my bike, my vocation, and on Billy's back, my brown suede jacket! In my imagination, I was Captain America. Then again, as Ferd's sidekick, maybe I was Billy. More likely, I was both.

I don't mind admitting that as a dreamer with a lifelong love of the philosophical elements of pop culture. I was more in awe of that biker movie than I was of the real-life bikers themselves. It did not escape my attention that Wyatt and Billy both end up dead, the result of their inability to put down roots like those they met along the way. The seeds of doubt about my aspirations had been planted.

I left my job at the toy factory at the beginning of 1969 and was supporting myself, however modestly, with the fruits of my cartel labours. Dawn was still at school, as was King Ferd. It was at that time that Ferd—God knows from where—came up with the idea of running for president of the student council. He had been king of the Hodads and was still the boss of the cartel, but he set his sights on student council president. In traditional terms, you could not find a less likely candidate. He was decidedly counterculture, with wild hair and a satanic little beard that made him look like Frank Zappa after a mild electric shock. It was also well known that, in the past year, he'd had trouble with the law of sufficient magnitude to get him into the Toronto papers. It's a testament to the pervasive atmosphere of dissatisfaction with the status quo that the student body of this new, middle-class, arts and athletics high school gave Ferd his presidency. I think the spirit of the times formed the restless student body into a raised fist and King Ferd was the upthrust middle finger. By the summer of 1969, the king had been elected president, and that coming fall, I was headed back to school as his unshakeable sidekick.

It's impossible not to acknowledge that the summer of '69 was the summer of Woodstock. We were half a million strong, descending on Max Yasgur's farm for what was to become the epic event of rock and roll history. The hippie myth was in its last days, but few of us recognized it at the time. This was Hendrix's last stand in America; he closed the show, the brightest amongst the firmament of stars, just as he had been at the Experience's Monterey debut. It's been said before that the lineage of the peace and love movement began at Monterey Pop, matured at Woodstock, and died at Altamont. To see a bright, hot culture emerge, go supernova, and become a black hole in such a short space of time was breathtaking to those of us circling in orbit.

I was not quite at the counterculture's nexus. I didn't go to Woodstock, nor did anyone I knew. At the time, I had never been out of Ontario, let alone across the border to upstate New York. But don't pity us. We were not music or sunshine deprived. Soon enough, we were to have festivals of our own. The constant in the stretch of the music landscape was change. In an attempt to embrace its roots and expand its horizons, pop music was broadening its influence and expanding its definition of itself. Gone were the days when, for all the energy and freshness, every record on the radio sounded like it was recorded within spitting distance of Liverpool. There were new sounds—country and soul and even jazz—seeping into the music once defined by two guitars, a bass, and drums.

The Toronto Rock and Roll Revival, which happened in September of 1969, was a patchwork marvel, with historical greats like Chuck Berry, Little Richard, and Gerry Lee Lewis sharing the stage with Chicago and Steppenwolf as well as exotic southern imports like Tony Joe White. The event's most historical highlight was the maiden appearance of the Plastic Ono Band. Eric Clapton, Klaus Voorman, and Allen White provided the backing for John Lennon and Yoko Ono. John was a vision in flowing hair and a white suit. Yoko, as I recall, wore a bag. In a classic reversal of the old Victorian ideal regarding children's behaviour, Yoko was not seen, but boy, was she heard. Her vocalizing from the sack was actually mistaken by some in the crowd as feedback and sent others crawling toward the nurses' trailers, their acid trips having turned from Technicolor to terrifying. But, make no mistake, this was art. Apparently.

John and the musicians prevailed. In keeping with the classic theme of the concert, they delivered a program of ragged but lovable oldies and, by virtue of showing up, made the day a life-affirming experience. The performance marked the first time I remember seeing the stands illuminated by the matches and lighters of the audience.

The lighter thing may be a cliché now, but with the Plastic Ono Band in front of me and the flames of the adoring fans on every side, the fresh and remarkable sight gave me the shivers as the refrain of "Give Peace a Chance" flowed over us. It was the first time the song had been played before a live audience, and there was magic in the air as we swayed to and fro to the music.

As unbilled performers, the Plastic Ono Band did cause the show to run long, but nobody was asking them to stop performing. By the time the Doors, the day's advertised headliners, hit the stage, it was nearing midnight. That was the year of Jim Morrison's Miami arrest for allegedly exposing himself during a show. The band's fortunes had suffered greatly from the fiasco with a string of cancelled dates. The Toronto date had not been cancelled, but I was told that the police were backstage that night with a signed warrant in the event that the Lizard King's lizard made a Canadian appearance. Due to the pressure from all of this, abetted by Morrison's drunken, belligerent state, the band was not at their best at the Rock and Roll Revival.

I make this point not on experience but on hearsay. I saw very little of their performance. My show companion, the beloved Dawn who was all of sixteen at the time, had a curfew. Her household deliverance deadline was being severely threatened by the fact that the show was about to hit midnight. We could envision her irate father hitting the proverbial roof. With immense reluctance, I caught what little of the Doors I could while walking backward toward the exit sign of Toronto's Varsity Stadium. Reality was, once again, crowding my buzz.

The year of Woodstock and the Toronto Rock and Roll Revival, as we know, was also the year of Altamont, where bikers, hired as security, were said to be the cause of the death of a fan who had come to see the Stones. Local bikers also served as security at the Rock and Roll Revival. Some of them were acquaintances and business partners of mine, and thankfully, we had no problems with the crowds or the police. But I was having troubles with my personal biker fantasy.

As the summer of Woodstock turned into the autumn of education, I was good and ready to go back to school. Somewhere in the passing months of true love, heavy movies, and plentiful acid, I had had another epiphany. I was a lover. I was a philosopher. I was a purveyor of the illicit ingredients of cultural enlightenment. Yes, I was all of those things. What I was not was a biker. I had gone too far down the road of beauty and flowers to be a chrome-hugging outlaw. And as the final affront, one of the very bikers whom I so revered had ripped me off for my beloved Billy-from-*Easy Rider* brown suede, fringe jacket. The die had been cast. Before I'd even secured a driver's license, I quietly sold my bike and moved on.

So, that fall of 1969, I was still dream-swaddled but back at school. The combination made me consider becoming a teacher. Not the kind that haunted our halls in haphazard ties, diamond socks, and impossibly baggy pants. I had developed an idea that combined my love of enlightenment and my determination not to stray out of the safety of high school. I wanted to be a philosophy teacher, a guru to the actively pubescent, a wise guide at the base of the mountain as the smooth-skinned seekers set out on their climb to adulthood. Okay, I know that philosophy was not taught in Canadian high schools of the era. But I thought it should have been, if only as an elective. I felt the times were a-changing, and I wanted to play my part. That may not have been a great plan for the long-term, but in the short-term, I was focused and motivated. I knew that, to teach, you had to have education beyond the secondary level, and I was determined to go to college. I buckled down and got the best marks of my life. By June, I had graduated from the four-year program and was off, I hoped, to college in January. For my part, I felt transformed from rebel without a cause to idealist with a purpose.

It was at that time that I began to read philosophical works and delve into the realm of the mystics, including Tarot cards and astrology. Socrates said, "Know thyself," and I was determined to do just that. He did not say, "Medicate thyself," but that was my method of travel. I was one among many who saw drugs as an agent of the revolution. I was convinced that what philosophers and mystics took lifetimes to learn was hidden in a single trip. I reasoned that I was under-prepared or not sufficiently disciplined enough to understand it. That, over time, was to exact its toll.

In spite of smooth sailing at school, things were not going so well at the green-roofed homestead. Though my oldest brother was gone, my three young sisters were growing and in need of space where there was none. I could feel the house straining at the seams, ready to pop a button. In fact, it popped two. My next younger brother had already started working, following in the pest control footsteps of my father, so he had an income. I did as well. I had just started a job at a toy factory—not the previous toy factory, a different toy factory. Psychology majors, insert your Peter Pan jokes here. But in spite of his two sons' demonstrated sense of responsibility, the old man was relentless. One day he told my brother and me to get our hair cut one time too many. We saw our opportunity. We told the old man that we were leaving.

And we did.

CHAPTER SIX
CAN'T FIND MY WAY HOME

So Ma's little birds—numbers two and three—left the nest, our head feathers intact. It didn't take very long to find a basement apartment, but finding a place suitable to our lifestyle was somewhat trickier.

Our new landlords, reticent from the start, were interested in nothing but the cash. We, in turn, were driven by the desire to sleep in a bed—a luxury that even our modest upbringing had never denied us. The uneasy alliance was not to last.

Roughly two weeks after we moved in, a friend arrived with a porno movie. He had scooped it from a stag party his father had hosted the previous night. It had to be returned in short order, before it was missed. With a parent-ruled environment out of the question for a screening, the nudie-flick borrower turned to the only ones he knew with a place of their own. Anxious to appear independent and more than a little curious about the entertainment, we foolishly agreed to host the film, the projector, and the projectionist. Now, in that pre-video, pre-cable world, entertainment of that nature was not as widely accessible, and strange as it may seem, it was not so much of a solitary activity. The word got out fast and wide.

Actually, we let it out. We were living modestly, but we were not short of acquaintances interested in illicit pursuits. The coveted yet clandestine event had attracted more than a few—just slightly more than a tiny basement apartment's worth, in fact. As the pink and curvy images played across the blank wall of our abode, it was not the sheer numbers that betrayed us but the startling volume of the enthusiasm. It was like a chariot race for the oversexed, as if testosterone could have been measured in decibels. Drawn by the animal roar, our landlady decided to investigate. The sight of many horny young men cheering images of overendowed and underclothed entertainers on the wall of her home was not a sight she was likely to forget or, as it turned out, to tolerate. All but two of the participants were rapidly dispatched to their homes. My brother and I were told that we were no longer welcome. We had two days to get out.

For the second time in as many weeks, we had to find new digs in a hurry. Surprisingly, we did—in the home of an immigrant family who manufactured drapes in the back half of the basement we were to call home. Our entrance to the apartment was private, but their access to their business facility involved a short trip down the stairs and across our living room carpet. But we were not in a position to be fussy, and as it transpired, they were not of a mind to be meddlesome. Likely understanding of how unattractive a situation they offered, they were very tolerant of our presence, our housekeeping, and our vices, which in my case included the sale of illicit drugs. The curtain workshop was to be our home for the next year.

So the glare of independence was waning, and the filtered light of reality was reaching through the tiny windows of our basement abode. With no parents to petition or blame, my brother and I were starting to feel the chill of having no one to rely on—no one but us. Our view of the world was becoming overcast, and the shapes of the clouds were familiar.

For me, the shadows began to take hold with the death of Jimi Hendrix. I know it sounds dramatic, but to me, Hendrix was a musical hero above all others. I loved his playing, which was simultaneously explosive and liquid. I loved his lyrics and his voice and the world that all three elements combined to create. Dawn and I saw the Experience at Maple Leaf Gardens in 1969. Jimi had been busted at the airport just a few hours before taking the stage, but he still managed to electrify the crowd. I was, without question, a citizen of Electric Ladyland, comforted by the possibility that I might never hear surf music again.

Hendrix was the first black artist that I truly took to heart. I suspect this to be true for many of my generation, but it was particularly important to me and to my worldview. I grew up in southern Ontario, but this was equally true of much of Canada: to say that black culture in the sixties was in short supply would be an understatement. The great black artists of the early and mid-sixties were infrequently heard on Toronto radio. Even those who got airplay—mighty Motown acts like the Supremes—played clubs not stadiums when they came to Toronto. Sure, Windsor, only a few hundred miles down the 401, had a taste-making powerhouse of a radio station, but their antenna was pointed south and west to Detroit, Cleveland, and beyond. We did not hear much of the great black music of the sixties in Peterborough or Toronto. This was not just a musical phenomenon. There was one black kid in my whole high school when I first came to Scarborough. I saw him in the halls and occasionally at the mall. He was too outnumbered to be a cultural influence. In an environment like that, Jimi was a revelation—a black man who eschewed the traditional sharkskin for satin, ruffles, and jackets with eyes on the front. His hair said freedom, and his music said magic.

A friend of mine told me that the first time he heard "The Wind Cries Mary" on the radio, he had to pull his car over onto the shoulder. He could not physically handle the prosaic act of driving with the poetry of Hendrix in his ears. I had no driver's license at that time, let alone a car, but I could relate. Jimi led me to the place where I felt I belonged. In the super highway culture of my youth, I aspired to leaning back at the side of the road, dreaming away on a rainy day. But then Jimi was gone, and within the year, we would lose both Janis Joplin and Jim Morrison. We had Hendrix's music, to be sure, but there would be no more, save a handful of tracks he had never intended us to hear. Someone had thrown a stone in the roomful of mirrors, and in a manner approaching slow motion, the options and opportunities were beginning to shatter.

My diversions, too, were growing darker. All of my substance discoveries began beautifully. But I cannot deny that time and repeated abuse was taking its toll—with me as it was with my heroes. My crowd had moved on from sampling our own wares—marijuana and LSD—to a recreational substance that we did not sell. We began to inject crystal methedrine. The practice started, as use of the other substances had, founded on lofty ideals. In the early days of that scene, meth, along with MDA, had a reputation as a love drug. We would sit up all night under its influence, discussing deep topics and attempting to resolve the great puzzles of the world. As an aspiring philosopher, it felt like a welcome tool to further my explorations. Dawn and I saw it as a drug of bonding and sexual enhancement. We did not abuse it—at first.

Sadly, as with all things artificial, meth's benefits deteriorated with time. Nights of philosophical rapping and physical rapture gave way, and something was lost. The roadmap became the destination. And in every sense, the means became the end. The greatest casualty was my relationship with Dawn. It's difficult to admit, but as much as we loved each other, we came to love the drugs more. Using became the central feature of the relationship. We were not alone in that; our friends were equally ensnared in their own ways. When I heard George Harrison sing that there was "a fog upon LA, and my friends have lost their way," I believed that he was describing a circumstance very near my own. But even in my high-test crowd, our intake as a couple was seen as prodigious. As time passed, Dawn's clandestine nickname amongst my acquaintances became Drugs Bunny. As I snickered, I wondered what they called me in my absence.

Their observation had the cruel ring of truth. The drugs were now the most prominent feature of Dawn's and my relationship. Our love was struggling. We were adrift, and it hurt. I started to drink on a very regular basis. The drink took over from the LSD, the MDA, and even the pot. Alcohol was, to our generation, the relic of a former, less-evolved era—the shame of uncool jocks and sloppy relatives. I was oblivious to the irony at the time, convinced that my speed sessions with Dawn elevated me above the narrow self-medicators of the past. But the late nights of love and philosophy had been replaced by the shared, hollow secrets of shooting up and sexual gratification. We still called it love, but it was empty and chilling. Our relationship was falling apart.

Through all of that, strange as it seems, I continued to attend community college and maintain my grades in the courses I completed. But school had necessitated leaving my job at the toy factory. My income was wholly comprised of providing the seekers of exotic substances with their hearts', or heads', desires. The cartel was long gone. I was nominally a student, but to the world at large, I was officially a drug dealer. As a post-secondary student of modest means, I had received a government grant and loan package intended to enable my continued education. In truth, it enabled me to secure some product that I parlayed into profits, thus facilitating both my education and my lifestyle. However, things were far from flush.

At that point, my old confrere King Ferd and I came across an opportunity to score a couple of pounds of quality reefer out of Rochdale, a legendary student residence in downtown Toronto.

For those unfamiliar with that fixture of Big Smoke counterculture, Rochdale was a large cooperative housing project located on Bloor Street at the edge of the University of Toronto's downtown campus. As well as a variety of housing units ranging from one- and two-bedroom apartments to ashrams (communal living spaces designed to house a dozen or so people), the eighteen-storey high-rise was the location of Rochdale College, the largest of some three hundred, tuition-free colleges operating in North America in the late sixties. The cream of Toronto's cultural class was often involved, especially in the early days.

But however qualified or talented its academic staff may have been, Rochdale's degrees were not granted in the traditional manner. Securing a bachelor of arts degree had some elements in common with the final stage of a sweepstakes. You had to answer to a single skill-testing question. Oh, yeah, you were also required to donate twenty-five bucks. As I recall, a master's degree was simultaneously easier and more difficult. You had to pony up fifty bucks, but just as with a traditional thesis, you got to pick a skill-testing question of your own. A PhD was a princely hundred bucks. It was assumed, at that point, that you had sufficient education that any question at all would have been presumptuous. You just paid and left with your degree. It was a freethinker's fantasy and a rebel's dream.

But, the times being what they were and human nature being what it has always been, Rochdale was also a narcotic officer's dream: an easy target and an advancement opportunity all in one big, poured-concrete monstrosity. Naturally, Ferd and I pulled up in front of

Rochdale on business of great interest to the latter group of dreamers. When we set eyes on Rochdale's grey and rather grubby doorstep that fateful day, it was not for the first time. We had been there before and were accustomed to the pitfalls one faced when acquiring product from that enclave of drug-savvy radicals. It was not a place for the faint of heart. For that reason, we often went as a team. But on that occasion, an associate who had arranged the transaction was to accompany us into the building. We decided that three of us entering at once would raise suspicion and paranoia amongst the residents. It was not the locals who should have concerned us.

King Ferd and the associate went into Rochdale, and I agreed to wait and watch at the Zumburger across the street. Ferd was gone for what seemed an inordinately long time. It's funny how, for all the experience you may have at this type of endeavour, the sensation of elongated time never changes. When Ferd did finally emerge, my mood did not brighten. He had a hand in each pocket, uncomfortably forming a makeshift pouch with the front of his coat. Whatever was cradled in that pouch was awkward and likely to generate adverse consequences when exposed to daylight. That recollection may reflect my state of mind more than reality, but I felt I could see the two pounds—one on each side—right through the jacket he was clutching so brazenly. To my agitated mind, he practically begged for scrutiny. I tried to shake the dread as we headed for the van, but as we arrived at its door, I noticed two men approaching with a sense of purpose. By the time we got the door open, I was certain that they were cops. On reflex, I spit out only two words.

"Ferd! Narcs!"

In the split second available, Ferd slid one pound under the driver's seat and flung the other into the back of the van. Ferd's instinctive reaction was to be hugely beneficial to me. First, the cops did not see me handle the pot and secondly, they saw the fling and missed the slide.

Even so, we were busted. We were handcuffed and taken to police headquarters, Fifty-two Division to be exact, for the first drug arrest of my life. If only it had also been the last.

With the efficiency and confidence that a pound in hand will bring, the police booked and released us in short order. King Ferd and

I drove back to my apartment, where the gang was waiting to partake of the spoils of our trip. In the course of our drive, I decided not to tell the gang what had happened. I was concerned about alarming Dawn, but I was also reluctant to admit to our peers that the police had nailed us. We slid the pound that the cops had missed out from under the van seat and went upstairs bearing gifts; we were Sensemilla Santas to our awestruck, festive friends.

Chapter Seven
I Fight the Law, Part Two

But I was not Santa. Santa, as far as I've heard, has never been in dire need of the services of a good lawyer. My dad's bug barrister aside, I was a novice at the lawyer thing. Naïvely, I set out with Ferd to find legal counsel. Ferd had heard of a lawyer named Clayton Ruby, who had been making a name for himself down in the Village. So we set out to engage him to defend us. He agreed to take Ferd's case (his parents were paying the bill), but I was referred to Legal Aid and an associate of Ruby's who worked there. David Newman was his name, and he had only recently begun to practice. But fear not, dear reader, that guy was good. That was the beginning of a professional and personal relationship that lasted throughout Mr. Newman's admirable career.

Many eventful months went by in the meantime, but let me jump forward to the trial for Ferd's and my Rochdale follies. Though years had passed since the affair of the purloined pants, there I was in a courtroom, once again being tried as the accomplice. But this trial was different. David Newman proved his worth as counsel from the moment the arresting officer took the stand. His opening question was, "You arrested my client because he was there, is that not correct?"

The officer denied it, as it was not sufficient grounds for arrest. Mr. Newman pressed on.

"Well, then, did you see him come out of Rochdale?" The officer replied that he had not.

"Did you see him with the marijuana in his hands, then?" Mr. Newman continued.

Again, the officer admitted that he had not.

Mr. Newman then asked the officer if the van in which the contraband was found belonged to me. The officer confirmed that it did not. Newman closed in.

"In the light of these facts, then, I'll state, once again, that my client was arrested because he was there."

The officer said, "Yes, I suppose so."

The judge said, "Case dismissed."

Ferd was not so fortunate. He had done everything that the officer had admitted that I had not, and it was his vehicle. So, even though his lawyer Mr. Ruby had the charges for the pound reduced to simple possession—a precedent at the time—Ferd got six months in jail. As for me, no incarceration was mandated, and regrettably, beyond "hire a good lawyer," no lesson was learned.

Although the trial described above was pending, it did not curtail my activities in the meantime. And the activities were numerous for someone with a pad of their own. Drawn by the unsupervised world of our apartment, my friends visited often and at length. Word spread, and before long, we were hosting crashers—many of whom we barely knew—for stays overnight and longer. These were locals on sabbatical from their parents as well as out-of-towners who needed a place to stay. Some visitors were female, but sadly, most were guys. On one occasion, a friend showed up with three guys from Detroit who needed a place for the night. We welcomed them, and in the course of discussing my occupation, they mentioned the five pounds of weed stowed in their vehicle downstairs. I offered my distribution services, and by noon the next day, the entire load had been sold. My guests were suitably impressed.

Two of those Motowners were suburban, long-hair types, but the third was something else altogether. Ringo was a striking, six-foot mulatto with straight hair to his shoulders and movie-star good looks. He was sharp, not only because of the platform shoes and satin pants that were very *en vogue* with the glitter rock bunch but also due to the cool way he carried himself. His attention to accessories set him apart. Like the ribbon on an impressive package, Ringo's neck sported a black velvet choker with a small cameo at its centre. In anachronistic parlance, that guy was *fly*. That side of Hendrix, we had never seen anyone like him.

As far as the other two were concerned, they seemed content to leave our business transaction as a one-off. But a sense of trust had been established. Selling five pounds of pot in a foreign country through someone you've just met is quite an accelerant. For my part, I was intent on forging a connection that would carry me to a new level. So I focused on Ringo, determined to go international.

One of the options Ringo presented was a product called peep, the Motor City slang name for PCP. It came in both pill and powder form, was less bulky than weed, and was less detectable by odour. For him, it was easier to take across the border. For me, it was a product with fresh potential in our market. He would supply, and I would distribute. Although unrecorded in the financial press of the day, a multinational was born. I had my second cartel.

We started modestly with Ringo's next visit—a delivery of one hundred tabs. Purchased from Ringo at five dollars per, I sold them at ten. Not a fortune made, but boy, those babies went quickly. Within a few months, we were importing a thousand at a time at three dollars per. I was selling them for five.

That was serious money by my standard, but, to be candid, things were starting to get away from me. Ringo was a wild man. I was still a student, remember, and all he wanted to do was party. I was struggling to juggle school, drugs, and international intrigue. The airborne objects were slippery, and my hands were unsteady. I was still not completely committed to the lifestyle. I still had remnants of the ideals and aspirations that had led me to drugs in the first place. But that life was neither deep nor philosophical; it was glitz. My pilgrim persona was not a ball I was prepared to drop.

I needed to find Ringo a new juggling partner. To that end, I turned my lucrative connection over to one of my buddies from the old cartel. He had left school to deal full-time and was more comfortable with the scene than I. He took Ringo as a supplier, and I became a humble sales associate. But I got my product at a damned good price.

The arrangement flourished for the best part of 1972 until an event pulled us up short. One of my field boys, a guy we had secretly nicknamed Duh Jerk had lined up a major buy with some gentlemen to whom he had sold a couple of hundred tabs a few weeks before. That time they wanted all he could get, meaning all I could get, which happened to be seventeen hundred tabs. Because of the quantity and the money involved, my old cartel buddy and I decided to accompany Duh Jerk to the transaction.

Neither of us had a car or a license. We normally took cabs everywhere, but for obvious reasons, that was not an option there. We solicited the service of one of our mobile friends. We picked up Duh Jerk at the local Dairy Queen and headed to a grocery store parking lot, where his buyers were waiting. I waited in the car with our wheelman while my cartel buddy and Duh Jerk went to the buyers' car. After a short time, one of the occupants of the other car come over to my window, complained about the count on their last buy, and questioned the accuracy of the package. I was convinced that he was a cop—his long hair looked like a wig, for god's sake. With every degree of cool that I could muster, I brushed him off. I claimed ignorance of the details. As he returned to the other car, I told my friend to get the hell out of there and regroup at the Dairy Queen.

I was still hoping that the buyers were not cops, but I was pretty certain that they were. But my partner was less sure, and to my absolute horror, he got them to drive back to the DQ to meet us. When they got to the Dairy Queen, the same rug-sporting dude came in and repeated his inquiries about the tab count. When I replied that I didn't know what he was talking about, he said, "I think you do," and identified himself as an officer of the RCMP. He was a Mountie, which likely accounted for the length of horsetail on his head. That line did not occur to me until later. At the exact moment of his identification, I was too scared to be clever.

While my bewigged nemesis was apprising me of the nature of his employment, his fellow officers were doing the same to my cartel buddy and Duh Jerk. I had seen it coming, but they had not. That did not make the handcuffs any more comfortable. They quickly searched our wheelman's car, and after finding it clean, took all four of us to the Fortress, RCMP headquarters on Jarvis Street in downtown Toronto.

We were all charged with possession of a narcotic "held out" to be THC and with trafficking in that substance. That, we learned, was because, unlike THC, PCP had not yet been designated a controlled substance. It was, therefore, legal for sale. Their case rested on the fact that Duh Jerk had sold it to them as THC, the active ingredient in cannabis, which *was* illegal to sell. Stick with me here. MDA, LSD, PCP, THC, and RCMP—if you're unfamiliar with the lifestyle, it's a lot to take in. If nothing else, you'll learn a variety of ways to rearrange the alphabet. We were booked and released. With a court date as our parting gift, we headed for home.

Once again, it was time to lawyer up. I retained David Newman; my cartel buddy hired David Humphries; and our wheelman got, of all people, Eddie Greenspan, a highly respected criminal lawyer just starting his career back then. I'm not sure who Duh Jerk got, as we never talked to him again. We saw him in court, of course, but as I recall, we did not wave.

Now, you'd think that the turmoil would curtail the illegal activities from which the trouble grew. But you would be wrong. I was mildly more cautious but otherwise undeterred. After all, I had legal bills to pay. So, the high life continued unabated. As a result of the Detroit connection, we began to meet more and more folks whom Ringo brought north to party. It was not long before we were invited south for reciprocal generosity.

Before the year was over, our local reputation as a party house, our guests, and the penchant that we shared for border-hopping brought us once again to the attention of the RCMP. That time it was my cartel buddy's home that was raided, and the Mounties came armed with a warrant for Ringo as well. Ringo was not there at the time, and through channels, we were able to warn him of his impending trouble on our side of the border. We never saw Ringo again.

That left my cartel buddy with two current charges, no cash, and nowhere to live. So my brother and I offered him the couch until he could get things in order or was ordered to jail. That was the winter of

1972. He eventually picked up a bed, shared my bedroom, and stayed with us until we moved out together almost a year later.

During his stay, the sister of one of the regular Detroit party girls turned up on our doorstep. Her name was Magdalena. She was very attractive young lady, and I hoped to convince her to stay the night. I offered to take her downtown to a nightspot we frequented, and she agreed. As my substance intake progressed that evening, I began to fancy my chances with her and invited her back to the pad. Upon our arrival, however, the excessive PCP intake had given me a bad case of the whirlies. I spent the night, as I often did, on the small mat in our bathroom, curled up before the porcelain goddess. In my absence, Magdalena crashed in an unoccupied bed, which is where my cartel buddy found her upon his return the next morning. In short order, they became an item. They were eventually married and remained so until her tragic death from cancer a few years ago. But their meeting spun my cartel buddy off onto a different path, which was to bring them both success.

Magdalena showed us another side of Michigan. She was well connected in Ann Arbor, forty miles west of Motown. Ann Arbor was the home of the University of Michigan and, as a college town, had a liberal, organic bent in contrast to our chemical-based Detroit connections. Magdalena had a marijuana source in Ann Arbor, where quality product was about half the price we were paying in Canada. All that remained was to get it across the border. At eighteen and while still living in her mother's Ann Arbor home, Magdalena took this upon herself. She stashed the bricks in the side panels of her 1969 Mustang fastback. It should be noted that the outer surface of each of these side panels was emblazoned with decals identifying the owner as Foxy Lady. Jimi would have been impressed. I sure as hell was. Ballsy Lady was more like it.

Foolishly, I thought that pot was too bulky and smelly and decided to stick to my more portable, concealable PCP, by then available in tabs or conveniently baggable crystal. So we pursued separate enterprises, buying by the pound and selling by the gram. Eventually, the happy couple became quite rich. Not for the first time, you may have noticed, I had picked the wrong horse.

I was soon to expand my international interests, however. Around that time, I met Plum, who was named for Little Plum, a cartoon character from his native Scotland. Plum was simultaneously a lively, mischievous sweetheart and a Glaswegian hard man. When I met him, he was working "security" for an MDA manufacturer. After that operation was busted, Plum came to work for us, bringing with him his connections for hash oil from India and Thai sticks from further East. I welcomed him, determined to keep up with every product that was out there.

That was not simple task. I was balancing school (yes I was still going), dating (although my relationship with Dawn was evaporating), and the chaotic life in a party pad. Then there were also the trials of clandestine commerce. To facilitate all of that, I had stopped taking all drugs—except peep, of course, and alcohol. And a bit of casual coke as it presented itself. Oh, and one other little thing: heroin. I developed a consumer interest in a specific type called Mexican Mud, courtesy of my thoughtful friends from Detroit. But to my good fortune, Mexican Mud was not readily available in Canada. I told myself that, because of the inherent danger, I was avoiding it. But truth be told, it was avoiding me.

What of our PCP bust, you may ask? Through the year, through a number of court appearances and some expert legal manoeuvring, my cartel buddy, the wheelman, and I were all acquitted on the charges of selling a substance "held out to be" on the grounds that we had not held it out to be anything. Because it was PCP and PCP was not yet illegal, we were found not guilty. Duh Jerk, however, in a classic example of karma, had told the cops that he was offering THC. He was convicted. Poor lamb. All of it was immensely frustrating to the police. They argued that my cartel buddy had acknowledged ownership, and therefore culpability, by affirming that the product was "my shit." But by using a euphemism in his acknowledgement, my partner had successfully avoided claiming that what he had was something illegal, despite his scatological terminology. Because owning PCP at the time of the arrest was not a criminal act, the cops were determined to prove that we said it was a narcotic by inference.

In his testimony, one immensely agitated officer exclaimed, "Well, we're not going to give up five thousand dollars for … jelly beans!"

To which my besuited lawyer, David, replied, "Well, sir, if you want to pay *me* five thousand dollars for jelly beans, I'll certainly take it!"

It was the third of December 1973, and for the first time in a good long while, I had no impending charges. I'll say it again, "God bless the child that's got his own."

CHAPTER EIGHT
IT'S A VERY, VERY MAD WORLD

When our lease came up, our landlords declined to renew. Surprised? I guessed not. The place had been the site of a continuous two-year party, and everyone in the building was glad to see us go. It's hard to blame them. Our door was regularly visited by a parade of folks in their pyjamas, often from a few floors down, telling us to turn down the music. I had one lady from the end of the hall tell me that she regularly listened to my song selection for a few hours before falling asleep. She was pleasant about it—we are Canadians, after all—but the message was clear: our behaviour, once again, was outside of what normal society found acceptable. We got the message, but our solution was not to tone it down, of course; it was to find a house.

We found a three-bedroom townhouse in Scarborough, just down the road from the police station. We reasoned that the cops did not sweep their own doorstep, and regardless of the quality of that logic, we were never busted there. But our crew was not without legal drama. By the time of my cartel buddy's arrest for the Ringo raid, PCP had been criminalized; there was no dodging of bullets that second time. He was sentenced to nine months and sent to Maplehurst detention facility in Milton, Ontario, also known at the time as Mickeyhurst or the Milton Hilton, because of its soft handling of the inmates. Easy go or not, my friend did not take to jail. He served five months, and he vowed to whoever would listen that he was not going back. He never did. Shortly after his release, he moved in with Magdalena and never endured involuntary accommodations again. I wish I could say the same.

So my old friends moved in together, and I moved in with Stewball. An old school chum, Stewball was a hard-working, union man, who earned a good wage and was not averse to spending his leisure hours in the pursuit that inspired his name. He looked solid to the landlord, and he was great company to me.

At about the same time, I applied to both York University and the University of Guelph and was accepted for the fall semester at Guelph. Though Guelph was one hundred kilometres from Toronto, I chose not to abandon the suburban Scarborough townhouse. I also decided against living on campus, reasoning that the partying would be a distraction. No, *really.* I had good intentions. But you can add my good intentions to the list of things that led me astray. I was very lonely in the drab little off-campus flat that I had chosen as an alternative. I missed the townhouse that I shared back in Scarborough with Stewball.

In order to afford both homes, I had to do a lot of hustling. That left little or no time for my required academic pursuits. On top of that, I found the university philosophy courses daunting compared to those in community college. College was much less formal and far less demanding. With philosophy as my major, I was required to take first semester courses in math. Plato wrote, "Let no man enter here who does not understand mathematics." The professors insisted on adherence to that principle. My first two compulsory courses were Logic and Theoretical Math. Tautologies and syllogisms made my head was spin, and not in the way to which I was accustomed. My weekend returns to Scarborough got longer and longer, until two months into term, I picked up my furniture and gave the key back to the landlord. After that trip back to Scarborough, I did not return to Guelph at all.

You'd think that that disillusioning university experience would have soured me on education. Not so. I still had a thirst for it. I decided to finish my three-year diploma at community college with an eye toward teachers' college. I'm not sure quite what I envisioned; perhaps teaching grade three classes the difference between Nietzsche and Descartes. It's hard to imagine now why I didn't realize that Plato and Play-doh don't mix. But in the interest of amassing credits toward a community college diploma, I lived out my lease at the townhouse with Stewball until he moved out with—you guessed it—his fiancée.

Prior to Stewball's departure, though, my pal, Plum, invited me to Scotland. Plum's life force was contagious. There was something in the way he carried himself that left those in his company intimidated and enamoured of him at the same time. He was a blend of the turbulent and the tender. He dressed in top fashion, but those who mistook that for femininity learned of their error the hard way. I was overjoyed when such a person invited me to Scotland and flattered by his willingness to introduce me to what proved to be rather a rough lot.

In Scotland, I met Plum's United Kingdom associates. They were as wild and hard as you could imagine. When I saw the film *Trainspotting* years later, I was bowled over by the similarities. But with no cultural frame of reference at the time, their behaviour was unprecedented and their accents close to indecipherable.

I was met by Plum at Gatwick airport. Before I even had my luggage in the trunk, I was given a big ball of opium and told to get it into me. I chose to swallow it in the light of the substantially less appetizing ingestion alternative. We hired a motor, as they say, and headed for Edinburgh to hook up with his mates and seek the local strains of savagery.

That night, I was taken to a curry shop, where we feasted like kings or ate like pigs, depending on your perspective. My massive meal included a lot of drink and another big ball of opium, which I consumed while I stuffed myself. As we left, I went straight to the gutter, where I divested myself of pretty much all I had taken in. Drained and emptied, I finally looked up from the pavement. The first thing I saw was the magnificent, historic Edinburgh Castle. I felt like a wastrel, throwing up in plain view of the ghost of Mary, Queen of the Scots.

One of the highlights of my Scottish adventure occurred on our way to meet more of Plum's mates, as if more were needed to add to the mayhem. En route to Glasgow, we were stopped at a makeshift police checkpoint. The police had spotted an unfamiliar face with the known perpetrators and had apparently gone to the trouble of closing the highway just to see who I was and what we were up to. It was my very own roadblock—another first. With police dogs at the ready, they had us empty our pockets and demanded my ID. Seeing that I was from Canada, they wanted to know what drugs I had brought into Scotland. Plum smirked, exclaiming, "Canada doesn't bring drugs to Scotland, you daft bastard; Scotland sends drugs to them!" The cops bade us farewell, or "fuck off" to be precise, and sent us on our way. But the encounter illustrated the notoriety of the gentlemen with whom I was travelling. I was a long way from the townhouse down the street from the Scarborough cop shop.

Roadside drama aside, the Scotland trip was initially as grey and drizzly as the weather. I grant you that December is not the month by which to judge a northern country, but the only time I felt physically comfortable was when I was high on opiates. I know that junkies lunge at excuses, but it was no surprise to me that there were so many users in a country so cold and damp.

As the trip progressed, I amended my harsh opinion to include "breathtaking." The company was fine, and the countryside was unforgettable. Plum and I travelled straight north from Glasgow for about two hundred kilometres along some of the most scenic and treacherous roads I have ever traversed. During the journey, I swear that Plum stopped talking only to lick the papers for his big hash joints. He was a spliff-rolling machine. Even so, I was introduced to the entire history of Scotland, from Rob Roy MacGregor and the tempestuous relationship between the English and Scots to the bastard clans that were, in Plum's view, bloody traitors. Never mind that over four hundred years had passed, he insisted that I know the conspirators from the loyal Scots. That was the Scotland that I needed to see: highland tales, harts on the hillsides, and hashish. It was wonderful, and Plum's company was even better.

I made it back for the Christmas holidays, but shortly thereafter, I was enticed to go to Las Vegas. I loved Vegas right from the start; I could not believe that a place like it existed. It was energetic, it was loud, and it was lit up like a Christmas tree—remind you of anyone? Back in the seventies, the city still had the outlaw, mob-run feel of its origins, founded as it was on the twin pillars of lust and greed. It was a male playpen: gambling, drinking, hookers, sports books, and icons live on stage. On that trip, I saw Elvis, but I could have seen Frank Sinatra, Dean Martin, or Bill Cosby—all of whom were playing that week. I've been back four times since, and the city has changed. Now, the scantily clad babes are on stage in lavish showrooms. In the seventies, they were on the sidewalks.

In the great tradition of Sin City, I lost all seven hundred dollars of my money on my first night. I had to call home to my cartel buddy for more. He wired the money along with a written dressing-down for my foolishness. He arranged for the girl at Western Union to read it aloud to me, which she did between snickers. I got another five hundred dollars, but the humiliation was free of charge.

Before returning to community college for the winter semester, I had one whirlwind trip to Jamaica. Jamaica, too, was a very different place than it is now. Bob Marley was just making his mark; he was not yet the saint, saviour, and it must be said, cash generator that he has become. The Rastas I encountered were a delight. I spent hours talking with them—philosophers all.

That was the most travelling I had ever done in such a short period of time. On my return, I went back to school. The rest of the year unfolded rather uneventfully. That's a good thing. I needed to settle down and pick up the missing credits.

But first, it was time to move again. Stewball was getting married, so I went house hunting. I found a perfect, three-bedroom house close to the college and convinced Plum and Kercules to move in with me.

Chapter Nine
Hello, Darkness, My Old Friend

Kerc and Plum were more than just roommates to me. The three of us had a real bond and were the closest of friends. Similarities in age and appetite forge remarkable kinships, the excitement and shortsightedness of youth being key ingredients.

You know a bit about Plum, but let me tell you more about Kercules. He was a close friend, an artist, an amateur musician, and a former Hodad from the old neighbourhood. He was a tall, blonde, handsome lad, who had a truly unique sense of humour and lived the life of the true bohemian artist. He had joined a band that was headed to California to chase the dream. He was back and gainfully employed, but the flexibility of a freelance artist was a good fit for the party house we envisioned.

So Kerc was freelancing. I was picking up credits and dealing. Plum was dealing as well, so our combined income could sustain a reasonable lifestyle. Mainly, we were dealing weed and hash, but I was still working the PCP, sourced from Detroit. Detroit was where I first tried heroin. For you hip hop and movie fans, we used to score in the legendary Eight Mile neighbourhood of the Motor City. I restricted my dabbling to Detroit, where I was introduced to Mexican Mud, the brown heroin I mentioned earlier. Back in Toronto, I was mostly just snorting, but if the opportunity to fix arose, I would stoop to the occasion.

On one such night, I was at a downtown bar called The Brass Rail, near midnight, feeling no pain. By the awesome powers of junkie radar, Bearpit, an old friend who had originally introduced me to Ringo, sniffed me out. He was in need of a fix; I was in need of a shred of sense—we were a perfect couple. I was easily persuaded that satisfaction waited in the form of some good *gau*, as we called heroin in those days. Not surprisingly, Bearpit knew where to cop. It's a testament to how uninformed we were about our poisons that I was unaware of the danger of mixing narcotics and drink. Unaware or too pissed to care—take your pick. I tied off, shot up, and passed out but not before uttering the classic line, "This shit is g-o-o-o-d … "

I left the bar at midnight. By one o'clock, I was in an ambulance. By morning, I was awake with a tube down my throat, a catheter in my penis, and an intravenous drip in each arm. To anyone with a Catholic upbringing, the symbolism of the human form in a four-point pattern with holes in each arm is as inescapable as catechism. Except Christ had a purpose. I was well and truly lost.

The doctor arrived. He told me to grow up and tried to show me that I had a lot to live for, that I was going nowhere with my addiction. I corrected his foolish assumption that I was an addict, pointing out that it was my first time shooting up in months. He stared at my arm in blatant disbelief. Instinctively, I looked at my outstretched arm as well. I was appalled. My limbs were full of inexplicable holes. I found out later that, in an attempt to revive me, my user friends had repeatedly shot saline solution into my veins, an old junkie trick. I may not have been addicted to heroin, but I was on that road with the best tour guides that ill-gotten money could buy.

Most hospital gift shops sell little T-shirts that say, "I was born in whatever hospital." They do not sell bigger ones celebrating an overdose. If they had, I might have bought one with the finger pointing up, saying, "Idiot on Board" or something to that effect. Had I bought one, I would have taken something away from my overdose experience. As it was, I took nothing. I should have learnt a valuable life lesson, but I didn't. I did learn that booze and narcotics are trains heading for collision on the same line. I decided to mind the trains. It never occurred to me to get off the track.

That year, I bought another motorcycle. It was not aspiration but practicality that prompted the purchase that time. I needed a means to get to college. I had disposable income. I needed a way to get around. My Norton Commando was my practical solution. For those of you who would suggest that a Volkswagen bug or a nice Pinto would have been more pragmatic—sorry, that was as practical as I got.

Ontario is blessed with good roads and beautiful lakes, and fortunately for residents of the southern urban areas, you don't have to drive far to find either. Summer had not yet arrived, but in Canada, you push the seasons before the seasons push you. One cool spring day in 1976, freshly minted Harley owner Stewball and I took to the highway on a particularly memorable trip. If only it had been memorable for the right reasons. Yes, we've been down this road before.

Setting off early, Stewball and I pointed the front forks northward. We were soon cruising through damp, glistening meadowland and farms freshly verdant from spring rain, Stewball entwined with a girl who was not his wife and me alone, free, and plastered, if you want to know the truth. Just as we hit Keswick, a resort town on the southernmost part of Lake Simcoe, the clutch cable on my Norton snapped. We pulled to a stop in the parking lot of a marina. Knowing that the bike was going nowhere, I convinced Stewball to head into town and see if he could get me a part or at least a tow. In the meantime, I settled down in the marina car park beside my disabled bike to wait. And wait. And wait.

The passage of time was modified somewhat by the part bottle of vodka I had stashed in the storage space under the seat of the bike. So I waited and sipped, sipped and waited, waited and sipped. It was getting dark and late. There was still no sign of Stewball or the girl who was not his wife. I decided to try to run-start the bike, which was a difficult process at best, but in the dark, by myself, and drunk, there was no chance. I ended up, bike and all, in a ditch. A very muddy, spring ditch. A spring ditch so muddy that, when I crawled out, my boots stayed in the muck at the ditch's bottom, as did my bike and any shred of dignity that a drunken man with a dead motorcycle might possess. It was all too much. Fresh air, exhaustion, and alcohol conspired to bring me to rest, passed out cold in the parking lot on the hood of a stranger's car, bootless and with my helmet still on my head.

Before long, I was awakened by a policeman. They took me to the station, where I was booked for control of a motor vehicle while intoxicated. I apparently regaled the policeman and his colleagues with a ceaseless, loud, and less than top-quality rendition of "Heartbreak Hotel." The performance went on in a continuous loop for what was, I'm told, hours. Thanks, Elvis. I had started the day as *Easy Rider's* Wyatt. I had ended it as *Andy Griffith's* Otis.

I was not a happy drunk. My bike had failed me, I had been busted, and Stewball and a girl who was not his wife had disappeared. As it turned out, they had not completely deserted me. True, the couple's mission to find a clutch cable was less pressing for them than it was for me. For that reason, they stopped at a roadside tavern on their way to the bike shop. There, Stew's bike was stolen. I'm not making it up. In his anguish over the loss, Stewball found solace in drink. Soon my bike, its owner, and its broken clutch cable were lost in the mist that forms when an overheated dilemma meets ice-cold beer.

Meanwhile, I was at the Keswick cop shop, entertaining the troops. They were anxious to see me out of there, so they told me that if I could find a ride home, I could go, and they'd see me in court. I managed to give them Dawn's number, and desperate to have the curtain fall on my unwelcome serenades, the police contacted her and asked her to come and get me. By the time the poor girl got there some hours later, I had fallen asleep and did not want to be disturbed. Remember, I had not called her, the police had. Instead of greeting her with gratitude, I was belligerent not only to her but also to the couple she had brought for moral support. In fact, I was so belligerent that my intended rescuers threw me out of the car not far from the outskirts of town.

So there I was, alone again, sloshed and without a ride, outside of scenic Keswick. I was not making much progress at all. I decided to walk a bit. Not far in the distance, I saw the lights of a modest motel, the kind with those little cabins meant to make tourists think they're cozy and independent instead of homesick and cramped. Ever a man with money in my pocket, I checked in to ponder my next move. I didn't ponder long, because I saw that a tavern was adjacent to that very motel. Clearly, I needed a drink. I ended up partying with some other out-of-towners who were also staying in the cabins.

The next morning, I went down to the bar, and who did I see sitting at the bar but Stewball and the girl who was not his wife. They had also stayed the night in the same motel, given that that was the place where his bike had been stolen. Yes, Keswick's that small a town. Stewball had called his wife, and she was on her way to pick him up. He had not told his wife about his lady friend. When his wife arrived, he told her that the girl was with me. First hurdle cleared. The next was not so easy. Stew's wife had arrived in his pickup truck. How does a three-seat pickup accommodate Stewball, one motorcycle, two female companions of divergent marital status, and me for the journey back to Toronto? Here's the answer: It does not. Stew, the babes, and my ailing bike headed back to Toronto. I went back to the motel bar. I proceeded to get good and pissed, worrying about how to get home. I was good and fed up with that town. In my volatile state, I had no trouble inflaming others drinking in my vicinity. My vocal assessment of our location as "backwater," a "two-bit hole," and a "fucking dump" led a local drinker to demonstrate his thoughts on the matter by punching me in the face. It was hard to blame him, but, of course, I did. Next thing I knew, I was in a widescreen, surround sound fistfight, not a one-punch quickie but a real barroom brawl that upended tables and actually spilled out onto the street, like we were citizens of Deadwood.

I don't remember winning. I do remember two black eyes, a bloody nose, and torn clothing—all of which were mine. Convinced that I'd had enough, my brawling buddy was dragged off by his friends. They left. What I should have done was crawl to a cozy cabin, lick my wounds, and sleep it off. What I did do was phone my friends in Toronto to tell them what happened. Then I sat down, drank some more, and waited for them to arrive.

Help was on the way. Not long after, a Volkswagen carrying five of my buddies including Kercules, Bearpit, and Plum, pulled up at the motor court. Overexcited and cranky from an hour in a Beetle, the five of them poured out like malicious clowns, armed with a baseball bat and two table legs, intent on punishing the bastard who had bloodied their pal. They asked me where he was. I pointed to the cabin where I had seen him last. We looked in a window to be sure. Astonishingly, we saw last night's brawler leaning over a bloody sink, attending to his wounds. My inflamed friends kicked in the flimsy door and laid an indiscriminate beating on the cabin's occupants.

Not surprisingly, our appalling behaviour alarmed either the owner or the hapless vacationers inhabiting the other cozy cottages. Someone had called the cops. Fearing incarceration, all six of us piled into the Beetle and headed for the highway. We would have made it too, except for the cruisers blocking the driveway and the officers, with revolvers drawn, who blocked our way. In short order, with my misguided friends but without our wooden sticks, I was back in the Keswick cop shop. Thanks to one of the table legs, I had a dangerous weapon charge added to my impaired driving charge from the night before.

It's odd what you remember from an experience like that. I said earlier that Bearpit had a habit. We all knew that, and he was certainly not the only user among us. But he was the only addict. I remember two things about our night in that cell: all of us witnessing heroin withdrawal—Bearpit's heroin withdrawal—firsthand for the first time. I also remember all of us laughing. He was our friend, and we laughed at his extreme discomfort. Such was the extent of our disconnection from the basics of humanity.

We were released the next morning and given a date a few months hence to appear in court. When that day arrived, the town was ready. Even a newspaper as small as the Keswick one could not ignore the tabloid instinct. We were likely the most appalling story to happen in a sleepy summer town for quite some time, but that didn't mean we couldn't be further sensationalized. They had dubbed us the Turquoise Gang, based on the southwestern native jewellery worn by much of our crew. The turquoise baubles came from Arizona, a prime exporter of pot at the time, so you can guess how we came to be wearing it. Fortunately, you can guess, but the paper did not.

At the courthouse, the locals were mightily impressed by the appearance of David Newman. They saw David as a high-powered Toronto guy, and the local prosecutor seemed to be in awe of his legal muscle. My trusty lawyer argued that a substantially impaired man

A Man of Substances

who is unable to start his motorcycle couldn't be considered guilty of impaired driving. He maintained that a bike of the size of a Norton Commando is not drivable without a clutch cable. I may have been *trying* to start it but "intent to drive impaired" is meaningless when the vehicle cannot be driven. I was acquitted of the impaired driving charge. As for the weapons offence—one of the truly shameful events of my life—the guy I had scrapped with turned out to be a friend of a friend, who was also in town from Toronto. Conversations were had, fences were mended, and the witnesses never showed up at the trial. The beating I took was considered punishment enough. All's fair in love and wooden sticks, apparently. The charge was dropped, but my profound embarrassment at my behaviour lives on. The ringleader of the Turquoise Gang went home, shackle-free but truly ashamed of himself.

After a simple road trip turned from bucolic to alcoholic, I stuck pretty close to home, our new digs on Dawes Road. But even at home, there were incidents. One typical night, the house was full of loud music, a roomful of revellers, and uninhibited dancing. The crowd was stomping to the tunes to such a degree that they were impeding the music. The repeated rhythmic foot stomps were bouncing the needle from the disc, and gravity was responding, returning stylus to groove in a series of highly amplified bangs. The dancers laughed at the unintentional chaos. The neighbours reported gunshots. It was not long before the street was cordoned off, and the SWAT team arrived, intent on crashing the party. I got a phone call from a friend who had just gotten off the bus at the local stop, asking what the hell was going on. That's how I found out about our visitors. I parted the living room drapes to see helmeted officers with riot shields coming up the driveway. They searched the house for weapons and told us to shut the music down and behave. Then, they left. The party continued, somewhat undermined by our uniformed guests.

Surely, you'll say, the sight of a SWAT team on the lawn would teach me something. I'll admit that the incident gave me pause. There was a lesson to be learned. I decided to keep my commercial stash at someone else's house. Kercules had a girlfriend with her own place down in the Beaches area, and I convinced her to hold my goods. I say that I convinced her, but it was likely the hundred bucks a week that turned the tide. She was sufficiently convinced to give me my own key. We both got used to the arrangement, and it was working beautifully. Then one day, with my judgement artificially altered, I took a customer over to her place—not into it but close. A few weeks later, he was busted, and I never heard from him again. But my stash house was busted just days after his arrest. They didn't get me, but they got my best friend's girl. Something had to be done.

We devised a legal strategy. I went on the stand at her trial and admitted that the goods were mine. Under the Canada Witness Act, you cannot be subsequently charged for admissions of criminal activity made on the witness stand in the interest of justice. I claimed to be using her place as a stash house without her knowledge. My pretext for being there was that she offered a quiet place where I could study. There was no evidence to the contrary. Her case was dismissed. The cops were not unhappy to see this nice girl's first offence dropped, but they were mightily annoyed that I had confessed and got off. They said that they were giving me just enough rope to hang myself. It took a while, but true to the cliché, I did.

I've admitted that my first overdose passed with the lesson unlearned. I can prove it. Not six months after my first, brief hospital vacation, I was entertaining a Detroit delivery guy, who had brought me my latest PCP shipment. He asked me where he could get some junk. I didn't know for certain where to find junk, but I knew where to find a junkie. I put a call in to Bearpit. I needed sleep, but I was anxious. Bearpit had not checked in, and I wanted my valuable delivery guy to be happy. I convinced him to stay overnight. He gave me some Valium, and I went straight to sleep. In the morning, Bearpit called. We met at his connection's house. Once there, I joined the gentlemen in their activity. I tied off, shot up, and passed out, but not before uttering the classic line, "This shit is g-o-o-o-d … "

I got to the connection's house at noon. By one o'clock, I was in an ambulance. That time, the paramedics could not revive me. I was dead for six minutes on the way to the hospital. Once there, they brought me back to life. I woke up in the hospital. It was in a different hospital with a different doctor, but he delivered the same message as before. That time, the doctor held up the little gold coke spoon that I wore around my neck and asked me when I was going to grow up. I had no answer for him—then or now.

Booze and heroin the last time, Valium and heroin the second—no apparent learning curve. I was approaching twenty-six, which was virtually the same age that Janis Joplin, Jim Morrison, Brian Jones, and my beloved Jimi had been when they had OD'd. They were dead; I was still alive. One other difference: they had accomplished something with the time they had been given; I, as you well know, had not.

I said after the first OD that I was well and truly lost. I was no less lost after the second OD, but that time, someone found me. My cartel buddy intervened. He convinced the same brother who had moved out of the homestead with me years before that I needed a change of scene. My brother, sensing the seriousness of our old roommate's concern, invited me out to Vancouver Island to stay for a few weeks with him and his new bride. I think he hoped that he could talk some sense into me. Heaven knows my God-given supply was running a bit low. My cartel buddy paid my way, and my brother and his wife put me up. How could I refuse? In short order, I was on a plane.

The thing about a change of scene is that, as the scene changes, you're supposed to change in kind. I had always thought of myself as a peace-and-love hippie type. But the thing about Vancouver Island is that's where the real ones are! I got off the plane in a renaissance print shirt, velvet pants tight as saran wrap, and platforms as tall as a modest Vancouver Island structure. In an organic town, I was a drycleaner's dream. It's not about the clothes, of course, it's about what's in them. And arriving at the site of my fresh start, what I had in my clothes were drugs. Not a big supply, just a pocketful, a friendly little walking-around stash.

Sadly, getting on the plane was more a matter of vacation than desperation. I wanted to please my supporters as long as it didn't mean actually having to change. I did not use heroin the entire stay, but I continued to be as high out there as I was at home. I didn't change my ways, just my poison. They gave me a chance, and I didn't take it. I needed something that they couldn't give. I needed the will to do it myself.

CHAPTER TEN
FOOL ON THE HILL

The will to do it myself. I knew what I needed, and knowing is a crucial first step. But it's a first step only, and alas, the will in question was not immediately forthcoming. What *was* forthcoming was the most harrowing year of my life.

Let's take stock. I was twenty-six years old and still living communally with a bunch of guys. Kerc and Plum were dear friends, and we had shared some astonishing times. But I was a diploma-bearing graduate of community college. The *Animal House* lifestyle was getting harder and harder to justify. As a future path, it seemed more like a dead end. Others had left the party path before me. Stewball was married, as were all my brothers. Of course, my cartel buddy had married Magdalena. I had no such prospects on my horizon.

Then there were legal matters. While my brushes with the cops had yet to end in incarceration as they had for King Ferd, my cartel buddy, and Duh Jerk, I was clearly in the crosshairs of the law. It was less a matter of cunning than it was one of luck. As a Vegas vet, I knew that luck deserts even the most loyal of suitors.

There were the overdoses. The experience of waking up in hospital—twice, mind you—would suggest to even the most clouded of minds that a change was due. And I did not have the burden of addiction to keep me from altering my path. I was no quitter, but neither was I a fool.

So I made a decision to break up the party at Dawes Road. I did so on the glimmer of hope that, by moving into a nice place on my own, I could stop dealing, get a real job, and get back together with Dawn. Yes, you read that right. We had been apart for ages, but she was the closest thing to a deep relationship that I'd had at the time. I reasoned that a change of address and a real job was the fertile soil that our relationship needed to reflower. She had straightened out, and I thought that she could help me do the same. I was counting on her will, not my own, but I did not see that at the time.

With the aforementioned intent, I signed a lease on a nice, high-rise apartment in Scarborough. Dawn was a registered nurse's assistant and was in the process of studying for her nursing degree. Generous fellow that I was, I offered her the use of my place as a quiet place to study, hoping that the uncharacteristic calm and comfort of my life would turn her head. She accepted my generosity and visited many times but almost always with a classmate and never past five pm. I was undaunted.

With the New Year came a legitimate job opportunity with a firm that my friend had just established. His new company printed and sold office stationery. I knew nothing about the industry, but being a recent graduate and a salesman of proven skill, I was hired without so much as a resume. I needed a car for the job and got myself a burnt gold, 1976 Cordoba Four Hundred four barrel. I had better wheels than the owner of the company. I called it the Golden Chariot. How did a guy with no assets, no credit rating, a brand new address, and a brand new job get such a car, you ask? Simple, I got my parents to cosign. I had left home years before, but apparently, I thought that their suffering was not complete. Thanks to their sturdy credit rating, I was mobile and embarking on a career, selling something about which I knew nothing. In that state of gormless grace, I went out on the road.

As I said, I knew nothing about the business I had entered or the product that I was trying to sell. Knowing the owner is not the same as knowing the job. I didn't know a business form from a racing form. One customer, after hearing my bumbling attempts to answer his questions, smiled cruelly, rubbed his palms, and sneered, "I love a virgin!" He may have been crass, but he was not wrong. I was serving neither my employer nor my customers well.

Some of this was my lack of expertise at my job. Some of it was the fact that I never stopped selling PCP—dealing was still my prime source of income. But the real problem was the PCP itself. I was living in a state completely coloured by my chemical state of mind. My worldview was mystical not practical. I felt transcendental forces at work in everything. I saw signs and portents in mundane occurrences. I was so far gone that I had counted the steps to my new apartment and assigned each stair a card from the Tarot deck. I'm not sure now why I did that, but the simple act of climbing the stairs had taken on cosmic significance. I saw myself as a PCP prophet, but in truth, I was dusted with drug-induced insanity.

None of that helped my bumbling performance on the job. It was skewing my personal relationships as well. A great man named John McDonaugh was my mentor at Centennial College. As a philosophy professor, he was a learned soul, but it was his personable nature that made him a great teacher. He became my trusted adviser and confidant during my time at the school, and given the number of years it took me to complete that three-year degree, our interaction was substantial. He knew something of how I earned my money. I had confessed to John about dealing marijuana but not PCP. His response had been that as long as my end, the completion of my education, was honourable, my means, an illegal but victimless crime, was justified.

But I'd achieved my end, and my means just kept on going. His approval was important to me, and I decided to visit him to show off the Cordoba, my Golden Chariot, as a benchmark of my progress. The idea that an overpowered Chrysler with a grandiose name would impress a dedicated, modestly paid, philosophy professor was preposterous, chemical logic on my part. But in my deluded state, not only did I think he'd be impressed, but I was oblivious to the possibility that he'd disapprove or be disappointed. He did, and he was. I took a shiny hunk of metal to impress the man who had introduced me to the great religions of the world. His reaction was succinct. Using the Hindi term for the soul, he said, "Looks more asshole than *atman* to me."

I was crushed. Nothing was going as planned. I was messing up at work. I was messing up with those I most admired. It was about time for the biggest mess-up of all.

In April, I headed the Golden Chariot toward Detroit to score a half-pound of pure PCP. I would traditionally pay for it in Detroit and have a runner deliver it to me at a gas station in Guelph so that I had no personal exposure at the border. On that occasion, my runner, a female junkie supporting a couple of kids, was sick and asked if I would mind picking up in Windsor, saving her the haul all the way to Guelph. It broke precedent, but out of sympathy for her condition, I agreed. I picked up the package in Windsor and headed back to Toronto. I stopped for gas in Guelph to fill up the Chariot. I could not resist a fill-up of my own and generously sampled from the bag of pure PCP.

On the way out of the gas station, I came across two hitchhikers with a gas cane walking in the direction that I was headed. Filled with the dust of human kindness, I offered them a ride. Their car was not far off the 401 highway and wasn't any great distance out of my way. As I dropped them off, it was growing dark. Thanks to the PCP, I'd inhaled at the gas station, I was growing dark myself. It was a short retracing of tarmac back to the highway, but I was soon confused. Then, I was lost.

I decided to climb a hill at the roadside to get my bearings. Such was the nature of high that I imagined myself a homing pigeon, cooing and turning in circles to determine my flight path. I know, I know, but it made sense to me. From the vantage point of the hilltop, I was able to determine my course, but as I descended toward the Chariot, I noticed that I had company. A police officer was standing by my car, writing in his little pad. I prayed that he had not seen me doing my wasted pigeon thing. On the final approach, I summoned what was left of my wits, hoping for a stellar performance to convince the cop that I was lost in only the geographical sense.

I pulled it off. He pointed me toward the access ramp to the Eastbound 401. I got in the car and pulled away. That sounds simple, but in my addled state, it was not. The crashing of cosmic forces in my head obscured the sound of my tires on the gravel shoulder. I approached the access ramp with light rain in the twilight sky and a half-pound of drugs in the trunk. As I followed the curve of the ramp, rain, panic, and PCP conspired to slide the Chariot, like butter in a skillet, into the awaiting ditch. I was sure that officer was right behind me. At that moment, paranoia was driving, and I was not. I grabbed the stash, tore up a hill, and dumped the drugs some distance from the precariously angled car. Upon my descent, I noticed that I had company. It was not the policeman, though. A couple of strangers who had witnessed my seal-like slide into the culvert had managed to push the car back onto the shoulder. By the time I got back to the Chariot, they offered good wishes and were gone.

I should have done the same. But I got in the car, circled around to be sure that I was not under surveillance, and came back for the drugs as if I was Moses and they were stone tablets. I ran up the hill again. On my third descent from the mountaintop, PCP beneath my coat, I noticed that I had company. It was a police officer. It was not the same one who had written in his pad and given me directions at hill number one. But I thought it was. Exhausted, guilt-ridden, and blitzed, I saw his presence as a biblical moment of reckoning. Assuming that I was already caught, I pulled the half-pound of PCP I had taken such pains to hide out from under my jacket and casually flipped it into the backseat.

The officer noticed. He asked me what was in the bag. The voices of the universe shouted in my head. He asked once again what was in the bag I had tossed in through the door. I looked as directly at him as is possible when choirs of seers are howling in your skull and replied, "The truth!" Satisfied that that explained it all, I crawled into the front seat and fell sound asleep. Even the sound of applause from the hands of fate failed to disturb my slumber.

Looking back on it now, I feel embarrassed and more than a little foolish. But if telling this story to you is difficult, imagine trying to tell my lawyer. It's hard, even for a guy as capable as David Newman, to free someone who was intent on getting caught. My spectacular run of legal good fortune was at an end. Thanks to my own self-destructive performance, I was not going to be able to weasel out of that one.

That was the rather spectacular end of my scheme to win back Dawn with good behaviour. It was also the end of my job as a salesman and the end of my life as a dealer of PCP. I looked around for a source of income before my inevitable incarceration. I had few prospects, so when a friend offered me a chance to work on a concert venture, I accepted. The event was called Sunny Days. There had been two previous incarnations of the festival. I had attended the most recent event the previous year.

Bear in mind that, in spite of my bust, I was still using PCP regularly and still strongly in its grip, which was a state of mind that elevates things to significance beyond their actual import. In typical grandiose intent, I imagined making Sunny Days a peace festival in the grand tradition of love-ins past. One of the first people I hired was Kercules. I asked him to use his considerable artistic skills to design a beautiful poster of cosmic import. If the apartment stairs could represent the tarot, you can only imagine my concept for a festival flyer. I envisioned a Gandalf-type character with thirteen stars coming out of his wand on a background rife with other symbolic characters. I was truly on the fringe at that point, having difficulty distinguishing between the doable and the delusional. But, thanks to Kerc, I got my artwork, and I started to disseminate the posters to Toronto and surrounding towns. I was on the road once again, hitting rock venues and local radio stations across southern and central Ontario in an effort to promote the gig.

The driving trips were tedious and lonely. Left to the perilous company of my own thoughts for hours at a time, I often got onto dangerous mental tangents. One of these was a game called Over the Hill and Hope, which involved driving at an accelerated rate over a blind hill, in spite of having no idea of what or who might be in your path on the other side. It was a way of wagering with fate, as I saw it. On one occasion, I came barrelling over a country hill with enough speed to feel the car lift at the crown. Just as I grabbed that moment of air, I thought I saw someone in my path. Reflex alone kept me from rolling the car. It did not keep me from taking out eight consecutive fence posts that edged a hapless farmer's field. By the time I had shaken off the impact and surveyed my damaged grille, the farmer's cows were at the spot were the fence used to be. By the time I backed up the car and got back onto the road, the cows were on the road as well. It was time to go.

Not far down the road, I encountered a cop. He flagged me over and, pointing at the damage to my car, inquired if it was recent. Desperate to avoid more trouble, I replied that I had been in an accident and was on my way to report it. It was a good answer, because the cop knew all about the collision. He had likely been called to clear the cattle from the road. He also knew that I was the culprit—as he raised his unseen hand into view, it held my front license plate. Although he had me dead to rights, he was very fair in his assessment. He told me that, as no one was hurt, I could clear up the whole incident by making restitution with the farmer. Not wanting to see the inside of another police station, I readily agreed.

I drove to the farmhouse with the cop not far behind. I pulled the crumpled Chariot onto the farmer's property and headed down the long drive to the house. I thought briefly about my grandparents' farm and the innocent havoc we had caused there as kids. I was welcomed inside. I sat at the dining room table, with the entire family as witnesses, and apologized profusely for the damage and trouble caused. I must admit that seeing that modest, hard-working farmer surrounded by his brood put me in mind of my childhood and another crowded dinner table. I felt a further flush of shame and enquired as to how much would cover the damages. The farmer quoted a reasonable figure. I quickly wrote a cheque and departed. Of course, I bounced that cheque. But that poor farmer never brought me to task. Once again, I escaped with only my Cordoba and my karma the worse for the transgression.

Because I was away so often, my apartment was able to accommodate a houseguest, one of Plum's buddies from Scotland. Petsy was involved in importing hash and hash oil from the Far East. He had been with me for about three months, and we got along very well. During his stay, it was not unusual to have importing acquaintances of his—fellow Scots—visiting us from time to time. They'd stay until I sold whatever product they brought.

Unfortunately the last of these drop-ins did not bring pot. He had gone to Asia for Thai sticks, but his supplier had been ripped off. With time running out on his visa, he had scored the only commodity that his supplier still had on hand: heroin. He had brought it to his old pal Petsy and, in turn, to me. This was a little out of my league. I was not a heroin dealer, and believe it or not, I still had some surviving principles regarding the product I was prepared to sell. PCP was not candy, but neither was it viciously addictive. I declined to sell the heroin, but I did not decline to sample the wares. I snorted a taste and was shocked by how powerful it was. Uncut Asian smack was a rarity in my circle. I wished the seller well and headed out on the road to a radio gig in North Bay.

I wish I'd never gone. I wish I'd shown the man and his China White to the door. I wish I'd warned my friends about how pure the product was. But I didn't. I got in the car and headed for North Bay. By the time I got back, Kercules was dead.

I beat two ODs. Kercules succumbed to his first. That beautiful, talented guy had been drinking, apparently, and he had snorted the China White. The combination took his life. I'm still haunted by the thought that, had I been there, I might have stopped him. I knew the danger of combining smack with alcohol firsthand, and I knew how powerful that batch of heroin was. But I wasn't there. I was in North Bay, hyping a peace festival.

My dear friend, roommate, and former Hodad was dead. I was devastated. I had to get out of the city. I rented a cottage on Pigeon Lake near the festival site. To work through my grief over Kerc, I poured myself into the mounting of Sunny Days. We booked top local bands like Max Webster and Teenage Head over three days on the first weekend of August. The event attracted over seven thousand campers and partiers, none of whom seemed to have any affinity with the lofty goal to which Kerc's poster aspired. I envisioned three beautiful days. I got nine circles of hell. There were fights and weapons and rip-offs and bikers riding roughshod through the crowd. The festival of peace became a festival of grease. Kerc's poster was an ironic reminder, and Kerc himself was gone.

"Wait," you say. "Wasn't this 1977? Why did you expect 1967, a 'Good Vibrations' event in a 'Pretty Vacant' world?" I don't know. What I do know is that the PCP mind-set had failed me once again. So with the disaster of the festival behind us, Plum and I headed back to Toronto, completely wasted, at about three in the morning.

Part way home, the Golden Chariot caught fire. Pulling onto the side of the road, I beat the flames with my leather jacket until Plum and I collapsed in uncontrollable laughter. My Chariot was a cinder, and my parents were on the hook. We walked to a nearby motel. It was full. We slept the remainder of the night on their deck chairs, lined up like fallen soldiers at the side of the pool.

The next morning, sobered up and riding home with a friend, I felt none of the mirth of the night before. I felt beaten, as if karma had caught up with me. I went back to the apartment that was to have been my fresh start. In the following days, I gathered up my things and sold them—furniture and all—until the place was empty. Then I slipped away while the superintendent slept and showed up with only my psychological baggage on the doorstep of the Birdhouse.

CHAPTER ELEVEN
A LITTLE BIRDHOUSE IN YOUR SOUL

The Birdhouse was a condominium in Thorncliffe Park, which was, at the time, a well-heeled area of a Toronto suburb called Don Mills. It was on an upper floor of a rather impressive high-rise near the lip of the Don Valley. It boasted an inspiring view. The vista out the windows was not the origin of its name, however. Its designation as the Birdhouse came from the nickname of its owner, a guy we called Kiki Bird. Over time, his moniker was abbreviated to Kiki, partially as a timesaver but also because, in its original form, it had too many syllables for the elegantly wasted to effectively pronounce.

Kiki owned the Birdhouse. He bought it in 1970, at a time when condominium apartments were a novelty. In that era, the idea of ownership without land was preposterous. But preposterous was exactly what Kiki was. You may remember that I used my student loan to partially bank roll my drug business. Kiki used his student loan as the down payment on the Birdhouse—seventeen hundred dollars, I believe, on a seventeen thousand-dollar purchase. It was an unorthodox use of a government grant intended to further his education. But Kiki already had an income. He sold dope and had been doing so successfully since the late sixties.

Let's take a detour for a bit, partially because I welcome a break from talking about my own misdeeds, but mostly because Kiki's story is worth it. Kiki grew up in the same neighbourhood that my family chose when we moved from Peterborough. He was a seemingly normal suburban kid through the first part of the sixties; he went to school, was a Cub Scout, and played house league hockey. He was a part of the Hodad crowd. We had been friends since I had first moved to Scarborough. We got into drugs about the same time, and he was a key part of my sales network during the first cartel. He went to Centennial College at the same time that I did.

But Kiki was not like the rest of the gang. He was a real individual with a different worldview than the rest of us. When we went to college, I took up philosophy. Kiki enrolled in fashion design. Try to imagine it—Kiki was the only male in an all-girl program.

The actual decade aside, the pall of the fifties still hung over a lot of our fellow students, as it did over the education system. The women's movement had made some inroads, but the establishment did not take female aspirations as seriously as those of men. Some of the course's young women may well have been destined for a future in fashion. But for many, the program was essentially home economics for the sartorially inclined. It's not uncommon, even now, for adolescents to enrol in courses for superfluous reasons, like studying art because you love to draw horses or taking drama because you're too flighty for bookkeeping. The administration knows that, but they're content to offer the classes and hope that something sticks. But it remains true that, in those days, a community college fashion course was designed as post-secondary education for girls who couldn't type.

Into all of this walked Kiki. He was male, yes, but he lived fashion and actually designed and sewed his own wardrobe. He had his boots custom-made to his specifications and had, at one time, owned an interest in a hip, downtown, boot shop. He wore frilly shirts and vests to the most modest of occasions. He switched to women's panties because they cut a better silhouette under his skin-tight satin pants. He was the real thing as far as his affinity for the apparel business was concerned. That, ironically, contributed to his status as an outsider. By his own account, the girls in his class hated him. He did little to court their affections.

On an overnight class excursion to Montreal, Kiki took it upon himself to run from room to room, dousing his female classmates with the contents of a fire extinguisher. When management intervened, he ran to his own room, locked the door, and launched the extinguisher out his seventh-floor window. He was immensely unpopular that day. He was also immensely high.

The Freudian implications of the fire extinguisher incident aside, there was much speculation within my crowd about Kiki's sexual orientation. We had the donning of girl's underwear on the one hand. But he had Playboy magazines in his apartment on the other, and you don't buy those to admire what the women are wearing. None of us knew whether or not he was gay, but there was little doubt that he was odd.

Odd was cool with us. The sixties were morphing into the seventies, and substances were being consumed copiously. Odd was actually more than acceptable; it was attractive. But Kiki really spun off the yellow brick road. Over time, he became the wizard of odd. He did strange things and spoke in a cartoon voice and made the rest of us, in our rock magazine threads, look like we were from the Sears catalogue by comparison.

Some of that served him well. Back when he distributed for the first cartel, his prime territory was the local plaza. He stood out like a well-lit store. Kiki was a walking kiosk—easy to spot and convenient to frequent. He was a bright guy, and his caricature approach made him efficient in dealing with customers; he was memorable but impenetrable. He was always good with money and, with the assistance of our accommodating government, the first homeowner in our crowd. The real secret of Kiki's success was his willingness to supply customers large and small. He would sell to anybody at any time. You knew where to find him, and he was always open.

So was the Birdhouse. Kiki lived in the midst of the straight world in his very own rectangle of strange. His condo was a remarkable collage of comic books and mail-order bric-a-brac. He had collector plates from the Franklin Mint and plaques with little swords on them and a miniature porcelain carousel, the horses for which arrived every month by mail. Additionally, Kiki collected old, eight-millimetre films and ancient vinyl records. Some of the more valuable artifacts in the Birdhouse had left upscale stores like the Art Shoppe and DeBoers without the benefit of a cash transaction. Kiki had acquired them from his customers in exchange for drugs, at far less than their actual value.

The surreal decor only added to the chaos. There were people in and out of the Birdhouse all the time. They were all treated equally or equally strangely. Many times when I visited the Birdhouse, he would stall a customer waiting for a pound while he haggled over five dollars with a guy buying a gram. Kiki's secret was markup; the smaller transactions yielded the biggest profit. That kind of thinking made him rich. And at least the customers had something to gawk at while they waited.

As time went on, Kiki was giving them more and more to look at. He was, like me, a devout disciple of the PCP we were peddling. A friend of mine visiting the Birdhouse to buy a gram was asked by Kiki to wait while he went to his stash. Due to the legal problems we all faced, Kiki had a policy of keeping his product in the storage locker located in the basement of the condo. He also had a policy of partaking of the product on each visit to the stockroom. I can't say for certain how many trips he'd made that particular day, but twenty minutes after his departure, he appeared at his own door with my friend's gram in hand. He was stark naked. He completed the transaction in that state. It certainly eliminated any haggling over price. Gram in hand, my friend departed with haste. In the calm of the elevator, he tried to imagine the reaction of anyone who might have been making a similar trip when Kiki had made his unclothed journey up.

That story made the rounds rather quickly, as you might imagine. The next time I saw Kiki, I asked him why he might do such a thing. He answered, quite simply, "Don't worry, I voted for Trudeau." I'm not certain if he meant that, as a supporter of our prime minister, he had a protector in high places or if it was his way of saying that he was liberal-minded (for those not familiar with Canadian politics, my apologies). Either way, the meaning of his reply eludes me still. Mind you, as the guy who told an inquiring cop that my half-pound of illegal PCP was "the truth," I have some inkling of the psychic state that inspired him.

Kiki was larger than life, but he was not big enough to elude the law. The very nature of his MO, in or out of his handmade duds, was a recipe for arrest. A permanent address with an open door policy, a varied customer base, and documented eccentric behaviour is a virtual bust beacon. And busted he was. In September of 1977, I was homeless, and Kiki was about to call a government facility home. He offered me a chance to move into his nest, rent-free, if I would take care of the place.

Taking care of the place involved touching nothing. Kiki was totally obsessive-compulsive about his stuff. If you did pick up one of his curios for inspection, you had to put it back *exactly* where you had found it. That was not as hard as it sounded, because each and every treasure had a laser-precise footprint in the Birdhouse dust. I said he was obsessive-compulsive; I didn't say he was good housekeeper.

My other key duty in living rent-free was to feed Kiki's tropical fish. Those things were humongous and very close to Kiki's heart. He took some pride in the size to which they had grown. His pride was of sufficient intensity that, when one of his finny friends died, he would pickle them in formaldehyde and put them in a jar. He kept those jars in a hall closet, should the need arise to authenticate the size to which they had grown. Frequent visitors were vigilant in ensuring that the topic never arose.

So with Kiki shuffled off to a government fishbowl, I was the interim lord of the Birdhouse and defender of the fish. Some of you with sharp memories will remember my exploits on the ancestral farm, with the chickens, the cows, and the pigs. Those with less efficient recall might remember my last encounter with the animal world, which left Old Macdonald's milk-makers all over a central Ontario thoroughfare. For those with such excellent powers of absorption as to remember *both* examples of my skill with God's nonbipeds, I will answer the question likely to stem from the task that Kiki set me: Every one of the goddamned fish was dead in a week.

Like Kiki's gill breathers, my stay at the Birdhouse after his departure was brief. I stayed only long enough to neglect the fish and to empty Kiki's freezer of every edible morsel. By the spring of 1978, I was back in a townhouse with Stewball. After growing up amongst seven siblings and living for years with Kercules or Plum or my brothers or someone, I found living alone excruciating. Stew's wife apparently felt the same about living with him, so Stewball and I were flatmates again.

But prison was on the horizon. I knew going in to the trial that David Newman's best efforts would not end in the case's dismissal. I had delivered myself directly into the hands of the law, wrapped like a birthday gift. I would have added a great big bow had I not been too high to tie a knot. On September 8, 1978, I was sentenced to two years less a day. That was the same day that Keith Moon died, which was of huge transcendental import to me in my PCP-addled state of the time, although I was not a gifted drummer and had never driven a vehicle into a swimming pool. I saw both Keith Moon and I cradled in the palm of destiny. The mystical significance then seems like mere coincidence to me now.

I'm not going to regale you with pages of prison wisdom. If you need it, treat yourself and rent *Shawshank Redemption.* I was assigned to a medium security prison in Guelph, the home of my momentary Alma Mater. It is true that I lasted longer at Guelph, the prison, than at Guelph, the university, but that, of course was not by choice. I spent the first few months making picnic tables that were to be used for the provincial government parks as well as at a new institution closer to home, the Toronto East Correctional Center. Just after my first Christmas behind bars, I got a new job as the assistant editor of the *Insider*, the joint's newspaper. After a few months, I became the editor. Good behaviour, you surmise? Superior journalistic skills, you ask? Nah, the real editor got released.

The position of editor was a good gig. In order to compile the news, I had a pass to go virtually anywhere in the prison. I made and regularly visited friends throughout the compound. I knew how to play bridge, and that became a great way to pass the time and meet some very interesting people. In the beigest parts of suburbia where I grew up, bridge was a game played by groups of parents in recreation rooms furnished with upright pianos and souvenir sombreros. I had picked up the game, not from my parents, who were more the square dancing type, but in the college common room. But the guys I was playing with had learned the game in the penitentiary. I marvelled at how far removed those games were from either the college crowd or the chip-and-dip set. The card skill of the prison guys could trump the best in either group—imagine how good you could get with little else to do all day. There I was, playing friendly games with the heaviest guys in the joint. All that and a chance to break free of my dead-end, sell-and-snort drug cycle.

My "bit," as we cons say, went by pretty quickly. Soon I was up for parole. I was also clean and sober for the first time in a long while. I foresaw smooth sailing: I was twenty-eight and a recent college graduate, and that was the first conviction of my life.

The waters were somewhat rougher than I anticipated. The first thing a member of the three-person parole board said to me was, "Well, Mr. McCarthy, you have been a pretty lucky guy."

Now, if you look back over the story thus far, his point is hard to refute. Bear in mind, too, that you know more details of my history than he did. He was referring to arrests for which I had been acquitted; unreported car accidents, lease violations, bounced cheques, and overdoses do not show up in the parole file. But at the time, I'll admit, I was taken aback.

"Well, I don't know about that. I'm *here,*" I said.

He pressed his point. "Well, let me refresh your memory." Then he recited the list: "1970: a pound of marijuana; absolute discharge. 1972: possession of a substance held out to be THC; dismissed; 1973: possession of marijuana; dismissed." He ran the whole rogue's role call, including that table leg thing from Keswick.

"I repeat, mister: you have been a very lucky guy."

I hesitated. I fumbled. I babbled something about the charges he had catalogued having been dismissed.

I had barely sputtered out the words when he said, "But where there is smoke, there is fire."

And that's when it came to me. With eight months of freedom on the line, I realized that, for all of David Newman's good work, I hadn't actually gotten away with *anything.* It may have taken a while, but I was finally being held accountable.

The parole board sent me out in the hall while they deliberated. It was a very long twenty minutes before I heard their decision. I had a good record inside, in spite of the obvious pattern of activities prior to incarceration, and it *was* my first conviction. In the end, they recommended that I serve a few more weeks of my sentence before being granted parole. But the lesson of the dismissed charges being taken into account in my reckoning was not lost. I was, like the man said, a very lucky guy.

But I wasn't free yet. Ten days before my release, the Guelph facility experienced the biggest inmate insurrection in the facility's history. It all started with some home brew made from potato peelings fermented in an emptied fire extinguisher. When it was time to go back to the cells, the surreptitious revellers declined. They decided that the schedule should change.

That is not how the joint works. There are rules. They are hard to change, and a bunch of pissed-up inmates are not going to do it at eleven o'clock at night. One after the other, the dorms and cellblocks went up in riot. There were fires and the breaking of furniture and general madness throughout. I was the inmate liaison committee representative for my floor; my peers turned to me to decide if we were going to join the riot. It was a tough call, as about a third of the joint was already up in smoke. I convinced my fellow inmates to wait. If the main floor that housed the president of our committee went up, then we would have to go. A mere ten days from release, I did not want any part of it. To paraphrase my probation board assessor, if there was fire, I was smoked.

The main floor did not go. My parole was safe, but the relief was short-lived. After about an hour, I witnessed one of the most appalling displays of human revenge I have ever seen—not from the inmates but from the guards. Fortified with outside police divisions, they marched through the halls in full riot gear, banging in unison on their shields. The rioting cellblock inmates were forced out of the common areas and back into their cells with high-pressure hoses. They were drenched and left like that for three days. They were the lucky ones. The inmates from dorms were escorted down to a "group hole" in the basement and doused with the hoses; the water was up to their knees. They, too, were left for days. They were given buckets for toilets and fed sandwiches that they had to eat where they stood. By the third day, the water was strewn with an armada of feces, litter, and uneaten food.

Only the unrelenting determination of the press to report the inmates' condition got the situation changed. In crediting the press,

I do not include myself; as of the riot, all of my editorial privileges were revoked, and I never wrote for the *Insider* again. The riot did not affect the timing of my release, but many inmates were still in the hole when I was freed ten days later.

Upon release, I was back with Stewball. I was grateful to be staying with him again. I was grateful, as well, to my cartel buddy, who had pulled my mates together and collected three thousand dollars to get me on my feet. Sadly, the list of friends who contributed did not include Plum. My Scottish roommate had overdosed in Damascus on the way to Thailand—dead on the way to his next big deal.

Having parted ways with me after the night of the flaming Cordoba, Plum had returned to Scotland to set up his next deal. He had been heading to Australia, but it was not a direct flight. The first stop was Damascus, and I'm told that his two Australian partners joined him on the plane. The ensuing flight was fuelled and propelled by Chivas Regal and mandrakes, a hypnotic sedative. Both were Plum favourites. As they disembarked from the pristine climate control of the plane onto the Damascus tarmac, 110 degrees of Fahrenheit hit them like microwaves hit chocolate. All three collapsed on the airfield. They were taken to hospital. The two Australians came around, but Plum never regained consciousness. Another good friend was gone. So how did I respond to the substance death of my second old roommate? By drinking with my new one.

When my friends had presented me with three thousand dollars upon my release from Guelph, their intent had been to keep me afloat. I used it to keep me floating. Stewball and I started every day with the crucial question, "What's it to be? A bottle or a box?" Our big decision was the choice between a forty-ouncer of vodka or a twenty-four case of beer. Sometimes, for variety, we'd pick up a mickey and down all twelve ounces between us behind the liquor store where we'd made our purchase. I'm not sure why. It might have been denial but it was more likely a penance for the frozen adolescence that was all Kerc and Plum would ever have.

Chapter Twelve
A Well-Respected Man

New Year's resolutions are part of our culture. Most people make them. Fewer people keep them. Somewhere, there is a landfill full of diet books, workout videos, and exercise machines to confirm this truth. I came very close to joining the ranks of the promise breakers. As of February 3, 1980, I was still pissing away the days with Stewball in a bottle-or-a-box torpor. On the morning of the fourth, I made my move. I roused Stewball to chauffeur me to the Manpower office.

Manpower, as the quaint prepolitical correctness of its name indicates, was an organization designed to put Canada's unemployed to work. Every day, jobs were posted to a large display. Each job had its own little card. I gamely read all the little cards. There were no openings for drug dealers, rock promoters, car destroyers, check bouncers, or drunks, but I was undaunted. I was determined to make a fresh start. One of the cards offered an opening with a managerial training program. God knows, I needed training; as far as the job market was concerned, I was barely housebroken. I was also terrified. I took the card and went to see one of the counsellors. The guy scared the crap out of me. Sure, he was just a regular guy doing his job, but that's what scared me. I had no experience with that guy's world and I understood the power he wielded over my future. For that reason, he was more daunting than any convict with whom I had shared a table. And he did not play bridge.

My fear was unfounded; he was gentle. He explained that Woolco, the company offering the training, was a part of the F. W. Woolworth Company, an old and well-regarded retailer. As a kid, I had frequented the Woolworth's in Peterborough. The counsellor said that the programme being offered was a good one and that all of their managers, regardless of their education, were required to take the training. I said that I wanted to be a part of it. The counsellor paused. Then he looked down for a moment and said, "There's one more thing." I asked what it was, and rather sheepishly, he pushed forward the job profile sheet. Without uttering a word, he pointed to the compensation. The salary was $3.75 an hour.

Let's pause for a moment. The counsellor certainly did, and I followed suit. I know that that salary seems outrageous in light of our contemporary minimum wage. But, given that I couldn't and still cannot see into the future, that's not why I paused. I paused because the half-pound of PCP that I had virtually given to the cops in my dusted, prebusted state had cost me three thousand dollars. Three thousand unrecouped dollars of my own coin, mind you. Had I been inclined to make this purchase from the wage I was being offered, I would have had to work retail for eight hundred hours. That's about five months under fluorescent light, wearing a clip-on tie. That was the cause of my pause. I had to do something, and I did.

I said, "I'll take it." I was on the straight and narrow and Woolco bound.

How did it feel? It felt good. As a trainee, I was acquiring applicable skills, encompassing every aspect of retail from the receiving dock to the ring of the register. From time to time, I even ventured into the parking lot to determine the status of the shopping carts. I was learning to be a manager of floor space, of goods, and of people. I felt a sense of pride in what I was doing and in the environment that was giving me the chance. But it didn't take long to put the tenuous nature of my position to the test.

About two weeks after starting at the company, I was summoned to the head office. I thought that that was it, my unrevealed criminal record had come to the company's attention. I headed off to face the music. When I arrived, I was ushered into a managerial office. The stern gentleman behind the desk had an open folder in front of him. The folder was my file. He shuffled the papers briefly and, lifting a page, said, "Mr. McCarthy, it has come to our attention ... "

Let me stop it there, simply to note that, once again, I felt the hand of fate. Once again, I heard the ominous voice in my head that had wailed "Confess!" when the cop had caught me running down the hill with the half-pound of PCP. But this time was different. There was no PCP, neither under my coat nor in my bloodstream. This time, with the mighty power of sobriety, I resisted the powerful temptation to fuck myself. With temple-pulsing restraint, I let the man finish his sentence.

"Mr. McCarthy, it has come to our attention that you have a community college degree. Can you confirm that this is the case?"

"Yes," I said eloquently. That kind of confession I could handle.

"Well," he said, "As that is the case, I can, by company policy, raise your trainee wage from three dollars and seventy-five cents to four dollars and fifty cents per hour. Congratulations. Of course, I will have to see the diploma."

And see it he did—the three-year diploma that took six years to acquire. Six years had just brought me seventy-five cents per hour. I told you there'd be math.

As a newly flush, college-graduate trainee, my first store assignment was in Agincourt, a part of Scarborough that was not very far from my old running grounds. I had been on the job for about six months when I spotted a familiar face coming up the centre aisle. It was my first love, the girl who had dumped me for my drummer. To be honest, I was not sure what to do. I still had feelings for that girl and, in the past, had misspent much energy trying to impress her. If that mighty effort had failed, what would she think of me now, on beige linoleum, beside a dump bin of paperbacks? I recalled the snickering of my first bandmates at the nature of my father's job. I felt a primordial shiver, followed by a shrill impulse to make a run for it. But I could not run. She had seen me. I considered pretending to be a fellow shopper, before imagining a nightmarish PA page, summoning me by name to the antifreeze aisle with a mop. I made a snap decision. Uncharacteristically, I decided to face her and, even more unlikely, to tell the truth.

She was wonderful and very supportive, congratulating me on the direction that I had chosen. That was my first test of the old meeting the new, and those few sentences of encouragement and approval meant a great deal. As I reflect on them now, it occurs to me that they also reflect the degree to which my direction had been out of step with those to whose company I aspired. But nothing this reflective occurred to me at the time.

I may have basked in my old flame's company, but the companionship of some others had become tiresome. Less than a week into the job, I had a blowout with Stewball. Over some minor matter, as I recall, he threw a fit. I, in turn, threw a punch. When I returned from work the next evening, the locks had been changed. Given the lifestyle that we shared, Stewball had done me and my prospects at Woolco a service.

I was not room mate-free for long. I hooked up with Buzzy, an old Peterborough chum, and another Peterborough native named Shoolong. Shoolong was a road manager for Frank Soda, one of the local headliners from Sunny Days. Buzzy was a minor coke dealer and a major womanizer. Those were my roommates for my journey down the straight and narrow. Boy, could I pick 'em.

We moved into a three-bedroom house in the Beaches area of Toronto. For all my good intentions, it was party central in no time. But, as a young man with retail aspirations, I rose every morning, got in my car, and went to work, regardless of the sins of the night before. **Still,** the sins were catching up. I was getting to work every day, but some mornings I'd open the store only to hide in the stockroom till I felt capable of interacting with humans. It was not completely unnoticed by my coworkers. One very early Monday, I arrived at Woolco, accompanied by a crushing hangover.

One of my coworkers said, "Big night last night!" It was an assertion, not a question.

"Do I look it?" I asked.

"Come on," he said. "If you opened your eyes, you'd bleed to death."

Bloodshot peepers aside, I was committed to my double life of raunch and responsibility and doing a passably good job of both. It was the commute between the two that was messing me up. To be blunt, I was driving when I should not have been driving.

One night, coming back from a concert in Peterborough, I was tired enough to consider shots from the bottle a prudent way to combat sleep. I was also speeding, or so the officer told me when she pulled me over. I took a Breathalyzer, and as we say in the impaired club, I blew over the limit. I was resigned to my fate until she insisted on putting me in cuffs. Bear in mind that, in 1980, a female officer was a rarity, and a solo female officer taking precautions while arresting a drunken male was a prudent course from her perspective—but not from mine. I lost it, ranting about her, her methods, and I'm ashamed to say, the unsuitability of her gender for the job at hand. I was lacerating and loud, blending vodka volume with the righteousness of the ripped. I was living justification for the cuffs that so offended me.

Once we got to the station, it was interesting to note that my inexcusable verbal abuse of the woman did not earn me the wrath of her male peers. Quite the opposite was the case. Beyond the smiles and snickers, they said nothing and even went so far as to offer me a lift home. It occurs to me now that, as a police officer, I was not the only kind of challenge that woman had to face.

Possibly in the spirit of my newly minted stab at respectability, I did not fight the charge. I pled guilty and was given a six-month suspension of my license. I accepted my conviction with dignity and humility. Then I drove myself home. I drove every day of that six-month suspension with no lesson learned. That is why, one year later, I was back in the same humiliating situation..

I completed my training in Agincourt and was assigned to another store at Yonge and Steeles. There, I met a girl who worked in personnel. We began to see each other. The relationship was developing sufficient seriousness on her part that she invited me to dinner with the parents. I went, hobbled by the combination of natural nervousness and my concern that the girl had more invested in the relationship than I felt it warranted. The combination led to disaster.

I got drunk at dinner with the parents, and—double disaster—I got pulled over on the way home.

Because of the proximity of that charge to the last conviction, I knew that it was a much more serious situation and that I was likely facing more jail time. I did not waste my lawyer's time and my money on an elaborate defence. I pled guilty and hoped for the best. I was very fortunate to receive only eight days in jail and a one-year license suspension. That time, I was determined to respect the sentence, and I did. I served the eight days on a combination of vacation days and weekends, so I never had to tell anyone at Woolco. As for the license part, I never drove a single day of the second suspension.

But the Beaches house was a long way from work. I was an assistant manager, a keen and ambitious employee—once sobered up from the night before. As such, I often worked from opening in the morning to closing at night. The prospect of the early hours and late nights on the subway and streetcar combination was weighing on me. Then, my girl asked me to move in with her. It was my first time living with a woman. For her, it was love. For me, it was a drive to work and a wait-and-see on the rest. It was my first real attempt at what I saw as the straight life. I had a real job, a bright future, and a live-in mate. I was behaving the way I thought normal people behaved, being good, socializing on the barbecue circuit, and trying to fall in love. I really tried. All told, I waited-and-saw for over a year.

Then, in January of 1984, I was promoted to divisional manager, a salaried position in charge of one of the three sections that comprised every store. I was given all the codes and the keys and responsibility for opening and closing the store. And what a store! I was assigned to the newly renovated, showcase store in Whitby, just east of Toronto. I was on my way.

So was my girl. Not long after I left the Yonge and Steeles store, she left me—for the manager of the store I had departed. But I had my division; I had my license restored; and I had my next car, a Camaro, for which my girl cosigned before she left me. Thanks, darlin'.

I loved working in Whitby, and I started thinking about moving closer to work. My boss at head office heard of my plans and offered me a financial incentive to take a divisional manager job at another store in Toronto. That was kind of a curveball. Honeydale was an older store in a rundown mall. But it was close to my apartment, the money was inviting, and the prospect of turning down my boss was not. Ambitious and determined to make my mark, I accepted the position at Honeydale.

Honeydale was no showcase. It was badly in need of refixturing, and it was faltering in the face of competition from a newer, cleaner, more attractive mall just across the street. I worked my butt off, but we missed our targets nonetheless. The store did not need me; it needed a saviour or at least a magician. If you've read this far, you know that I'm not Houdini, and I'm certainly not Jesus. What I was, though, was discouraged. I had given my best, but I felt my career dream fading. My store was doomed, and there were whispers about the state of the company as well. I started looking elsewhere.

Actually, I did more than look. In 1988, I made a flying leap into the unknown and put a down payment on a stretch limousine. That was August. By October, I had bought another. Three weeks later, Honeydale looked up, and I was gone.

When my mother heard that I had left Woolco, she cried. If only I'd had that much foresight.

Chapter Thirteen
Let the Good Times Roll

Okay, I jumped some juicy details. How could a Woolco employee afford to buy two stretch limos? Woolco pay cheques did not fund the limousine acquisition. Weed did. Did I neglect to mention that? I suppose I did. I think it's time to rewind and dig into the details. Because in those very events are the seeds of my ultimate undoing.

In the fall of 1985, after roughly nine uphill months at the Honeydale store, Buzzy from the Beaches unearthed an enticing connection for Mexican pot. He sought my expertise and my partnership. I accepted. Retail professional *and* cannabis importer both? The combination was not as strange as it would first appear. My journey and the culture were moving in parallel. By the mid-eighties, driven by the baby boomers among us, society was starting to blend elements of the so-called counterculture into the grind of daily living. In many households, well-heeled or otherwise, you bought a home, you bought a car, you brought home the groceries, and you brought home a dime bag. Weed was slowly but surely replacing the martini culture of a previous generation.

For media proof, I offer the movie *Poltergeist*. He sells homes in a suburban estate. She's a housewife. In the evenings, with the swimming pool construction crew gone and the kids safely in bed, they retire to their bedroom. And they smoke a joint. That movie, produced by pop culture guru Steven Spielberg, came out in 1982.

I'm telling you, pot and traditional society were not strangers in 1985. Buzzy, the very man who brought me the pot opportunity, was apprenticing as a stockbroker. Having difficulty imagining a stockbroker on drugs? I'm not, because I didn't know many who weren't. Plenty of them were buying from Buzzy.

Buzzy's business was cocaine. His powder came through a guy his friend Dutchie knew—a guy in Mexico named Pedro. Pedro's connections were, in turn, sourcing the coke from Columbia, but they also had a local sideline in high-grade, seedless Mexican pot: *sensemilla*. The quality of the product was unusual; grass of that calibre was usually Asian like Thai sticks or Jamaican like lamb's breath.

It was not *largesse* that moved Buzzy and his partner Dutchie to share their Mexican pot connection. Neither of them had the kind of distribution network required to move the quantity of marijuana involved. That's why they came to me. I was a little rusty, but I knew whom to connect with whom. My first stop was Shadow, a guy who had a cartel of his own that had recently encountered setbacks when his shipment had been hijacked. I knew he was looking for alternative sourcing. He was the jump-start that we needed. We asked for his help, and Shadow was in.

The first lot available to us was a single bale, which weighed in at thirty pounds. We took the bale to an industrial unit at the north end of Toronto, used for the storage of theatrical props and lighting. As soon as we cracked that bale open, I knew that we were onto something. The moment the air hit the pot, the pot hit back. It gave off a thick, skunk-like aroma that snaked around that warehouse like a ghost with a fresh house to haunt. We danced with the aroma for a few moments and dug in. The product had very few seeds, and the buds were full and long, an exotic, flared variety, known rather indelicately as "wife beaters." We bagged our bale into half pounds. Not long into the process, the scent of the product gave way to the smell of serious money.

Calculators ready? Here we go: Dutchie needed fifteen hundred a pound to make things work at his end. I figured that, in order to take care of Buzzy and I and the guy who lent us the prop warehouse, I had to get seventeen hundred. I approached Shadow and made him the offer. It was quite a jump from the Columbian numbers to which Shadow was accustomed; that stuff came in around a thousand per pound. But, by virtue of the limited quantities available, this was more retail than wholesale, and his days as a major wholesaler were over. I knew a lot of the players myself, but I was still pulling manager's hours at Woolco, and Shadow was short a supplier. I thought that he would jump at the chance.

He didn't jump so much as shuffle. Thirty pounds was a mere fraction of his former volume, and our product was too pricey by his standards. He had come in as a favour to me, but the partnership was not to last. Shadow was used to running the show, but it was Dutchie's connection, and for that reason, Dutch had the right to the top spot. My days with King Ferd had taught me that top dog is also top target. I didn't care whose ass was in the big chair, as long as I saw a sufficient quantity of money and adventure. There aren't many thrills in the Woolco staff meeting.

But we put aside the initial friction and pushed that first deal through. Our conduit just south of the Canadian border was Buffalo Bill. Bill was mighty impressed with the rate at which the product moved and the accuracy with which the money was paid. Within a week we had another thirty pounds, and we repeated the process. The shipment had the same benefits and the same drawback. Shadow was not happy about the price, and he and Dutchie were tussling for position again. At Woolco, if there's a spill in your section—manager or not—you man the mop. Putting my retail experience to work, I decided that I would have to step in.

It was only thirty pounds coming up every couple of weeks— chicken weed by Shadow's standard—and everybody was weary of the friction. I asked Shadow to step back. Then I called up every old connection I could trust and got them excited about the product.

One of my first calls was to the legendary Kiki. He had his eccentricities, but he also had money, and as they said at Woolco, "sales hide sins" (and you wonder why I lasted so long!). Kiki still did business out of the Birdhouse. He was only too happy to pick up five pounds, stash it in the storage locker, and dole it out, as required—clothing optional. Yes, he still transacted by the gram or by the pound, whatever the customer could bear. At the Birdhouse, the customer was always right.

Not long after I took full control of distribution, Kiki's buying habits changed. Instead of his regular five pounds, he began asking for ten pounds and then twenty. I had known Kiki for a long time, but his recent fondness for freebase had me concerned that he could not be relied upon to pay for quantities of that size within the two-week cycle that was our standard business practice. He hadn't stiffed me yet, but he was taking way more product than his small customer volume could bear. He was paying in small bills as well, suggesting that his transaction style had not changed.

In the interest of our friendship and my own skin, I demanded to know where the quantity of product was going. Kiki explained that it was going to one man, a large fellow who reminded us of Sydney Greenstreet, if that great actor were less fastidious with a razor. I remembered the gentleman from a previous Birdhouse visit. We had come to call him the Fat Man, originally for his physical size but eventually for his wallet. Kiki believed that the Fat Man was good for the money, but I was still uncomfortable. Why was he buying large quantities in small bills? Our dealers' code gave me no right to approach the Fat Man directly. So I waited and kept my eye on the situation. I did not have long to wait. Kiki was unravelling, and he found himself owing me money with no means of payment. That seemed like a problem, but I saw that it was not. I offered Kiki a way out of his predicament. I offered to buy the Fat Man.

That worked on many levels. Kiki was free of his debt, I was free of a credit risk, and the Fat Man was buying direct—a situation warranted by his volume anyway. So for the princely sum of thirty-eight hundred dollars, the Fat Man became a direct distributor for the cartel. He told me that most of his stock went north of the city, so he was not infringing on current territory. It was a good move.

Once I knew him a bit better, I quenched my curiosity and asked about the small bills. I asked him why, even on forty thousand dollars of merchandise, he paid only in small bills. He smiled and said that Kiki's quantities were not big enough to get into his large stash. Apparently, the Fat Man had almost a million dollars in fifties and hundreds, buried in a fishing rod tube somewhere on his distribution route. He said it would take a mighty big deal to have him go to the trouble of exhuming the tube and fishing out the big bills.

It took me a few years, but I did eventually see some of the Fat Man's buried treasure. But for now, an investment of thirty-eight hundred dollars had eliminated a major headache. The Fat Man often told me that he was the biggest bargain of my life. He was right.

Few of my associates were as exotic as the Fat Man, but there were plenty of others—guys as well as girls, working street level from Toronto to Belleville and beyond as the business grew. Among them was a guy called English. He was an associate of Shadow. Unlike Shadow, however, English was not thrifty with his earnings. He lived large and spent large. He loved Manchester United and had been known to follow them around the world. He drove a Lincoln and told time by Rolex.

I knew English before Shadow had worked with him, so I was free to engage him without the obligation of a user's fee to Shadow— so says the strict code of contraband to which we adhered. English serviced downtown Toronto and was one of my top distributors from the start of the new cartel. Other associates covered eastern Ontario and northern Ontario, as well as Scarborough and the Beaches, but English was the most serious earner among them.

By 1986, I had taken the reigns of the operation. By spring of that year, we were taking delivery of thirty pounds every two weeks. I had been using my employee discount at Woolco to buy suitcases for the pot deliveries, until one day when I heard a conversation about how we had the most successful luggage department in the country. I decided that prudence was in order, and we switched to cardboard cartons that we ordered from an industrial supplier twelve dozen at a time. The volume elevated nary an eyebrow in an industrial context, although I doubt that too many other customers were paying in cash. The boxes held ten half-pound bags, and by the summer of 1986, we were shifting about 120 pounds a month. Buffalo Bill sent up two roughly thirty-pound bales every load, and we got a delivery every second week. That gave me enough time to box 'em, distribute 'em, and collect the money.

And oh, baby, did I have money. I was still living in a rent-controlled apartment in the west end—easily the richest person on the block. I bought a stereo. Ten thousand dollars later, I was the loudest person on the block as well. I bought an extensive array of patio furniture and the best barbecue that I could find. My pond was small, but this fish was loud, comfortably seated, and well fed.

At that point, I was making about forty thousand a year at Woolco and about ten thousand a month tax-free from my extracurricular activity. Times were good. It was hard to maintain perspective and discipline at Woolco. I was making more than the store manager, even before I cashed my pay cheque. I was earning big and spending bigger.

My next splash out was one of the dumbest expenditures of my life—bigger than a barbecue, slower than a TransAm, and heavier than the realization that Dawn was gone. It would have been better to let Mohammed Ali blacken one of my eyes while I offered Mike Tyson the other. But instead, I bought a couple of limousines.

Chapter Fourteen
I'm in Love for the Third Time

When you are graced with disposable income, your first indulgence is usually for personal comfort. I was textbook here. I indulged in regular and expensive vacations, for instance. But vacations are vapour; the moment you step back into the terminal, your very arrival erases them from everything but memory. We all try to fight this with souvenirs and snapshots and hideous approximations of local apparel. But soon enough, the mementoes are dusty, the ill-advised outfits remain unworn, and nobody wants to see the photos anymore, assuming that they ever did.

There are other personal comforts, of course—other things larger than holiday mementoes. Although things like my monster stereo or my barbecue and my patio furniture are fine, they too have their limitations. That stuff all stays hidden inside the house or behind the backyard fence. It only announces your station to the small group of people you invite across your doorstep. In my line of work, that group was smaller than most.

Another way of manifesting the disposable part of disposable income is to hit the town. You can splurge on drink and drugs, food and drink, entertainment and drink, or just plain drink. And I did. But if vacations are vapour, immoderate nights on the town wind down to something even less appealing. I will assume your familiarity with the biological and physical by-products of those pursuits and will spare you their mention here.

So, what next? At that stage of the consumption cycle, the ordinary nouveau riche soul buys real estate and cars. Both are substantial expenditures, but they're also conspicuous ones. For most, that is the intent: to show your wealth. But for someone in my position, the very source of my wealth dictated that undue attention should not be invited. I drove a nice car, but I bought it used. I had a house full of great stuff but lived unassumingly in a neighbourhood most would vacate as soon as was financially feasible.

So the limousines were perfect. They were huge, ostentatious head turners, but here's the trick: they were also a business. Everyone who throws around major cash while averting the attention of the cop and the taxman has to be able to point to a source of that income. If that source has asymmetrical revenue in the form of hours booked and tips received, you're less likely to attract attention for living a cash-fuelled lifestyle. That's why the limos were perfect. The reasons why they were less than perfect will soon become evident.

So I had the vehicles, and with my partners (there are always partners, right?), I had a business. I also had eight years of classic management training in the employ of one of the continent's longest-standing merchants. Last, and far from least, I had $140,000 of rolling stock. I proceeded to get an office, determined to run this thing in a professional manner. I sublet part of a west end industrial unit that Dutchie was using for his straight enterprise, a fire retardant company. So I guess I didn't have to worry about the place burning to the ground, but by the end, I might have welcomed it. Those were early, optimistic days for my partners and me.

One of those partners was Buzzy from the Beaches. He was still on the pot payroll as a thank-you for the original import connection—possibly the world's most generous and longest-running finder's fee. I told him that he was expected to show up at the office and put in some effort. With his cash cow at risk, he agreed. We called our enterprise Moonlight Limousines. It's okay; I'll give you a moment to savour the irony. Just before New Year's, we were ready to roll.

We had no sooner begun than a deal arose on a third vehicle, a calling card limousine built to order. It had been built in Canada but delivered to the United States to promote the manufacturer's wares south of the border. It was a stretch Chevy Caprice classic, and it was dressed to the nines. It had every conceivable feature of the day, including a bomb detector. Not a sought-after option in Canada, I grant you, but that thing had been built for Chicago, where your client pool might well include Bad, Bad Leroy Brown. Of more interest to Canadian aficionados of excess were the spoke wheels, continental trunk, leather upholstery, console bar, TV/VCR/CD player, and moonroof. Whether it was a Molotov cocktail-proof moonroof was never specified.

The sales company had not met with the success they had expected, so it was up for grabs for forty thousand American dollars. We certainly did not need another car; wedding season was over, and proms and graduations were months away, but the deal was too good to resist. We offered no resistance whatsoever. Perhaps we should have. When time came to bring our purchase across the border, we found that we owed the Canadian government import duties of ten thousand dollars and sales tax to boot. After the financing charges and exchange rate were tallied, our purchase came to sixty thousand dollars Canadian, less than it was worth but also less of a bargain than it had originally seemed. So there we were, in the doldrums of January, with a 30 percent increase in monthly payments. Without the underground spring of cartel cash, our business would have died of thirst. What was a legitimate businessman to do? Easy answer: Buzzy and I grabbed a flight to Las Vegas.

Don't take us to task. Our destination was a limousine convention, and we actually went to the show floor. There were astonishing vehicles on display, from a stretch Lamborghini to a Lincoln with a hot tub. Great for a moonlighting coke dealer, maybe, but way beyond our marijuana means. Then again, maybe you should take us to task. The sales rep of a major manufacturer at the show offered us an excursion to a spot of local interest. In short order, we were in a limo on the way to the Chicken Ranch.

The Chicken Ranch had been formerly located in Texas. It's the titular establishment in a Dolly Parton movie you may want to pretend you've never seen. You know, with the cheerful, apple-cheeked whores and Burt Reynolds grinning like he thought his career would survive the film. You may ask why I would relate a story this crass and unflattering, being the refined soul that I am? This embarrassing adventure was the source of personal revelation for me.

When you arrive at the Chicken Ranch, you can't help but notice the heliport and the electric fence, neither of which was featured in the movie, as I recall. The housemistress, whose name was Madame Gator (thank you, any of you who think I'm clever enough to have made this up), hands out what I can only describe as a menu and rings a bell to assemble the available girls. I had no compelling feeling of moral outrage at that point; I did choose a "partner," and I did accompany her to her bedroom, although *workshop* seems more accurate terminology in hindsight.

Once there, I stalled a bit, claiming to need a drink before proceeding—a declaration that has preceded a great many events in my life. Three triples—they only served triples—later, we went back to her place of business. But in spite of my well-chosen young lady, and, I swear, in spite of the triples, I had no enthusiasm for the prospect of having sex in that way in that place. I paid, I tipped, I thanked her for her company, and I climbed back into the limo that had brought us in the first place. It was in that shadowed moment that I had my epiphany: I had come face-to-face with a limitation as to what I was prepared to do in pursuit of a good time.

It was not the first odd sensation I'd experienced in the days after quitting Woolco. The carnival aspect of my life had continued unabated. But in the absence of the daily grind of the commute, the store, the staff, the customers, and the commute home again, I had felt a stillness that made me uneasy. I was the lone carny on the carousel, leaning on the mirrors at the great machine's central axel, staring without empathy at the colourful animals—wooden and human—as they spun by. I did not enjoy the sensation. It embraced invisibility and promoted reflection. I had no appetite for either.

Back in Toronto, reality hit hard. Monthly payments on three vehicles, the office lease, the support staff salary, and assorted overheads were taking their toll. To give you some sense of it, the auto insurance for the first year on the first limo was nine thousand dollars. Business was slow. In those early months, too many "rolling hours" were logged by the owners and their friends. Suffice to say, passengers getting a free ride empty a lot of decanters and burn a lot of upholstery. It's one thing to launder money but quite another to have the rinse cycle chew it to bits.

In an attempt to conjure up some business for the limo company, I opened Moonlight Promotions. The idea was to hark back to event promotion and to incorporate the limo service as a service supplier to the entertainment events. Moonlight Promotions started promoting bands and booking a variety of acts through 1988 including very successful shows with Rick James, Humble Pie, and Mick Taylor.

Mick Taylor's tour was after his brilliant stint with the Stones ("Brown Sugar," "Tumbling Dice," "Wild Horses," "Honky Tonk Women," and "Bitch," anyone?). He played a sold-out show at the Spectrum, and we were treated to a truly fantastic performance. The next night, he had a show in Brampton, so when it came time to pick him up at the hotel, I went along, riding shotgun with the driver. Mick and I snorted coke together as we drove out to the show. To anyone looking for this story's key celebrity moment, that was it. I've met a couple of celebrities in the limo and promotion businesses, but no one on a par with the Man-Who-Made-Keith-Richards-a-Rhythm-Guitarist. Next time you hear the Stones' "Can't You Hear Me Knocking," bear me in mind.

Bear in mind also, that Moonlight Promotions lost as many as we won. We booked Flock of Seagulls, the post–Winwood Spencer Davis band, and even Steppenwolf. All of those failed; not miserably, but they were unprofitable nonetheless. The small consolation was that Moonlight Limousine got paid, but, in truth, show business was not the strength of the limo ledger. My promotions got the limo company service contracts with MuchMusic, Yamaha Music, and the Toronto Argonauts. Those types of gigs were impressive on paper, but corporate contract work is highly discounted, and by the time you pay the driver and the gas pump, the overhead absorbs what little is left.

The real money in the business was with the real folks' weddings, anniversaries, proms, graduations—and those are mostly in the summer and the fall. We made it through the winter of 1988, so with Real Folks Season on the horizon and a few months of a real business on booking sheet, I decided that it was a sufficiently prudent time to make the second of the great purchases of the affluent. I got into real estate.

The market in Ontario was rising fast in the first half of 1988. I was determined to get in before things got out of hand. I bought a little cottage in a lovely spot at the edge of a Chemong Lake. For those of you who do not know the area, the nearest town to Chemong is—ahem—Peterborough, my birthplace. I know, I know, I didn't just buy a cottage; I bought a ticket to a Freudian field day. So I was a landowner. I went up once or twice, but it wasn't what I had expected. It had a stillness that made me uneasy, a quiet that courted reflection—uh-oh. I didn't actively dislike the place, but I felt a strong desire to court something else.

Just after I bought the cottage, my Cobourg friend Gordon, with whom I had worked promoting the Sunny Days festival events, called me for a favour. His girlfriend Patti and he were taking their son into Toronto to see a show based on the music of Billy Holiday called Lady Sings the Blues. The occasion was the boy's sixteenth birthday. Gord was hoping that I would offer the use of a limousine, and in exchange, he offered me a ticket and a date with his sister. I always liked Gordon and Patti—Patti in particular. I readily accepted.

The play was good, and we went to eat afterward, but I was tremendously drawn to Patti. We'd met before, but that time, something seemed different. I was feeling a one-to-one attraction that I had not felt in a very long time. I was certain that Patti was feeling it too. They were all staying in town at Gord's sister's house that night, so I offered to take Gord, Patti, and their son for lunch the next day. I arranged to pick them up in the limo and drop them off at his sister's after our meal. We had a wonderful but mildly unsettling time. During the entire meal, I was convinced that there was electricity running between Patti and me. It seemed astonishing to me that Gord was oblivious to the sparks that shot across that table.

I decided to face the issue and, in a private moment, asked Gord if he would object to me calling Patti to ask her out. Gord said he had no objection. Perhaps he reasoned that a Toronto/Cobourg romance was doomed by distance. Perhaps his possessive edge had been worn smooth by the gentle lapping of luncheon beverages. What Gord knew was that his relationship with Patti had changed, that the intimacy was gone, and that the core of their current relationship was the son they shared. At least, I assume that he knew this. Patti certainly did. And I knew it, because she told me.

What I knew from Gord was that he was in another relationship, one of sufficient seriousness to have produced two children. On our night out, he told me that his other relationship was about to bear fruit for a third time. It will not surprise you that he had yet to share that news with Patti.

I recognize the temptation to view this mess as daytime network stuff. But I ask you to resist the cheesy organ music you're imagining. This was not a soap opera; this was my life. I was an incorrigible, arrested adolescent, perilously close to my fortieth year, and I had found a wonderful woman. She seemed to feel a reciprocal attraction. To my utter astonishment, I was falling in love.

One of my first acts of courtship was to offer Patti the use of my cottage for her summer vacation. I was given to understand through one of Patti's friends that she hoped I might show up. Believe me, I needed little prompting. I was anxious to see if our initial sparks were more than flirtation.

Clearly, I was not the only one still assessing the situation. Initially, Gord had been sceptical that my interest in Patti had a future. But, in the face of obvious chemistry between Patti and me, his casual blessing soon turned sour. Not long after our first conversation about my intention to pursue her, Gord phoned me and demanded that I never see Patti again. In my most conciliatory tone, I agreed not to see her if that was her wish. I assured him that I would pursue the relationship no further if Patti wanted to break it off.

But that put Patti in control of her own destiny, and it was not what Gord wanted to hear. Let's just say that he professed his commitment to change my mind in the strongest of terms. I think you may have surmised by now that I'm no quitter. I've stuck with some of the most toxic influences on my life long after they passed prudence or even common sense. If I had the tenacity to hang on with the bad, I sure as hell was not going to give up on the good. And as far as my life has gone, this was, unquestionably, the good.

The summer of 1998 with Patti was the best of my life. Ours was a cottage romance. She lived in Cobourg; I lived in Toronto. We met every weekend at Lake Chemong. I counted the days. The week dragged until I saw her. I recognize that feeling for the cliché it is, but if love can't revel in its own clichés, it should call itself something else. I called it love.

Patti and I were classically opposite in many ways. She was a seasoned, small-town nurse, and I was … well, if you've read this far you've got a pretty good idea of what I was. You probably have a better idea than she did at the time. But she loved me.

We progressed very rapidly—at light speed, considering my romantic history—to the point of wanting a child, my first and Patti's second. We set a wedding date for the fall of 1989. To the long list of dodgy things that I was or had been, I was about to add two worthy of pride: father and married man.

Chapter Fifteen
Nice Day for a White Wedding

But life is never simple, right? To my utter frustration, my personal life was blossoming at the very time that both the cartel and the limousine business were beginning to falter. The problem in both cases was consistency. I've already talked a bit about the seasonal element of the limo business, but the inconsistency in the pot business was new to me. There are supply blips in any enterprise, but for the first time, we were seeing three weeks and even a month without a delivery. When there had been shortfalls in the past, the stutter had been offset by an increase in the next delivery or a reduction in time between shipments. Now, there were no make-goods, and the machinery sat idle.

The part of the operation that I controlled was finely tuned and reliable. The product would cross the border in a specially equipped station wagon with enough space in a false bottom under the car to accommodate up to four thirty-pound bales. Once on Canadian soil, the wagon would be tailed by one of our own vehicles. Without ever making contact, they would follow the shipment to Bolton, a small town just north of Toronto. The clean Canadian car was there to act as a decoy, to divert police attention should the need arise. The tail driver was instructed to drive erratically to draw the cops away from the shipment or, in more extreme circumstances, to ram anyone intent on hijacking the goods. Fortunately, neither tactic was ever necessary, but we were prepared had trouble arisen from either side of the law.

Once safely in Bolton, the payload would be unloaded into the safe house where the United States driver would rest and enjoy Canadian hospitality before recrossing the border. I would arrive at the safe house before eight the next morning and have the load transferred to my car for the drive to the industrial unit. The product was loaded into my trunk in plastic garbage bags—nothing tricky or Hollywood there. We used that same theatrical storage warehouse mentioned earlier for years without any problems. There, we would weigh it and box it in five-pound lots of ten half-pounds per box. To make a tedious task more amusing, we would make a game out of seeing who could get closest to perfect weight in a bag before putting it on the scale. We did that so often that our unmeasured accuracy became quite consistent, but we continued to play, just to break the monotony.

Once packaged, I would deliver the goods to the territorial vendors like English and the Fat Man in daylight, always sober and usually wearing one of the ties that had been policy at Woolco. Just as the cops dressed counterculture to try to catch us, I would dress "straight" to foil their tendency to profile. That may seem crazy, but I never got busted wearing a tie. The delivery process was wrinkle-free, save for the occasional grousing of vendors when they were given less than they wanted.

Unfortunately, our supply situation gave my associates more and more to complain about. We started to hear bits and pieces—rumours really—that our source suppliers in Mexico were having avarice problems, drawn to the superior profits and simpler handling of a hotter product. That product was cocaine. The street demand for coke was skyrocketing. The price for blow was down a bit, but the introduction of crack brought coke to a new and massive downscale market. No wonder the Mexicans were losing interest in weed.

With a precision distribution system sitting idle, I had two choices. The most obvious one was to go with the flow and get into the coke business. Call me old-fashioned, but I was uncomfortable with that option. I'll be the first to admit that I've used cocaine. I've used heroin too but had never even considered selling it. Somewhere in there was a line. I was prepared to snort it but not to cross it. Maybe close observation of Kiki's downward spiral gave me pause. Maybe the fact that the coke crowd attracted scary guys with scarier guns brought me up short. Call it lack of nerve if you like, but I like to think of it, like the Chicken Ranch incident, as a moral watershed. Those among you who question my courage have no grounds to question my judgement. Within a few short years of moving from smoke to blow, our Mexican suppliers started to disappear. Their story hit the international papers when they turned up dead in the desert, irrigating the scruffy, local plant life with their own blood.

The second option, the one I chose, made much more sense. I started to consider alternative sources of product. With the calibre of organization that I had built over the past few years, individuals with goods to sell often approached me. Although I may not have done extensive business with them previously, they were usually prepared to front the product and waive payment until the goods were sold, knowing I had the right people in place to move it safely.

So with Dutchie's connections drying up, I started to shake a few trees and look up some old supply contacts. With the exceptions of coke and heroin, I was open to product diversification. I became involved with kilos of hash that I was getting at a very competitive price. The product was unique to my market and did not compete with regular pot sales. The hash came in a number of varieties with exotic names like Romeo and Juliet, 777, and Mazar-i-Sharif, the latter named for the town in Afghanistan from whence it came. Every time I hear the city named in the war news, I think of hashish. I remember another load that was labelled Freedom Fighters—that would have been during the Afghan struggle against the Soviet Union. As well as the hash, I was also getting oil that originated in Jamaica. Whatever I got went straight out to my soldiers.

But I was starting to hear tales of homegrown weed. We even managed to get a hold of a bit for distribution. It was not available consistently or in any quantity, but what we came across was pungent, potent, and revered by the serious smoker. We never dreamed that the stuff was grown in Canada; we didn't think that a sufficient growing season was possible that far north. I knew someone who kept his small domestic operation secret for years out of concern about poachers or, worse, imitators. But a secret that big could not stay hidden for long.

My own secret was the dire state of my limo business, which was in the glassy calm of the '88–'89 winter season. Moonlight was in distress; without the cash infusion from the marijuana business, it was heading clockwise and south like a soap bubble in a draining sink. I was not prepared to accept this at first. The limos were my front, my flash, and my baby. I was desperate to keeping the business from cascading down the bent pipe. My solution was characteristically shortsighted. To save Moonlight, I spent cartel money that was not mine. I covered it up for a while with claims of outstanding debts and nonexistent inventories, but Moonlight was heading for the sewer, dragging me behind it like the shoes on some newlyweds' getaway car.

I use the image intentionally. I had a honeymooner's mind-set in my personal life, after all. Heading into 1989, I had stopped all luxury purchases, shelling out only for essentials. Everything else went to Moonlight—everything but the down payment on the sizable engagement ring I bought for Patti. In the face of all pragmatism and fiscal peril, I was a man in love. My romantic reveries involved not just marriage and parenthood but financial redemption where Moonlight was a target for acquisition and I got out alive. In the meantime, Patti and I had a near-dreamlike Christmas break at the cottage—warm, happy, and oblivious. Her blithe perspective was understandable; I had shielded her from of my fiscal turmoil. But my determination to ignore the rumble of disaster is harder to fathom. I've always had a gift for convincing folks that I had the answers. Apparently, I was just as adept at convincing myself.

Early in 1989, two events reinforced my optimism. The first occurred when Yamaha Music, a Moonlight corporate client, sponsored a national rock music competition called the Homegrown Show.

Here's how it worked. A radio station in each Canadian province ran a contest open to unsigned bands in their jurisdiction. The ten winning bands were flown to Toronto, housed at the prestigious Royal York Hotel and showcased in a massive concert held downtown at the new Convention Centre. The authorized limousine service for the event was, you guessed it, Moonlight. We picked up the bands and attendant bigwigs at the airport, took them to the hotel, and shuttled them to the convention centre on the night of the event. Among the celebrities was the evening's host, a fresh, young Canadian comedian named Jim Carrey. We also provided service for the president of Yamaha Music and guitar guru Rick Emmett, then singing and playing with Triumph. Rick was one of the show's judges.

Homegrown was a huge boost for the flagging fortunes of Moonlight, and it fell felicitously in the middle of the January doldrums that threatened to bleed the business dry. But beyond the financial windfall, I still remember the pride I felt watching the resultant TV special and seeing Moonlight's name in the scroll at the end—the closest I've ever come to a screen credit. Alas, my bankers were less enthusiastic.

I mentioned that two things buoyed my optimism. Homegrown was one. Can you guess the other? Here's a hint: it weighed five hundred pounds and crossed the border without incident in a single blessed month. Yep, the dope drought ended in one almighty flash flood of product. Now, even by our standard, five hundred pounds was a lot of weed. That meant accelerating the usual two-week cycle between loads; every week, we got a shipment of 120 pounds or more. We'd been starving for product, but this was more akin to gluttony. How did we manage that much? We just did. By the end of the month, if you will pardon an expression that I swear I use without smirking, the smoke had cleared. Not a bud was abandoned, not a leaf was left. All that remained was the fifty thousand dollars that created a noticeable lump in my pocket.

That is where optimism tripped me up. Even though the cartel balance sheet was awash with crimson, the drought was over, right? Nothing to worry about there. I was about to be married. I looked to the bright side, obsessively, relentlessly, foolishly. I put thirty thousand of the fifty toward my cartel shortfall and twenty thousand on a house. I only saw the potential for sunshine. After all, I had a matrimonial home, and the spring prom season was just around the corner. Things could have been said to be looking good, if you squinted hard enough.

But here's the thing: the limo business was never a standalone success, even in its finest hour. It floated on the stream of contraband cash, and the deadly drought was not over. Sadly, the Five Hundred-Pound February was an anomaly never to be equalled. From that point on, there was never enough weed for the need. I was the owner of a circus, and the centre pole of the big top was about to snap. The wheels were falling off the circus wagons. I see this now, but what did I see then? I envisioned the limo king, his bride-to-be, and the entire wedding party pulling up at the chapel ... in a fleet of cabs. No, no, no! I hung in and booked all three of my limos for the impending nuptials.

Our wedding was a highlight of my life. I'm a noisy guy by nature, but I treasure no memory so dearly as the silence of our two hundred guests as my bride walked down the aisle. She was stunning without question. And it's entirely possible, given my circle of friends, that many were stunned in another sense entirely. But regardless, the bride Patti gave them cause for wonder. Her golden hair fell in curls down the back of her long, white dress. You think that's corny? Tough. It's also true. I was in a state of complete happiness in the aura of my bride, oblivious to anything but her.

After the wedding, a lot of our friends stayed in town and had a massive, well-fuelled barbecue in our honour the next day. Or so I'm told. By 6:01 am, we were airborne for Jamaica. Among our numerous stops, Negril was of particular interest to me. It is the heart of *ganga* country and had long been on my wish list. It will not surprise you that it was not on Patti's. She did not know that my interest was professional as well as personal, but as we had been given accommodation in Negril and the use of a car as separate wedding gifts, she agreed to go. The roads in and around Negril are narrow, winding along the contours of the coast with scrub brush on one side and a long drop into the ocean on the other. My Cobourg bride never put down her rosary during the entire drive. Hopefully, that is not the only thrill she remembers from our two-week honeymoon. She probably remembers the Trivial Pursuit marathons as well.

Back home, I carried my lovely new wife across our threshold. That was a joy and a privilege. But other things that I carried across that threshold were heavier and more ominous.

The limo business had flat tires all the way around. It was not a matter of our cars or our drivers or, as I told myself, our management; it was the business as a whole. Toronto was awash with limos. One of the models in our livery was one of one hundred and twenty identical cars sold into the Toronto market. I remember events at the newly opened SkyDome where I lost count at 150 limos around the facility's perimeter. Competition was ridiculous. At the airport, it was not uncommon to head for the cabstand and find a stretch limo waiting, hungry for will-call business. The market was beyond saturation.

As for my dream of selling the company and getting out clean, that's a laugh. I put Moonlight on the block, but there were no takers. By 1990, limo companies were being offered cheaply to anyone foolish and starry-eyed enough to be interested. So I staved off disaster by taking on a partner. He brought expertise and a limo of his own into the mix. We paid off the other partners and moved the business into the basement of my new Oshawa home.

But don't mistake this pairing for prudence. Convinced that the future of the business was in less ostentatious transportation, we bought two more cars, each one foot longer than a regular town car and designed for airport service. When not booked, they were fuel-efficient enough to be used as our personal vehicles. Fare thee well, TransAm; I was going conservative. I even drove a few airport runs myself. Yes, I actually went into the trenches. Times were changing.

I should mention, joyously, that Patti was with child. With parenthood on the horizon, the trenches never looked so good.

But despite a new partner, a home office, and the more modest vehicles, Moonlight continued to sink. I continued to search for someone prepared to take over my presidency, my financial woes, and my partnership. When I finally found such a man in my new partner, I virtually gave him the company just to be free of the debt. Yes, you read that right; I gave away Moonlight Limousine. Considering that the balance sheet showed the business to be worth substantially less than nothing, I thought that I got a bargain.

So my legitimate cover was gone but not for long. On August 1, 1990, I started the second real day job of my life at a video distribution company. Twelve days later, our daughter Alexandra was born. Six days after that, I celebrated my fortieth birthday.

I was joining the regular world—fifteen years behind.

Chapter Sixteen
I See My Lights Come Shining

So, once again, I was trying on the straight world's shoes. Gone were the fantasies of Moonlight Dancer, my cleverly named thoroughbred horse, breezing across the finish line and flipping an insolent tail at Northern Dancer as he pranced into horseracing history. My yacht, Moonlight Mist, never left dry dock—or maybe she did, but it was with some other captain's fanciful name sprayed across her well-crafted stern. My fleet of limos—well, they were real, but my giveaway of the company aside, they were soon to return to the lessors from whence they came. The Moonlight dream was dust. But do not favour it with precious tears, dear reader. I was alive and well. My beautiful, loving wife and I had a new daughter, a treasured gift from God of our own. And, glory be, I had a real live job.

Of course, I still owed more money than a small municipal government. I knew that I had to address my debts, so I arranged to face my debtors. A meeting was called with Buffalo Bill, our United States supplier whom I had never met face-to-face, and Dutchie in the fall of 1990. The intent was to assess our current situation, to try to resolve the shortfall, and hopefully, to move on without personal injury or hospitalization.

The meeting was cordial, considering the fact that I was acknowledging a $220,000 shortfall. Dutchie and Buffalo Bill were willing to work with me. I was given time to facilitate repayment.

We all shook hands and promised to stay in touch. I believe that that is the difference between working in the green trade and the white trade, between dealing marijuana and dealing coke. Had I done what I had done in the latter culture, I would be dead.

I went home, feeling like a man who had flattened down between the tracks and narrowly missed the impact of an express train. My hair was dishevelled, and I was outwardly intact, but the truth was that I was profoundly shaken inside. Maybe I sensed that, despite having narrowly escaped the express, a slow freight was just over the horizon.

I came out of that meeting knowing that I could keep my house, but I had to sell the motorboat, the cottage, and my TransAm. I sold the car to Kiki of all people. I don't know whether he even had a license (not that it ever stopped me), but I do believe that he never drove it. It sat in the underground garage of the Birdhouse, gathering dust like all of his curios. It became one more of his treasures.

At home, my wife was on maternity leave until after Christmas, so the year ended in sweet, domestic tranquility.

I had started my job with the video distributor in August, but not wanting to repeat the mistake of the printing company, I never went out on a sales route till after New Year's. I set aside my arrogance in order to learn the nuts and bolts of the business. We sold new videocassette releases to rental outlets. We assembled and sold inventories comprised of both new and used product to stores that were just opening, facilitating that process and making their start-ups more cost efficient.

We also had a small video duplication lab in Kitchener, enabling us to manufacture and sell product for which we had purchased Canadian rights. Finally, we developed a business selling used videocassettes, sourced from the very rental retailers who were our customers in the previous dealings. Those cleaned up, rewrapped beauties were euphemistically known as "previously viewed" or, my personal favourite, "previously enjoyed," which was a mighty stretch in many cases. We sold them in bulk lots to mass merchants. You've likely seen them in big bins that prevent your cart from navigating the aisles without a pilot's license. Our first big push was—you guessed it—at Woolco. Allow me to take a personal bow for that one. My head office contacts and knowledge of their inner workings allowed us to expand our modest presence there. We were soon a listed supplier with dedicated merchandising space. Woolco should take a bow too. My experience there had taught me the benefit of actually *doing*, as opposed to *pretending* to do, the job at hand. My new boss paid me well and leased me a van.

I had no further use for the last of the airport town cars, so I sold it, the last vestige of the limo debacle. No, make that the second-to-last vestige. I also had to humble myself further and declare personal bankruptcy. I had no choice, really. The leasing companies would not recognize my transfer of the company to my partner, and they were coming after me for the unpaid arrears on the vehicles. I was the signatory, after all, and he was not. I discussed it with me wife and also with my boss and concluded that the prudent thing was to declare, as they say, which I did to the tune of seventy-six thousand dollars. Under the bankruptcy, my two seventy thousand-dollar town cars were sold off, one for eleven thousand dollars and the other for six. What made that all the more painful was that I still had my shortfall with my contraband partners to contend with, a shortfall that was born of my foolish determination to keep the limo business afloat. I felt like I'd stepped into a puddle that had an open manhole underneath.

But I was determined to find my feet. I had a good job, a wonderful wife, and a brand new daughter. My life was blessed, but it was not exactly of the cookie-cutter variety. When my wife's maternity leave was over, she had returned to work in Cobourg, a fair hike from where we lived in Oshawa. She was a small-town girl, and to be honest, the combination of a tremendously responsible nursing job and five-day-a-week commute was wearing her down. Because of our financial situation and the location of my new job, moving to Cobourg was not an option. So we did the next best thing. It was decided that she and my daughter would stay at her mother's home in Cobourg through the week and come home from Friday night through Sunday. It was not an ideal option, but it was an increasingly common one where the pressures of career and finance bite into the apple pie of traditional home life. It also served to keep her unaware of my dire situation.

Financially, of course, she knew that all was not rosy, but I was determined to hide the ugly details. She was unaware of the extent of my debt and the illegal manner from which it had originated. Having her home only on the weekends facilitated my task. I concentrated on my video job and enjoyed my expanded family from Friday through Sunday. I reasoned that the holes in my week would enhance my chances of getting a fresh start.

In my free time, I renewed some old acquaintances and pondered ways to get out from under my debt. In September of 1990, those two pastimes converged when I paid a visit to my old cartel buddy. We had not seen each other much in recent months, but he asked me over, saying that he had something of interest to show me. When I arrived, he said that he had a couple of girls that he'd like me to meet. Amused by my reluctance and discomfort, he took me to a room where, with great fanfare, he introduced Franny and Cloney. They were not flesh-and-blood girls—they were plants. Marijuana plants. *Female* marijuana plants.

Now, at that point, I had worked with marijuana for over half of my life, but I had seldom seen marijuana that was not dried up, ground up, or processed. To be candid, I found the sight of two plants that looked like they'd be at home in a vacant lot to be underwhelming. I saw yard work; he saw the future. The plants were called mothers. My cartel buddy envisioned a concealable indoor nursery for their progeny, nestled in a building missed by the unsleeping eye of the police helicopter or the passing patrol car. What he was looking for was a nondescript location, and he asked me to keep my eyes open for a site that fit the criteria.

I thought of Dutchie. Any enterprise thrown in his direction helped me by simultaneously demonstrating cooperation and reducing the burden of my current debt. The idea of product produced locally, impervious to the whim and brevity of a Canadian growing season, was attractive, and Dutchie was interested. The next person I approached was Buzzy, who, to my surprise, showed me some plants his rock and roll friends had been cultivating. They were in a basement closet under a four hundred-watt bulb. That was low yield, personal-use experimentation, sure, but it was also the beginning of an industry. Once again in the history of human endeavour, market need and entrepreneurial ingenuity were about to join hands and dance.

To say that Dutchie was interested might be an understatement. He called the very next day with news. Not only had he found a location, but he had also found a live-in sitter for our babies, the rooted clones that were our first step. So we had a plant source, we had a location, and we had an attendant. What we didn't have was money. In order to execute our brilliant plan, we needed rent and utilities money and fertilizer and, of course, lights—powerful, expensive lights.

Amongst my immediate crowd, everyone else had also crashed when the imported pot had dried up. We had all invested—and I use the term ironically—in straight enterprises. I had my limos, and Dutchie had his fire retardant. BB, our partner from the Bolton part of the import chain, had invested in an ultralight airplane venture that … um, didn't fly. Collectively, it seemed when it came to legitimate enterprise, our big ideas led to bigger disappointments. Our entrepreneurial disasters had spawned a joke amongst our crowd.

> On its maiden flight, BB's ultralight crashes and burns. Dutchie comes to the rescue to douse the flames, but his fire retardant doesn't work. G arrives by limo to rescue his friends from the flames. They jump in the limo to make their escape, but as they pull away, the wheels fall off, soaking all three with freshly poured alcohol from the minibar. The car stops. The flames do not.

The joke had many variations, but the punch line was always the same: three crispy critters.

Our entrepreneurial history was appalling. I see that now. But what I saw at the time was a way out of crushing debt. To my regret, I did something that began a financial nightmare that is with me even now. I borrowed more money. From a bank? Not a chance; I was freshly bankrupt, and besides, what would I have told them it was for? From family? Hey, if you've read to this point, it will not surprise you that my family, even those most near and dear, considered me a lost soul. The prospect of lending money to me was my family's equivalent of taking cash, soaking it with vodka, and setting it on fire. Without the benefit of fire retardant, I might add—unless you count pissing on the flames. Nope, family was out.

But I needed cash, I reasoned, to get me out of the hole I'd dug by borrowing cash from the cartel; it was cyclical reasoning at its finest. So where do you go when your life has left you in a hole? You go underground. The first person I thought of was a regional distributor from the cartel who had not blown his earnings as many of us had. That guy we called the Spinner.

The Spinner was a volatile gentleman. He taught wrestling and was a practitioner of the martial arts. He had a brown belt in karate. Karate is a reactive art not a proactive one. The idea is that you use your skills for defence and not offence. That is a founding principle of the discipline. Legend has it that the karate powers-that-be refused to give the Spinner his black belt, although he had earned it, because they found him to be too violent. That is the guy from whom I chose to borrow money. But his temper was not the only attribute that made being in his debt ill-advised. People accuse banks of gouging; I was going to pay that guy 10 percent interest … per month!

Once again, I know, I know. But here's how I figured it: I assumed that the grow cycle for the plants was three months. If I borrowed thirty grand from the Spinner at 10 percent interest per month, at the end of the three-month cycle, I would owe thirty-nine thousand dollars. I calculated that I'd be able to pay off at least half of the principal, with the other half coming off the next run when the start-up costs would not be a factor.

Seems solid, right? The Spinner was still reluctant. He was good with money, or at least better than those of us who blew or lost our cartel profits, and was not convinced of the superior viability of this venture compared to our failed ones. But I was persuasive, because I believed. Spinner coughed up thirty Gs.

I took the money to Dutchie. In accordance with my vow to erase the shortfall debt, I gave him half. Honourable, you say. To that, I add rash and shortsighted. Look at it this way: I gave Dutchie fifteen thousand dollars. What I did not give him was the obligation to pay interest on the fifteen thousand dollars. I had fifteen thousand dollars left to fund my part of the grow house venture. I also had the interest obligation on thirty thousand, in effect giving me a three-month debt obligation of nine thousand dollars on fifteen thousand dollars of working capital. That is where my brilliant scheme started sliding irreversibly into the pit. I was compounding myself into the ground.

Armed with our indentured cash, a location, and a willing live-in caretaker, though, we were ready to grow. But nothing is easy; this was our maiden voyage, and the sea was fraught with reefs. The house itself was not too bad; it was a modest, anonymous, suburban bungalow. It had a basement of sufficient size and construction. You do not want a basement that is finished. Rugs, drop ceiling, panelling, or even painted drywall are all impediments to the process and also have the additional drawback of retaining evidence of the manner in which the facility was used once you're gone.

It may not be true in nature, but when growing indoors, poured concrete is your friend. Our location's open basement ceilings made the wiring and watering needs simpler to accommodate. On the outside, our chosen place was isolated on a quiet road in the northwestern suburbs of Toronto. Back inside, the upstairs was furnished, giving the illusion of a normal residence. On one wall was an inexpensive painting of the Riviera. As is my wont, I named the place, and I named it for the painting. Given the homely nature of the structure and its surroundings, I will admit to some intended irony. But at the same time, be assured that my aspiration to grandeur was mixed in there too. The Riviera was our first grow house, and it began a tradition of naming each location that lasted nearly the length of the venture.

We were in the early stages of the setup when I got a call from one of Buzzy's rock and roll friends. He had progressed from the plants in the cupboard and was partnered in a grow house with a prominent and eccentric Canadian musician, famed for his unusual instrumentation and mysterious stage attire. The performer was less famous for his sexual orientation, and that secret caused him some grief. A dramatic lover's quarrel, misinterpreted by neighbours as two men in violent conflict, brought the cops to his door. Under police pressure and in fear of seeing his entertainment career unravel, the local rock star turned in his grow house partner. Under the duress of being fingered, that guy quickly tore down the part of the operation the cops had not found and arrived at my door, armed with five lights, 250 babies, and best of all, expertise.

I say *expertise* advisedly, because we, the original partners, had none. A granny with a flair for delphiniums knows more about plants than I did. Shoolong, my doorstep refugee from the rock star bust, was inexperienced in the grander sense, and he was self-taught, but he was, nonetheless, a budmeister. To be labelled a budmeister, one has to know the entire operation of growing the plant. That would involve the ability to clone the original cuttings, to root them, and to transplant them into a larger pot. The budmeister oversees their vegetative cycle and, finally, knows when and how to bloom them. He—we never had a *she*—determines when the plants are ready to harvest and executes the correct drying methods to produce the saleable product. We needed his skill.

Shoolong contributed his lights to the venture as well, giving each player in the ever-ballooning partnership one light under which to harvest his portion of fortune. My personal lack of expertise added greatly to the wonderment at the process we witnessed. Those babies grew to be four feet tall, and like the diapers on their human namesakes, they were full and stunk beyond belief. I was delighted by the novelty of the experience. Less delightful was the realization of how little of the abundant foliage is actually saleable.

At harvest, you take 80 percent of the plant and throw it in the garbage. The root, the stalk, and all of the fan leaf (virtually all of the leaf on the plant) go straight in the bin. All that remains is colas, popcorn bud, and calyx leaf. You put those components on a screen and dry them, losing another 80 percent of their original weight. The rest is marketable. So, typically, a four-foot plant yields less than half an ounce of useable product. On our virgin run, the emphasis was on the *less* part.

So yield expectations are a key part of the profitability equation. No one imparted that gem of weed wisdom to me or to my partners. We, not knowing any better, doubted the integrity of our budmeister, of our growing stock, of each other. It took me a long time to realize that that was about an average indoor yield and that the results had more to do with light and time than with incompetence and treachery.

I've heard growers boast about one pound per plant, but that's only true if you have one plant per light. In the end, it's not about yield per *plant* but yield per *light*. It's also about the time it takes to get there. If you leave the plant under light longer, you will increase the plant's yield. But you'll also decrease the number of harvests you'll have over the year.

How do you win in that scenario? You don't. What I know now is that—number of plants be damned—the best you're going to get is two pounds per light in a ninety-day growing cycle. There are ways to cut the cycle down to sixty days, and we used them as we learned them, but I defy anyone to get more than two pounds of sellable pot per light in a sixty-day period.

Okay, Bong Botany 101 adjourned—for now. But let's apply what we learned to the situation my partners and I were in. The Riviera was a five-way enterprise. Overall, the entire grow-to-product process should have taken us three months: thirty days of veg, sixty days of bloom, followed by the harvest. However, the inexperience of our new team and the fact that this was the first setup in that house ballooned the process to five months. There were five partners and five lights. We got a pound each. My pound was worth three thousand dollars. In the process of producing three thousand bucks of product, I owed, beyond the principal of course, not the expected nine thousand but fifteen thousand dollars in interest, thanks to the five months to harvest. At the end of my first tour as a grow-op entrepreneur, I owed a further thirty thousand plus fifteen thousand minus three thousand: forty-two thousand dollars.

That is not, by anyone's definition, an astute debt-erasing strategy. Clearly, our beautiful entrepreneurial model needed a serious face-lift.

CHAPTER SEVENTEEN
WOKE UP, GOT OUT OF BED

It was time for a reckoning. Let's run down the list. Here's what we had: partners (too many); debt (too much); product (not enough); expertise (just enough to get by). Here's what we needed: more lights; less overhead; a bigger yield; and, for the sake of both prudence and economics, a new location.

There's one factor that is a little too complex to reduce to a list item. The disappointing yield from our first harvest led Dutchie and I to dark thoughts about our budmeister. Our concern was not only his depth of expertise but the depth of his honesty as well. Dutchie and I shared suspicions that both assets were in short supply. Was the poor crop the result of incompetence or thievery or both? Our own lack of expertise as to what the yield should have been left us with doubts.

Also missing from this list of wants and needs is the one thing I had in abundance: blind, knuckleheaded optimism. In spite of having bled money in the pursuit of the first harvest, I still believed that I could make it work. Every visionary, schemer, and lunatic has a secret element that sets him or her apart from peers and competitors. Mine was hope.

Back in college, I had learned the inscription that Dante says is on the gates of Hell: "Abandon all hope, ye who enter here." I had not abandoned hope; I still had a pocketful. In a spectacular moment of circular reasoning—neither my first nor my last—I deduced that if I still had hope, the gates of hell were not my current location. Considering the fractured nature of this logic, it's somewhat surprising that I was correct. I was not *quite* at the gates of Hell. But I was on the highway, and the mighty metal doors were only a few expressway exits away. I was driving in their direction, certain that hope was hellfire-proof. This, I admit, is a marginally poetic way of attempting to candy-coat the unthinkable.

I found another location, and I borrowed more money. The new location was the White House. It was a typical, suburban Scarborough bungalow, as unremarkable as any of the neighbouring residences that mimicked it on either side. It was on a major thoroughfare and had all the appearance of ponderous normality at street level; we confined our clandestine enterprise to the basement. Other than the hide-in-plain-sight benefit, the White House had one distinct advantage over the Riviera: a "friendly" landlord. I use the term to describe a sympathetic rent collector willing to overlook the location's activities for either a piece of the action or an extremely high rental fee.

In that case, our landlord was to become an active participant in our venture. Her name was Kitkat, and she had been a successful operative for us in the days of the import cartel. The house was smack in the middle of her old distribution territory, and—wait for it—she owned it! The advantage of a sympathetic or participating landlord is clear; the friendly landlord is one more layer of legitimacy between you and the authorities. On top of that, you minimize the cash outlay, because you can pay your way with the harvest. In our financial state, that was mighty enticing.

But a friendly landlord is also a partner. The Riviera disappointment was a vivid lesson in the Four Ps: Partners Pinch Profit Potential. Dutchie and I decided to downsize. We had our own lights, so we didn't need equipment partners, and we decided to reposition the Riviera's babysitter, Crispo, as budmeister. Our suspicions regarding the low yield at the Riviera motivated us to part ways with Shoolong, our erstwhile expert. Crispo was keen to develop his skills as a budmeister and was further enticed by the promise of a bigger payday than the paltry sum he had gotten as babysitter at the Riviera. But if Crispo wanted full partnership, he would have to earn it by proving his worth as a budmeister. We promised him partnership once the enterprise arrived in the black. Neither Crispo nor Dutchie nor I were fully aware of how far off that would be.

So we had six lights—two each for Dutchie, Kitkat, and me—and Crispo was on the payroll as hired expertise. All we needed was capital. It seemed imprudent to go back to the Spinner. At our next meeting, he would be expecting cash, not a pitch to borrow more. I was already dreading having to tell him that I had no way of paying him out. My dread was well founded, as it happens, but more about that later. Bypassing Spinner for the new loan, I approached a gentleman I'd known for a number of years.

Alpha was a big guy, not fat-guy big but hockey big. He was a former minor league defenceman, and he knew how to hold his own in the corners, equally skilled with stick, glove, and elbow. Such was the extent of his skills that he once received a police escort out of an out-of-town arena after death threats from what seemed like half the fans in the rink. Since leaving hockey, he had made his living as a ticket scalper, and with the help of a few highly placed friends at Maple Leaf Gardens, he was at the top of his trade. He had ready cash, and he was a nice guy, but, once again, he was volatile. I do love a challenge. Actually, when you believe in the dream you're selling, salesmanship comes naturally, or it does to me. I got Alpha to lend me thirty thousand dollars, the same amount that I had squeezed from the Spinner. Unfortunately, it was also under the same draconian terms.

So, with cash, a better location, and fewer partners in the mix, all that remained was to talk to the Spinner and tell him that I didn't have the thirty thousand dollars that I had borrowed five months before. But I did have the fifteen thousand dollars of interest that had accrued on Spinner's thirty thousand; I took it right off the top of Alpha's loan. I know, I know, paying off interest with a loan that has interest of its own is … well, I didn't study business in college, did I? I'm a philosopher, not a mathematician. Come on, I gave you a Dante quote. Cut me some slack!

At any rate, I approached Spinner with caution, because of his reputation for being volatile, but I wasn't overly concerned, because I had fifteen thousand in interest to offer. What I ignored was the fact that it had been five months since the loan, and I was supposed to have returned, money in hand, in three. I had also forgotten that the Spinner had not shared my enthusiasm for the enterprise in the first place. Initial reluctance multiplied by a 66 percent payment delay did not temper his temper.

I met him in a parking lot. We got out of our respective cars and cased the surroundings like movie mafiosi. I quickly explained to him that all was not well but that I had a solution that I assumed would be satisfactory to both of us. It was immediately obvious that I had assumed wrongly. From the moment I told him that I didn't have the entire forty-five thousand, he began to engage in exaggerated gesticulation the likes of which I, and I'll assume you, would find unprecedented in adults, especially adults in a public parking lot.

The strange and, frankly, scary flailing of extremities was accompanied by fragments of barked dialogue that ran along these lines:

"What? No fucking way! This is not … no! Oh, no! This ain't fucking happening! I don't give a fuck, because …. This is not fucking happening!"

During this swear-saturated soliloquy, he began to rotate on his toes and to pummel his karate-trained fist into the palm of his opposite hand. Then he cocked his right hand as if preparing a punch, only to have his left hand grab the right and push it down to his side. Then, as the monologue continued, he would spin on his toes some more.

"This is …. FUCK. I don't give a … because this is not fucking … because I am not gonna … Whoa! FUCK THIS! Because I don't give a fuck, so … FUCK IT!"

None of that was from Dante, but believe me, it was hell just the same. And it went on for about five long minutes. I could not get a word in, but honestly, had I been able to get a word in, I'm not certain what it might have been. "Fuck" was certainly spoken for.

So I let him sputter and swear and spin for what seemed a much longer time than the five minutes it likely was. Eventually, his left hand successfully contained his right, his toes finally gave out, and a brief period of silence ensued. I took that opportunity to do what few would when confronted by a flailing, ungrammatical, and furious individual: I offered to buy him a drink. Traditionally, it is considered imprudent to ply a madman with spirits. But you may be astonished to hear that, in that instance, it seemed to work. Drink in hand, the Spinner paused to realize that he was not going to get his entire wedge that night. He took the fifteen and reluctantly agreed to a three-month extension for the rest. Plus accruing interest, of course.

What may further astonish you is that that was not the only time that I witnessed the Spinner unwinding exotically in the face of unrealized expectations. But let's move on; to lunatic and angel alike, I prefer to dole out the disappointments one at a time.

So then I had fifteen thousand dollars, and we were off and running at the White House. We needed to do better from a yield point of view than we had at the Riviera. So, it was time for a little science again.

What you're trying to do in any artificial growing situation is to replicate the conditions that a plant would experience in the outdoor environment. You want to facilitate the plant's maturation and thus produce bud as quickly and efficiently as possible. Cannabis, in its natural habitat, typically experiences two growing seasons. That means that it takes a plant in nature four months to get established and a further two months to come to full bloom. But in an indoor environment, the plant can be tricked into blooming every three months, yielding four crops a year instead of two. In fact, using a two-room technique, one to establish the plant and one to induce the bloom, it is conceivable to have six harvests per year. This takes meticulous cultivation and is a yield that only an experienced budmeister can achieve.

Of course, we were a long way from that level of expertise at the White House. We were acutely aware of the effort it took to achieve even the modest results that we were getting. At the White House, we continued to use a process called *bioponics*. That means that we grew our plants not in traditional soil but in a substrate that just held the plant in place while it was fed by the chemicals in our watering solution. We would typically fill pots with this nonsoil mix and plant a rooted cutting in each pot. Fifty pots were arranged under each thousand-watt bulb and exposed to eighteen hours of light per day for the first month. The lighting was on a timer to conserve human resources and ensure consistency. After thirty days of eighteen-hour light exposure, the plants would be about eighteen inches high. At that point, the light cycle was reduced to twelve hours per day for a further sixty days. That was the bud cycle, and there was no way of shortening that time frame.

"Whew," you may well be saying. At first, I didn't care about any of this either. My line to my people was, "I'm strictly in sales." But as the challenges of the growing process became apparent in measly yield and doubts regarding the expertise and honesty of my peers, I started to absorb the process. Slowly and reluctantly, I was becoming a budmeister.

But as far as my boss and my wife and the straight world were concerned, I was still the assistant national accounts manager at the video distribution company. I was doing well in the world of entertainment software. I was able to hide the clandestine side of my existence, but I was not able to make it go away. I was responsible for six thousand dollars in interest per month—three for the Spinner and a further three for Alpha. Although things were working out better at the White House than they had at the Riviera, no amount of optimism could disguise the math. As I watched the crop grow, my hope began to shrivel. We were nowhere near being able to produce a crop that would address my obligation to make good on six thousand a month.

The second crop was harvested on schedule in the first week of May. I was convinced that Crispo had done the best he could, given his knowledge as a budmeister. We got the grow cycle down to three months from five, and we got about three pounds per partner.

I owed thirty thousand dollars to the Spinner, plus nine thousand in interest for the three months. And I owed thirty thousand to Alpha, plus nine thousand in interest for the same three months. My piece of the harvest got me nine thousand dollars. You guessed it, folks; it's tally time. At the end of my second round as a grow op entrepreneur, I owed thirty thousand plus nine thousand plus thirty thousand plus nine thousand minus nine thousand: *sixty-nine thousand dollars.* I was pretty freaked out. Bear in mind that I still had the original debt to Dutchie and Buffalo Bill that had sent me down this road in the first place. I did not see any way out, and my previous "way out" had actually driven me backward.

We know what Dante said was on the Devil's gate. It's said that the inscription over the transom of Plato's study read "Let no man enter here who does not understand math." That phrase, too, was absent from any doorway in my consciousness. But I didn't need Plato to tell me that I was sinking fast. I needed a miracle.

One day, I realized that I had seen my salvation at the dinner table the previous Christmas. My newly minted miracle maker was a high school friend of my wife's who had joined us for the holiday dinner. That woman was going through a divorce and was struggling with the pragmatic details of her situation. The subject of her home came up. Her husband had moved out, and she was paying the bills alone. The place had electric heating, and her hydro bills were outrageous. It was located on a secluded road that was tricky in the winter. The isolation discouraged commuters, and the lack of a lake or river nearby made it a poor choice for recreation. The worst element of all, from a seller's perspective, was the electrical baseboard heating. The bill could run upward of a thousand a month during the winter season.

This is a huge disincentive to a buyer and prospective homeowner, but to a grower, it's a gift. Sudden, substantial hydro usage is one key indicator the police use in identifying a grow operation and justifying a search warrant, but with that place, the history of high electrical use was already there. The electricity draw from the lights would not be as obvious. It was, indeed, like a miracle. Every single shortcoming the property had as a real estate investment made it a better prospect as a grow op location. I was interested at the time of the conversation, but in the light of my current predicament, I could barely contain my enthusiasm. In a friendly and casual way, I offered to go up north with my wife's friend to take a look at her "problem." Grateful for another perspective, she agreed.

When I saw the property, I knew it was perfect. She desperately needed to get rid of the place, and now, I was just as desperate to have it. But I stayed calm and casually proposed to see what I could do. I offered to talk to some friends of mine who were interested in real estate and to see where we could go from there. But really, I knew where I was going. I saw the snow sparkling, and I heard the trees whisper, and I knew that this was my shot.

Chapter Eighteen
A Very, Very, Very Fine House

I was a desperate man at that point. I was in mid-ocean, and the raft I'd devised to save my life was sinking faster than the ship I'd been forced to abandon. I had more pressure, more responsibility, and more debt than on the day I had first laid eyes on the lush, green forms of Franny and Cloney. Despite my increasing expertise in our secret science, my knowledge was not reassuring. Quite the opposite, in fact: I was beginning to realize how much space, how many lights, and how few partners it took to yield the kind of harvest that was going to save my skin. So forgive me if I looked with lust at the Chalet, yet another inanimate object, as the vessel of my salvation.

First off, it was a beautiful building, an upscale prefab home known as a Viceroy, designed for the discriminating soul who seeks Shangri-La by plopping a European ski cabin into the Canadian woods. It had a sunken living room with an eighteen-foot ceiling, a fireplace, four bedrooms, and best of all for our purpose, an unfinished basement and electrical heating throughout. It sat atop a hill on seven and a half acres, four of which were manicured lawn and hedges, twenty minutes outside of Cobourg. You could see Lake Ontario from the south side of the house if the day was clear and you were standing on tiptoe. Outside, there was ample parking on the side of the house that was hidden from the long, winding driveway. The drive led out to Sky View Road, which ran along the southern extremity of the property. Sky View was not visible from the house, nor was the house visible from the road.

The property, being more or less pie-shaped, had only three full sides. Shelter Valley Road was the property's western border. The northern border was, if you can believe it, Highway 401, known to the rest of the country as Southern Ontario's contribution to the Trans-Canada Highway. That may seem like a detriment to seclusion, but it was not. Anyone approaching from the north would have to park on the highway—vastly dangerous and sure to attract attention—only to have to traverse a substantial ridge that hid the house from the swish and rumble of the nation's main thoroughfare. The small remaining border was a farmer's field that hosted a modest herd of horses.

At the bottom of the hill on the southwest side ran a stream that eventually meandered into our Great Lake. On the other side of the stream, which was still Chalet property, was about three acres of rough, unkempt ground with a small pond and sumac trees. That scrubby patch was destined to be a crucial piece of the puzzle.

It was, in short, a dope cultivator's paradise. The asking price of paradise was $169,000. That was a bit high for the recession-squeezed market of the time, but Dutchie and I were what real estate types call motivated buyers.

My plan involved Dutchie and I offering $160,000, including a nonrefundable deposit of $20,000. The twist was that the closing date was not to be for twelve months. I was characteristically optimistic that our efforts would produce the remaining $140,000 in that time. In the meantime, we offered the owner $1,000 per month in rent over that period, which was not applicable to the purchase price. The owner, who bought into the tale that we were speculating and planned to use the twelve months for renovation, agreed. After all, the monthly thousand bucks solved her mortgage crunch, and she still had the $20,000 if we couldn't come up with the $140,000 in twelve months' time. Her position was relatively safe, but, once again, I was gambling on a future that was far from assured. You may notice a pattern.

The deal was set to close on May 1, 1992. The Whitehouse crop would be harvested by then, and we knew that we would need it to have any chance of meeting the deposit. We were also playing for time. Dutchie had convinced me that one of our yield problems was the nature of our stock. He proposed flying to Amsterdam to procure seeds of other, more resilient and fruitful strains of cannabis. In keeping with the fairytale nature of our ambition, we called these seeds the "magic beans."

At this juncture, it seems prudent to convene another class of Bong Botany 101. Or maybe at this point, we've progressed to 201. You be the judge.

Our efforts thus far had been with a variety of marijuana plant called Purple Indica, a plant found in nature that had been neither modified nor crossbred. It did not have the benefit of scientific tinkering to maximize potency, yield, or even pest resistance. Those qualities and others were being enhanced in greenhouses around the world. Particularly well known were the greenhouses of Amsterdam. Many varieties were being bred there, and once a year, they would hold a competition called the Cannabis Cup. The winner was the plant that excelled at certain criteria set forth by the judges. Dutchie had read about all of this in scientific publications such as *High Times* and, of course, *Playboy*. He was determined that the best smoke that science had to offer be an integral part of our operation. I found the idea attractive; maybe that was the secret as to why our yields had been so low and the buzz only mediocre. Clearly, we were in dire need of magic beans.

To that end, Dutchie, who spoke no Dutch but was fluent in French, flew to Amsterdam where pot cultivation and sale is controlled but nonetheless legal. That April, he spent about a week partaking of the sights, sounds, and even the smells of the historic town, before returning with a small bag of seeds and some promotional literature. Dutchie had selected three strains for our operation. Here's what the brochure said about each:

> Northern Lights: Indica strain, grows to six feet, blooms in sixty-five days. Yield per plant of five ounces.

> Big Bud: Dwarf Indica strain, grows to four feet, blooms in sixty days. Yield per plant of four ounces.

> Shiva Skunk: Dwarf Indica strain, grows to four feet, blooms in fifty-four days. Yield per plant of four ounces.

This was why we called them magic beans. In comparison with the yields we'd had up to that point, those numbers seemed the result of witchcraft. To recap, the Riviera harvest had yielded a third of an ounce per plant. We didn't know at that point how much the Whitehouse setup was going to yield, but I knew that it was only going to be fractionally better than the Riviera before it. As it turned out, the Whitehouse yield was about half an ounce per plant. If the Amsterdam brochure was to be believed, I had found not only the way out of the pit but the road to the mountaintop as well.

All we had to do was buy the Chalet, grow the pot, and get rich. That's all. If you wonder what the substance is that's dripping from the last sentence, it's irony. Believe me, there's more where that came from.

Okay, eyes back to the blackboard again. I know there's no diploma at the end, but bear with me; the magic beans demand it. Before the advent of the sorcerer's seeds, we were planting clones or cuttings. Those are cut from mother plants, where the mom has sprouted a node and a new leaf. Not surprisingly, the cuttings are called babies or, more often, kids.

Incidentally, a mother can be either a male or a female plant, and the cutting always mirrors the gender of the parent. But before your head explodes, be assured that mothers are typically female. In a grow operation, the males are used primarily in the crossbreeding process or tossed. There; point made and natural order restored.

Back to the main point. The cuttings or kids are placed in a shot glass that is filled with rooting gel. You leave them in the gel for about the time it takes to cut the next kid and then move the first kid to propagation tray, a forty-eight to seventy-two compartment grid of tiny, potting indentations. Each indentation has been filled with soilless mix that's been moistened with water and a growth enhancer called SuperThrive. Our formula was ten drops of SuperThrive per litre of water and about one litre of water per forty-eight-compartment tray. The tray, the rooting gel, the SuperThrive, and the soilless mix are common plant nursery products.

Once a tray is full, the kids are misted, and a transparent hood about six inches high is placed on top of the tray to trap the moisture. From there, the tray is placed under fluorescent light and left until rooted. Before rooting, the cuttings take on water by osmosis through the leaf. That's why you must have at least one leaf along with the node on each clone. No fertilizer is used until a root appears at the bottom of the stem. This typically takes nine to fourteen days. The hood is lifted for daily misting. The process also serves to provide fresh air and inhibit mould. Once fully rooted, our cuttings were transferred to a four-inch pot and placed under a thousand-watt, metal halide, grow lamp that reflects the blue end of the light spectrum.

Whew! Growing from cuttings is a ton of work, *ja*? Guess what? The seed process is even more involved, because you have to grow your mothers from scratch.

To do that, the seeds go directly into four-inch pots and are left for fourteen days under eighteen hours of light. Then you switch them to twelve-hour light for another fourteen days until they can be sexed, a step that's unnecessary with clones, which, if you remember, always reflect the gender of the parent. The sexing process is the responsibility of the budmeister, who can differentiate between the seed clusters of a male plant and the seed receptor hairs of a female. Once sexed, the male plants are usually destroyed, and the females go back under lights for eighteen hours a day to become mothers. Then, and only then, can you run the cloning process from the top.

I'm not trying to write a how-to here, I'm trying to illustrate that the seed process has different requirements from the cloning process that we were used to. Those requirements affect not only the way you proceed and the length of time the procedure takes but also the layout you need to facilitate the process.

The Chalet's unfinished basement had three rooms. We envisaged one room for the mothers and two grow rooms with a twelve-light capacity between them. In short, in our new magic bean world, the Chalet basement was perfect for our needs. But we had no Chalet yet.

Our seller was not the problem. She had agreed to the twenty thousand down; she had agreed to the thousand-dollar a month rent. She even agreed to keep the utilities in her name as long as we agreed to pay the bill directly to her along with the rent at the first of each month. Not having to change the billing name was a real plus for us. Given the juice we were planning to burn with the lights and ventilation, we wanted as little scrutiny and as few eyeballs as possible on that bill. Our next hurdle was the twenty thousand down. Dutchie and I had nine thousand each in product from the Whitehouse crop, but I had my loan interest to pay as well, so I was still miles away from my down payment target.

It was time to put on my salesman suit. I prepared a presentation kit comprised of the real estate appraisal of the house complete with survey, water sample, and pictures both inside and out. To that, I added a schematic that showed that we could safely install fifteen lights and execute our intended basement activity without damage or detection. As the metaphorical ribbon on the package, I included the hybrid seed brochure, complete with those tantalizing yield estimates in black and white: four to five ounces per plant.

My pitch in hand, I went to see the Spinner first. This was less bravery than pragmatism. I reasoned that if the Spinner murdered me, I wouldn't have to worry about telling Alpha that I didn't have his money. My plan was to give the Spinner all nine thousand dollars from the Whitehouse crop, taking care of the interest owed. I hoped that would reassure him enough to bankroll the Chalet project. I demonstrated the viability of the scheme as well as my trust in him as a partner by taking him to see the Chalet. Generally, you don't conduct tours *to* or *of* your grow locales, given the preponderance of betrayal amongst illegal associates. But to Spinner's credit, he never betrayed my trust, as much as I may have shaken his. He loved the Chalet when he saw it, partially as an ideal grow location and partially as equity should the science go wrong. Did I mention to the Spinner that there would be other investors? Um, no. Feel free to take a moment and wag your finger here.

My next stop was my old pal, King Ferd. I showed King Ferd the package and explained that I was looking for ten thousand dollars in startup costs. I offered 10 percent a month interest, and he bit, more to help a friend than as a savvy business investment. I say this because, at that point, Ferd's buccaneer days were behind him, and he was pretty much legit.

Speaking of legit, the startup costs that I pitched to Ferd were only startup in the broadest sense. Nine of Ferd's ten was headed to Alpha's pocket as payment for the interest on the Whitehouse loan. I figured that that was the only way I could get Alpha to invest again, and I needed Alpha's coin to make the Chalet deal happen. Remember though, that Alpha had yet to see a penny over the three months since the Whitehouse launch. When we met, I quickly peeled off the nine thousand in interest owed (thanks, Ferd!), but the cash was barely in his pocket when I launched my pitch. I showed him the land survey. I showed him the layout plan. I showed him the seed brochure. I topped my pitch with my newly minted catch phrase. I told him that "when this is over, you won't just be *thanking* me, you'll be *blessing* me!"

Now, given my upbringing's substantial and involuntary exposure to Catholicism, I should have known what a blessing was. I think it's only prudent to point out, however, that at that point in my twisted personal cosmology, the concepts of *blessing* and of *curse* were intertwined and, arguably, interchangeable. In their dealings with me, my investors saw little to suggest otherwise. But this is hindsight. In the heat of the pitch, between the dollars and the dope, I think that it's fair to say that my high-interest associates saw only green.

Alpha was the first recipient of my punchy new pitch line, a single sentence with interwoven layers of bombast, unconscious irony, and unadulterated bullshit. It seemed to work. My pitch completed, Alpha had only one question: "How much?"

My answer was, "Twenty thousand dollars more."

Yep, that's right, the very twenty thousand we needed to put the Chalet purchase in motion. So, I had done it. I paid Dutchie's half of the purchase deposit, bringing my original debt to Dutchie and Bill to two hundred grand.

We were off! We had our ideal location: a beautiful, practical building on plenty of land, with the perfect balance of seclusion and quick access to a massive highway full of anonymous traffic. But there were still challenges ahead. There's a song on the second Roxy

Music album called "In Every Dream Home a Heartache." Our Chalet dream had a its own heartache as well. Although I had succeeded in securing the Chalet, I didn't have a dime to outfit it. We needed a ton of stuff, from lights and wiring to exhaust fans, vapour barriers, and gardening supplies. We needed bodies to man the operation and cash to pay the rent and utilities. In short, regardless of the heartache it would bring at harvest, we needed at least one more partner. At that point, we had Dutchie and me as the property partners, and Crispo, our budmeister, as a harvest partner. Crispo was to be the live-in babysitter, and we agreed to let his girlfriend stay at the Chalet as well. But none of us had cash. In desperation, I approached a former girlfriend and offered her 20 percent of the crop for ten thousand dollars in advance. She accepted.

So here's how it shook out: Dutchie and I each owned 50 percent of the property and 30 percent of the crop. Crispo owned 20 percent of the crop as budmeister and babysitter. My ex owned the remaining 20 percent of the crop, and we had her ten thousand for setup. We had the human resources and the cash, but our harvest was to be carved into more, and smaller, pieces.

So we set to work straightaway to get the equipment and have it set up. I called a friend who was an electrician, and he agreed to wire us. He became the semiofficial electrician for the cartels once we set a standard price for his work, one pound of goods for every ten lights he hooked up. Our fifteen-light setup cost us a pound and a half off the top of the first crop. The fact that he wasn't going to be paid until harvest assured us that he was available for troubleshooting throughout the first crop.

Our three basement rooms were converted into a mother and nursery room and two grow rooms. The mother room had three metal halide lights, called fat boys, which were considered best for vegetative growing. That room also housed a rack of fluorescent lighting over twelve trays that were capable of growing 860 cuttings at a time. In the spirit of diversification, the surplus cuttings were intended for sale. The primary grow room, the largest of the two, housed eight high-pressure, sodium lights, called long boys, which were used for the bloom cycle due to their reflection of the red end of the light spectrum. That room held four hundred pots. The smaller grow room, lit with four long boys, held two hundred pots. That room also had a squirrel cage fan that vented twenty-four hours a day out a window under the front deck.

The other basement windows were blacked out with black plastic, and the area under the deck itself was covered by wooden lattice topped with a black plastic tarp. We even covered the stairs into the basement with a trapdoor, hoping to avoid detection or at least impede casual exploration. Our electrician was mightily impressed with our setup, and I can still remember his line, "You only have one problem here: what to do with the fucking cash!" Alas, there is no historical record of Fate fulfilling the prophecy of electricians.

Despite the extent of our renovations, the whole project was executed quickly; the clock ticks loudly at 10 percent per month. But in spite of our rapid setup, several factors handicapped our haste. First, we were working from seed, and the sexing and cloning of six hundred plants extended our cycle. It also took us into the summer months. The natural heat and humidity of a southern Ontario summer made the heavily lighted, breezeless basement rooms unbearable to the crew who had to work in them. It was also an impediment to the natural development of the plants. We had oscillating fans in each room as well as our externally venting squirrel cage model, but it was a whisper against thunder. Marijuana will not grow once the temperature exceeds eighty-five degrees. In an effort to retain moisture, all the juice runs to the roots where the plant is cooler. Fertilizer is no solution. Overheated, overfed roots clog with undissolved salts that act as a fire retardant when the product is dried.

In an effort to avoid that phenomenon, we ran eighteen-hour light cycles when we could have run twenty-four. But the heat was still brutal down in that basement—fans be damned. One benefit of the shorter cycles, however, was a reduction in electricity consumption. This reduced costs as well as helped to keep the utilities bill from attracting official attention. We even kept the lights off in the bloom rooms from ten in the morning until four in the afternoon to insure that our neighbourhood meter reader never witnessed the numbers tumbling like the counter on the deaf, dumb, and blind kid's pinball machine.

Another twist in the timeline came with the discovery that the Northern Light strain grew at a much faster rate than the other two magic bean varieties or even our original Indica Purple stock. The Northern Light plants were getting too tall for the room. Our solution was to transplant the Northern Lights to a spot outside, down by the stream amongst the sumacs. They thrived in that location, and I was all for moving more plants outdoors. But it was a partnership, and I was outvoted in the interest of caution and focus on the already substantial task at hand. It was also kind of late in the season by that time, and that skewed the vote. My personal debt pressure made the decision not to expand outdoors frustrating, but I had to be content to bide my time.

By September 21, we found ourselves at our first harvest. It was the best crop so far. The smell of it alone was intoxicating. Shiva Skunk derives its name from its aroma, but despite the aromatic similarity to the discharge of our furry black and white friends, I thought the stench was wonderful. It smelled like victory. The crop looked impressive too; both the Big Bud and the Shiva Skunk had grown massive big colas and were getting harder every day. But there was little time to savour sights and smells. The fifty-four-day bloom cycle of the Shiva Skunk gave us six days to harvest and replant; we had to have the next crop ready to keep the cycle cost-effective.

We were up to the task. Crispo, his girlfriend, my ex-girlfriend, and her husband joined Dutchie and I in clipping the plants and hanging them to dry on wire strung from wall to wall in the upstairs bedrooms. We had four-by-eight screens on the floor on which we dried the smaller bud and the "shake," or loose bits. I remember lying on the floor under our tightropes of THC, pondering the buds and thinking that they resembled rocket-propelled grenades. They were also quite phallic, but don't expect me to admit to pondering that.

The bliss was short-lived. When we had finished hanging, there was a lot of pot in those two rooms. But I knew from experience that a harvest dries out to 20 percent of its cut weight. I tried to hold on to the illusion of success. I was physically exhausted from the harvest, but I held that dream tightly in one hand and my vodka in the other, praying for deliverance in the morning.

None was forthcoming. The harvest weighed in, still slightly wet, at twenty pounds. That's sixty thousand dollars. My share was eighteen thousand dollars. In claiming that share, I had amassed a further forty-five thousand dollars in debt. What next?

The first thing I did was replant. I didn't know what else to do. We had the next crop ready to go up just before October. I hoped that the small act of continuity would be of some help with the investors. I rehearsed every possible excuse: renovations, summer grow, first crop from seed, and the standard startup stutters of any new venture. I also drank as much as I could before the meetings, feeling a desperate need for Smirnoff armour.

Loins sufficiently girded, I went to see the Spinner. I brought three pounds of product along with one thousand dollars. I was supposed to give him forty-five thousand. Spinner favoured me with the usual gyrations and plenty of cursing, but he calmed down pretty quickly as I trotted out my litany of laments. The fact that I actually had no idea why we hadn't achieved the promises of the sales brochure must have been outshone by the bullshit. The Spinner signed on for another season. I was astonished, and in truth, so was he. But that was the first time that I had to carry over the interest as well as the principal. That was the moment where the math began to spin out of control.

I met with Alpha next. I owed him a staggering seventy-five thousand dollars. I gave him five thousand. He expressed his concern very loudly. He genuinely scared the shit out of me. Not all of it of course—I seem to have been blessed with a surplus. Besides the fear, I actually felt sorrow. Alpha was a friend. Even in my most hucksteresque moment, I had never intended to disappoint him. He took the five thousand, and I left in one piece, but he was very clear in his expectation: regardless of my other obligations for the next harvest, he wanted the lion's share.

My last stop was King Ferd. I had only four thousand left, and I gave it to him. Now, the fifteen thousand I owed Ferd was a far cry from the seventy I still owed Alpha, but King Ferd had been a friend virtually since childhood—I mean, he was a Hodad! I wasn't physically afraid of Ferd like I was of the other two, but shorting him made me feel very small.

I may have been diminishing, but my debt was not. My financial obligation was a moving target, and we all know that a moving target is harder to hit. The only way I knew to survive was to become a moving target myself. I turned my attention to our fresh new crop.

Chapter Nineteen
Gimme Money

My life away from the lights was my refuge. I managed, through a vigilance not always in evidence elsewhere, to keep the nightmare of my clandestine life out of the family home. Certainly, it was evident that we weren't flush, but the bills were paid, and life was good. Part of that stability came from my determination not to use our family income to relieve the debts I was amassing extralegally. It was an uncrossable line for me, remarkable in a life of boundaries crossed, crisscrossed, and crossed again.

The fact that my family was home only on weekends allowed me to cry my tears all week and put on a cheerful face as my family pulled into the driveway. *Put on* may not be the best description. I dearly loved my wife, and I lived for my two-year-old daughter; there was nothing forced or false here. Even the trials of a weekend-only marriage and the boundless energy of a two-year-old seemed endlessly desirable and adorable to me.

My job at the video company was also progressing well. By then, I was the national accounts manager, and I felt respected by my boss and those who reported to me. But there too, there was trouble on the horizon. Our business of selling used goods at attractive prices was about to be buffeted by the winds of change. Not content to sell the videos to a retailer who reaped the rewards of the consumer rentals, the studios that made the films in the first place were expanding into the sell-through market. The studios reasoned that selling twelve copies at thirteen dollars was better than selling one copy at seventy bucks. They ran trials with a few monster hits: *Beverly Hills Cop, Raiders of the Lost Ark*. The public responded favourably, as did the mass merchants.

It was the beginning of the end for independent and small, chain video rental outlets. For us, it was a double shot: soon there would be fewer rental outlets to open, and our mass merchant goods were being returned to make space for the shiny new releases from the studios. The disappearance of our entire customer base would only be a matter of time. But as that Christmas rolled around, we were still seeing big orders from the likes of Woolco, Zellers, and Kmart. We felt a bit like Santa, but the harder truths were still to come. Unlike Mr. Claus, we were about to see the bounty of Christmas go back up the retail chimney and make an unwelcome arrival back on our North Pole doorstep.

But at home, I was warm and oblivious. The tree was up, the fire was on, my wife had the week off, and it was baby's third Christmas. I wanted that week to last forever, because I dreaded what lay in the man-made jungle just a few miles out of town. The crop that had been planted in October was due to come down right around Christmas Day. Harvest was delayed, not only because of the holidays but also because of the dread.

Let me explain something here. In agrarian culture, the harvest is a time of great celebration. In agrarian counterculture, it should, by rights, be the same. But looming over our every harvest was the cursed brochure that Dutchie had brought from Amsterdam. Let me requote: "four to five ounces per plant." That simple promise had fuelled my optimism, my revenue speculation, and my borrowing strategy. But at this point, I was starting to see it as Dutch duplicity; as Netherlands nonsense; as plain, old, good-for-the-tulips horseshit. No crop we had ever harvested had even approached the yield promised in that Amsterdamned pamphlet. Every single yield had brought a chain of disappointment, recriminations, and logarithmic debt. For that reason, I succumbed to insurmountable dread before each crop hit the weigh scale.

But hit the scale it did. We got twenty-four pounds, our best yield yet but nowhere near four ounces per plant. We got two pounds per light or twenty-four pounds in total. That translates into $72,000. My share was seven pounds or $21,000. It was time for my dreaded tour of the investors. In other words, it was time to get my ass kicked.

I saw the Spinner first and gave him $15,500 dollars. I did this in the form of five pounds and $500 in cash. That left a balance with Spinner of $40,000. The nut kept going up, but the payoffs were getting more substantial. It's worth noting that Spinner's original $30,000 was well paid off by then. But who's counting? Certainly not the Spinner.

I had two pounds of my portion left. I sold it and contemplated the fate of the $6,000. I owed Ferd $14,300; I gave him $300 just to keep an even number. In Ferd's case, of course, we were friends from way back, but it must be said that there was a conscience at work here. He saw my tailspin, and he did not want to accelerate my downfall. Ferd offered to cap the interest. He said not to worry about it. But I did; I felt bad—but not bad enough to decline his offer.

Alpha was in Las Vegas for the holidays and was not returning until after the Super Bowl. He knew the timing of our harvest and had invited me down after New Year's. He wanted to wish me a Merry Christmas and to kill me in a foreign country if I didn't have his money. That is an exaggeration, but I was reticent to make the trip. Alpha's number, three months of interest on $70,000 dollars at 10 percent a month, came to $91,000. I had $6,000. Remember that I had promised Alpha the lion's share of this crop, but that's hard to do with only $6,000 left. I decided to grab every illicit dollar I could get my hands on. In the last few months, out of desperation, I had been dealing small quantities of imported product as a sideline to the grow operations. I had a bit of money in hand from that enterprise. Dipping imprudently into that stash, I managed to assemble a total of $11,000. It would have to do. I boarded a plane for Las Vegas.

Alpha was booked into the Las Vegas Hilton and had been there for about two weeks. He had flown back for a few days over Christmas, but he had the room booked for a month. He knew when my plane was getting in, so I wasted no time in arriving at his hotel. He was in the midst of preparing what I can only describe as a tailgate party inside his gorgeous and quite substantial suite. He seemed happy to see me but even happier to get down to business. I gave him the $11,000 and an involved explanation as to why I thought we were not getting the four ounces per plant promised in the brochure. He seemed so anxious to begin his party that he accepted the money and the explanation in short order.

But I was not out of Alpha's clutches. He threw me a garish sweat suit and demanded that I put it on. He also told me that it was required apparel for the rest of the weekend. The apparel was something called Zubas, an aberration of the mid-nineties that had started life as workout wear but had become the uniform of bodybuilders, sports nuts, and anyone who might lack sufficient powers of self-assessment in front of a full-length mirror.

All of Alpha's crew had to wear the costume, and each suit was heavily embellished with the logo of an American football team. I was chosen to represent the Pittsburgh Steelers. The intent was to look cool. The result resembled an NFL clown convention. I was appalled. Had it come to this—that I was to resemble a football-obsessed children's entertainer? Where was the cool guy in the bell-bottoms and the handmade boots? Up to his neck in debt and ill-advised logo wear, it would seem. I felt like a puppet, but to be honest, I was so relieved to escape physical harm that I would have worn a Dallas cheerleader outfit had Alpha asked.

That night, the whole crew—twenty strong and draped in our thematic Zubas—went to the casino. The next day was more structured. Alpha had a plan. We were instructed to arrive at his suite the next morning with the wastepaper basket from our rooms filled with ice. Alpha's bathtub was already full. All the curtains in the suite were taken down and replaced with NFL team flags. Then the room's two couches were stacked on top of each other as were the two couches from the adjoining room of the suite. The back legs of the upper couches were propped up by stray furniture from around the room. The makeshift bleachers were then positioned in front of the television, which was the biggest one available in those days, even in Vegas. At that point, room service started to arrive, a haphazard train of carts brimming with pretzels, chips, and dips.

Once unloaded, the hotel staff departed and out came Alpha's *pièce de résistance:* a smokeless barbecue. This last innovation elicited awed and raucous praise from the twenty Zuba'd guests, and in short order, to the absolute cacophony in the suite was added the sound of sizzling meat. The collective volume was deafening, the spirits were flowing, and the richly scented smoke of sausages curled up toward the pot lights. What happened next is exactly what you'd expect when a supposedly smoke-free barbecue is in full blaze in a supposedly nonsmoking room. The neighbours did not call the falsely advertised cooker's manufacturer to complain. They called security. Then, they pulled the fire alarm.

Try to imagine the scene. It was ten thirty in the morning, and I was already drunk, but I can still see it as clearly as sausage smoke will allow. The fire alarm was wailing. People on our floor, and possibly others, were racing for the fire exits. Firefighters arrived at the door. Alpha greeted them, wearing his Zubas and eating a wiener. Amid the mayhem in the hall, there was a big furor followed by small assurances, and the hotel staff and firemen left. Ah, the power of a high roller in Vegas.

Alpha's vision had been curtailed, but no, it had not been stopped. He moved the barbecue to the fire escape. This time, there was no alarm, and there were no firefighters. But there was a very large cop, with a very large gun and a fist the size of a Christmas turkey. His pounding on the door was as loud as the fire alarm. At the officer's insistence, a Zubas-clad jester was dispatched to get the boss, and Alpha was invited into the hall for a candid conversation with Vegas' finest. He returned shortly, shaken but not stirred. Dispatching another bozo to fetch the barbecue, Alpha called for hot dogs all around—this time from room service. The tailgate party rolled slowly to a full stop, and I was on a plane home the next day, Zubas safely stowed in my suitcase, never to be worn again.

I had one more investor in the Christmas crop. In coming up with eleven thousand to take to Alpha in Vegas, I had slid some money from an import deal. I mentioned this earlier, somewhat disingenuously employing the phrase *dipping imprudently,* as I recall. This, I admit, is merely a euphemism for my actions at the time. What I did is more accurately characterized as *sticking my hand in the till.* The till was, in fact, the property of an importer named Philby.

Philby was a big guy—six feet two and about three hundred pounds. Born in England, Philby had come to Canada when he was about twenty-five. He had arrived with quite a history. Independently wealthy since the seventies, thanks to a substantial inheritance, Philby had dabbled in band promotion and management with some success. That gave him access to exalted places, but his personal wealth freed him from the sycophantic tendencies of other denizens of the realm.

Legend has it that, during his association with a band called Spooky Tooth, he was invited to the hotel of Eric Clapton, for whom Spooky Tooth was opening. Also in attendance, so the story goes, was George Harrison. It's said that a rather inebriated Philby had approached Mr. Harrison and asked him why he was playing silly religious shit instead of great songs like "Taxman." George did not consider the question for long. His bodyguards deposited Philby in the gutter outside of the hotel before you could say "My sweet Lord."

I believe that story to be true. Philby was loud and sometimes abrasive, but he travelled his own road. He lived well and had a large apartment in the prestigious Manulife Centre in downtown Toronto. He also had another two floors above it. It was there that he grew clones for his outdoor marijuana enterprise.

Although his clones were produced in an apartment, he detested the indoor business. As a smoke connoisseur, he believed that the best bud could only be grown in the sweet Lord's sunshine, its thirst slaked by heaven's cool rain. I had a growing interest in the outdoor concept myself, particularly after seeing how well our Chalet castoffs had thrived down by the brook amongst the sumacs. I decided to regale Philby with the rosy story about the Chalet opportunity. The eventual point of my story was to inform Philby that his compensation for the hash that he had fronted me had morphed into a partnership in the Chalet enterprise. His money was gone, or as I more delicately put it, it was "not immediately accessible." Call it involuntary investment, if you like; it's not a fundraising concept that's likely to catch on. But Philby was an adventurer, and intrigued, I suspect by the outdoor potential of the Chalet, he gave the reconfigured partnership his blessing.

So, by the time I got back from the Zubas Zoo in Vegas, we had another crop under the lights, and I had yet another investor, Philby, to answer to. We took the crop down in March 1993. The results were no better than the Christmas crop, but by then, I had Philby to pay as well as Ferd, Alpha, and the Spinner. All from my seven-pound share.

Look, I know that it's obvious that it was not working. I know it now, and I knew it at the time. The Chalet was not going to solve my financial problems. The crops were not improving, the closing date was looming, and my partner list was increasing. But even so, I saw no sense in abandoning it—at least not until the vendor came to take the Chalet from us. I was already in conversation with her. The May closing was not far off, and I was determined to get an extension, at the very least to get one more crop out and the building cleaned up before we had to vacate. But our seller was not swayed. Her divorce was final, and both she and her ex-husband were unwilling to wait any longer for their money. So, blindfolded traveller that I was, I put in another crop and prayed for divine intervention.

I didn't exactly get it. One day, not far from our deadline, I paid a visit to the Chalet to see how we were progressing, as if looking anxiously at the plants would speed their development. I pulled up the drive and parked around the back. Mine was the only car, but it was not unusual for Crispo and his girlfriend to be out during the day. I let myself in and headed straight for the carpet-covered trapdoor that led to the basement. I headed down the stairs. The mother room was first, and everything was as it always was, the plants standing stoically captive in the strong, artificial light. I proceeded to the small grow room. It seemed so much bigger. That was because it was empty. With disbelief driving my steps, I bounded to the big grow room. It was empty too. No crop, no lights—even the goddamned fans were gone. I ran back upstairs and checked the bedrooms. The minimal furniture was still there, but Crispo and his girlfriend's personal belongings were not.

My babysitters had fled. My one thousand plants—pots and all—were gone with them. I stood astonished and wordless, mere days from having to deliver $140,000 to the legal owner of the Chalet.

CHAPTER TWENTY
RIDING THAT TRAIN

Needless to say, the Chalet caper was an inside job. Dutchie had seen the same shortcomings to the enterprise that I had. It was the same gun for the both of us, even if I was staring down the barrel, and he was just worried about the splatter. But from his perspective, I wasn't much closer to paying the debt to him and Buffalo Bill, Chalet or no Chalet, and the yields were not going to get any better. The situation disturbed him as it did me, but we had different solutions. With May 1 just weeks away, I decided to soldier on and hope. Dutchie decided to take the babies and run. I discovered later that he had another grow operation that he had not told me about. Obviously, Dutchie had decided that his effort and our plants would serve him better there.

My first reaction was something of a cliché. I was suicidal. I had no money, no crop, and no hope of keeping the Chalet or, possibly, my life. But thoughts of suicide passed very quickly. If you have people ready to kill you, why do their job for them? I decided to live, or to try to, and to do so I was going to have to turn shit into shoe polish.

First things first, I was determined not to lose my deposit on the Chalet or, for that matter, the Chalet itself. I knew that the $20,000 down payment on the property was a real asset. With that in mind, I approached an old and trusted friend of mine, Big Ben. Ben was a real estate guy, a professional landlord. He often speculated in real estate, and I was sure that he would see the value of an arrangement.

To that end, I drove him out to the Chalet, gestured grandly around the acreage, showed him around the main floor (with the trapdoor closed and covered) and offered to let him in at $140,000—a good deal for the property. Big Ben saw the wisdom of adding the Chalet to his portfolio and, given the down payment that I'd sunk into the place already, he was prepared to put my monthly rent toward a lease-to-buy arrangement for half ownership as long as I was responsible for the utilities.

So the Chalet was saved. But that was only one of my problems. Let's pause for a moment and reconsider one particular flaw in the enterprise thus far. You might argue that any list would have to start with unbridled optimism, but I'll fight that notion with all the passion of, well, an unbridled optimist. As ill-advised as it may have seemed at several key points in the past, my blind belief in the path was what was keeping this thing alive. But let's set that aside to consider a more tangible flaw.

It's clear to me now that the primary impediment to personal profit was the number of slices being made in the pie. I've said it before; I'll say it again. I had too many partners. I'm not arguing their values as investors or, in some cases, friends, but the knife was hitting the pastry a few too many times. The Great Cannabis Abduction of 1993 may have cleaned out my crop, but it also dispensed with Crispo and Dutchie. As terminal as the midnight plant grab may have seemed, it also increased my portion of any future business.

The other, overarching flaw, of course, was the suffocating payment cycle. The merry-go-round of outstretched hands, deserving though they may have been, was a terrible drain on an ongoing enterprise's financial resources. I was paying rent, utilities, and supply costs, and the investors were getting the profits. I reasoned that I needed a free run around the circuit to get back in the game. But in a bizarre and ironic twist, the runaway harvest had helped me there as well.

I reconsidered my approach to the investors. In the place of the cheery, don't-worry-the-next-crop-will-do-it approach, I did a one-eighty, rehearsing my poor-cuckolded-G-whose-partner-let-him-down face until I had it perfect. My arguments sufficiently polished, it was time to face the Captains of Usury.

It was delicate work. I had to characterize Dutchie as the traitor, but I was concerned that I might put him in physical jeopardy. There was a lot of money at stake here, and Dutchie's flight was only a reaction to an untenable situation and my ongoing obligation to him and Buffalo Bill. I had to tread lightly—never a core attribute for ol' G.

I went first to the Spinner and did some spinning of my own; it was my first crack at the woeful tale. I had a chilling moment when the Spinner suggested that Dutchie was a worthy recipient of "one in the fucking ear." I knew that the Spinner was not referring to a wet forefinger. But I also knew that Spinner's style of conversation often involved flights of fantasy never intended for realization. I chose not to take a chance, though. I calmed the Spinner by assuring him that he would be compensated for the lost crop. That was a ridiculous notion that I had little intention of honouring; who reimburses investors when a stock tanks? But it removed bullets from the conversation. Next, I trotted out the Cinderella story of saving the Chalet, dancing deftly to the bright future ahead with fewer hands in the till. Spinner agreed to stand fast.

I ran pretty much the same story past Alpha, although, as a seasoned business guy, I didn't have to promise him restitution for the purloined crop. I assured him, though, that the interest clock was still ticking. In my instance, the Doomsday Clock is a more appropriate appellation.

Philby, too, accepted the delay. He had not been in line as long, so it was easier to convince him that the prize was not moving farther away. The Chalet's future grows were what he had signed on for anyway.

King Ferd was, of course, a prince. I swore that he would recoup, and though he may have doubted, he accepted and wished me well. Ferd became the first investor to set a cap, in that case at twenty thousand, and the only one to suggest it willingly.

So I was missing a crop, but Dutchie had gallantly left me the mothers. I was also short a budmeister. But I'd been through the cycle enough times and with enough lacklustre results that I knew just the man for that job. I made a call along the lines of "Come, back, Shoolong; all is forgiven." I offered the same cut Crispo had been getting, as well as a piece of the resale revenue on any extra clones he could produce. I also showed him the Chalet. He signed on that afternoon.

The first order of business was to cut clones. As we waited for them to root, we took the time to re-establish the grow rooms. Shoolong had six lights from his last project, so I had to buy just six more. We were back in business by the first week of June.

Unfortunately, the reversal of fortunes in the video trade meant that, by the end of the year's second quarter, my straight job was gone. The company could not overcome the Christmas returns, and in the face of the competition from the major studios, we went bankrupt. I managed to hook up with another video company, building inventories for a mid-size chain. I worked there for only a few months, delaying the inevitable. By that point, it was apparent that a fifty thousand-a-year day job was not going to address my problem. Just as I faced the reality that I needed something bigger, something bigger that way came.

The newest addition to my gallery of scoundrels was a rough Irish drinker we called the Kid. I met him through a friend of Dutchie's. That may seem odd, but it's not. Dutchie despised the Kid. They were bitter ex-partners—he had been Dutchie's coconspirator in the industrial grow operation that was secretly running parallel to our partnership at the Chalet. The unrealized promises of the notorious pamphlet had corroded their relationship as it had mine with Dutchie. I've been told that Dutchie conspired to have the Kid introduced to me as a form of vengeance. The Kid had money. I needed money. Dutchie was supposedly convinced that, if I partnered with the Kid, I would be the Kid's financial ruin—such was Dutchie's love of us both.

The Kid had a reputation as a hands-off guy. That annoyed a lot of people, Dutchie included. A grow operation is very labour-intensive; cutting, planting, watering, and harvesting is hard work, and your hands get dirty in a very literal sense. The Kid's hands were clean; he kept them in his pockets. But, ah, what deep pockets they were! And I had just the project. The demise of one of the video companies with which I was associated had left vacant a large industrial space in the suburbs just north of Toronto. Voila! The Kid and I were in the industrial grow op business.

I set up an office in the front of the unit, just as a legit tenant would. We left receiving open, but we drywalled the rest of the warehouse and painted all the glass—doors and all. Rent was five thousand a month, which was a bit steep but not uncommon for the premium paid to a landlord with eyes closed and an outstretched hand. By the way, we called the front company Moonlight Promotions. The old dreams die hard.

The Kid had twenty lights from his last operation, and he had his own electrician. I was to reimburse the Kid for half of his investment at harvest. I had Shoolong cultivate a thousand kids, and he came onboard as budmeister for 20 percent of the yield. We had everything prepped and the lights up in the first week of June. The place came with a ten thousand-dollar air conditioner unit on the roof. We convinced ourselves that that would be our hedge against the heat drawbacks of a summer grow. We were wrong. The lights looked beautiful, but the place was an oven. Still, with twenty lights at the Beaver Lodge, as we industriously named it, and twelve lights at the Chalet, I felt that I had turned the corner.

One real plus to the Beaver Lodge was my growth as an apprentice budmeister. With two locations many miles apart going up and coming down on a roughly synchronous schedule, Shoolong was stretched pretty thin. And the Kid's hands, as I've said, were untroubled by soil or fertilizer. With the sound of the Doomsday Clock in my ears, I jumped in up to my elbows in dirt and water.

The industrial was not the only thing I did on my summer vacation. I knew Sir Gilley from the limo days—he had been a partner at one point—and he was a long time associate of Dutchie's. Gilley had approached Dutchie about an outdoor opportunity, but Dutchie was not interested. Sir Gilley, not to be dissuaded, came to me for clones. I had been convinced by how well the orphan Indica plants had flourished at the Chalet that there was a future in outdoor growth. I talked to Shoolong and decided to jump in with both feet. I told Sir Gilley that we would supply clones but that we also wanted to be partners. Maybe outdoor was to be my path of debt dissolution.

Unlike the Kid, I was ready, willing, and anxious to get my hands dirty.

I got them dirty all right, and I got my back broken and pretty much every other uncovered body part feasted upon by bugs. The secret locale for the planting was near Napanee, Ontario, a few miles into the woods and inaccessible by car. We had to carry everything—plants, soil, fertilizer, water—through the woods to the site. The bags of fertilizer alone would reduce a tough guy to tears. Then there was the digging, the planting, and the watering. We never stopped, even to eat. The black flies, however, ate constantly. And the horse flies ate what the black flies left.

Bug banquets though we were, we successfully planted fifty kids each in the wild, and then we left them to Mother Nature. We were so exhausted by the end of the two-mile trek back to the cars that we could barely speak. The entire mission took about ten hours. It was the hardest I've ever worked in my life, before or since. So traumatized were we by the reality of brutal physical work that we never went back until harvest.

All of that was on top of the summer duties at the Beaver Lodge. Shoolong and I put a great deal of effort into the Lodge, and by September, the crop looked promising, even though we fully anticipated the heat to affect the yield. Just before the harvest, Shoolong and I were there to water, when we noticed a guy up on the roof. Shoolong smirked and suggested that he was looking for the skunk. In a very literal sense, he was. The owner of an adjacent unit had registered complaints about the incessant odour of a skunk and called a maintenance guy from the company that supervised the buildings. The owner of our unit got a call the next day, asking him to let them inspect the facility on the suspicion that a family of skunks had taken up residence inside.

As the crop was close to coming down, I asked the owner to buy us a week. The maintenance people, in the absence of a life-threatening situation, agreed. As it happened, that weekend was a long one, with Labour Day to be exact. I had a total of three days.

Rather inconveniently, the Chalet was coming down at the same time. Shoolong and my ex, who was still a Chalet harvest partner, got a couple of guys we trusted to help, and the Chalet came down in record time. Next stop, the Beaver Lodge. We brought the guys from the Chalet in for that one, as well as two other guys I knew. The Kid was in attendance as well, but he barely did more than watch. He was there to keep an eye on the crop. Note that I said an eye and not a hand or even a finger.

We only had the three days, but I wanted the marijuana out of there by Sunday so that we could clean up, take the lights down, and return the space to some semblance of normalcy. The two guys I hired turned out to be useless; it's hard to be productive with a beer in one hand and a cigarette in the other. I never hired them again. But the job got done, and the maintenance inspector never found a thing. Of course, what we were actually doing never occurred to him. He was looking for an animal; it never occurred to him that the stink might be a plant. His solution was black and white, when the real culprit was a dark, sticky green.

We had two more crops in, eighteen pounds from the Chalet and twenty-four from the Lodge. We trimmed and dried the Beaver Lodge yield at the Chalet. It was a necessity that time, because of our ungracious exit from the Lodge, but it became the standard in future. The Chalet also proved useful as a composting site for the soil and trim from the Beaver Lodge crop. I instructed my crew to dump the remains by the stream, where we'd thrown the other soil from grows at the Chalet. In a few years time, that gully took on the appearance of reclaimed land. That afforded us detection-free disposal, which was yet another advantage of our secluded Viceroy paradise.

By the time Shoolong, the trimmers, the Kid, and my ex each got their shares, I had eleven pounds from the Chalet and nine from the Beaver Lodge with the Napanee outdoor yield still to come. First, though, it was time for me to ride the investor-go-round. I had twenty pounds to divvy up, totalling $60,000. The first big bite had to go to the Kid, about $10,000 right off the top for my share of the overhead he had fronted at the Lodge. That left fifty thousand, but because it had taken five months for us to come to fruition after the plant heist, the interest rates had far outstripped the yield.

I'll go over how I distributed the cash, but the bong bookkeeping segments of this story are coming to an end. I haven't given you a numbers report in a while, though, and an overview is necessary to understand the weight of my chains. I owed Alpha a total of $135,000. I paid him $20,000, leaving me with $115,000 owing. I owed the Spinner $75,000. I paid him $10,000, leaving $65,000 unpaid. Philby was up to $67,500. I paid him $12,500, so that I then owed him $55,000. As King Ferd had voluntarily topped out, I let sleeping dogs lie and just avoided waking my old buddy up. On top of all that, I had kept up with the Chalet monthly payments, and even though I could barely afford it, I put $5,000 down toward the mortgage under my deal with Big Ben.

It was time for another nature hike at the Napanee location. Shoolong, Sir Gilley, and I headed for the woods to harvest the outdoor. It was late in the season, so the bugs were less of a problem, but our initial view of the crop stung nonetheless. The first 150 plants we came upon were a total disappointment, not even worth harvesting. Before planting, I had worried that our plants were a bit immature for the mighty whims of Mother Nature, but I had hoped for the best. A large portion had not survived.

Disappointed, we hiked up the weather-ravaged hill to survey the rest of our planting. At that point there was an angelic choir and a heavenly beam of light. Possibly. What is certain is that I looked out over about a hundred healthy plants with huge buds, the like of which I had never seen. From that Napanee hilltop, I saw for the first time what a true outdoor crop might yield.

Were we finally seeing the four-to-five-ounce plants of the well-worn brochure? We each had hockey bags, and we proceeded to rough cut our own plants and load the harvest into our bags. The biggest plants were, indeed, about four ounces each, the holy grail of the legend. Back at the Chalet, after the final cut, dry, and weigh, my haul was two pounds. Praise be and hallelujah, I had seen the promised land.

One valuable side benefit of the trek through the woods with Sir Gilley was a conversation we had about indoor setups. Gilley had been the prep carpenter for a few of Dutchie's ops, and he claimed to know building techniques that could keep our "skunk" problem from troubling us. I filed that revelation away, intent on tapping Gilley's expertise in the very near future.

The debt clock was ticking, and never one for the slow, measured decision, I decided to set up, once again, at the Beaver Lodge, armed with new expertise. We had, after all, survived our skunk scare unscathed. Why not return to the scene of the crime? First, though, I had to sell the idea to the Kid and Alpha. The Beaver Lodge really was a good location; it was anonymous, it was spacious, and we knew how to configure it. I reasoned that, with Gilly's design improvements incorporated into the new setup, our skunk problem would not reoccur. But the renovations required money on top of the cash it would take to do a normal setup. I know you'll think I'm nuts, but I decided to go to Alpha.

It was important to Alpha that he not be taken for a fool—more important, I think, than the money itself. I approached him when the twenty thousand I'd just paid was fresh in his mind. He knew that a large part of that had come from the Beaver Lodge, and he could see the advantage of having it in operation again. But I explained that the Kid was willing to finance only half; he was not willing to front the whole thing. There were risks there. We'd already drawn attention to ourselves, but I was convinced that, with our new techniques, it would not happen again.

There was another risk. Shoolong would not be returning. It was time to step up and take the reins—or the clippers, or the watering can, or whatever metaphor you deem appropriate at this point. I had decided to budmeister that one myself. From Alpha's standpoint as well as my own, that could be seen as good news. It meant one less partner to pay. Here's the deal I offered Alpha: for an additional $20,000 cash from him, I would reset Alpha's debt at $200,000. At that point, I owed him $115,000, and the fresh $20,000 should have taken it only to $135,000. But here's the catch: under my deal, I was to pay Alpha no further interest.

That was not as rash on my part as it might seem. I knew the yields that I could get out of both the Chalet and the Lodge and had plans to further expand capacity. I also no longer had Shoolong to pay. Finally, three months of interest on $135,000 was $41,000. That brought the total close to $200,000 anyhow. I reasoned that it was worth the bump up to be in pure payback mode with my biggest lender. Alpha, possibly tired of my quarterly excuses, accepted the deal.

With Alpha's fresh $20,000 in hand, I called Sir Gilley to bring his expertise to the Beaver Lodge. It should be said that Gilley knew more about it than I did, but there were several principles—negative pressure, moisture control, proper use of roof fans—that even Gilley had yet to learn. But he did upgrade our operation from the skunk farm of a few months before. When Gilley was done, we used the Kid's electrician again. We ordered the clones from Shoolong; he had them for us by the first week in October. We were back up and running with thirty lights, and the place looked marvellous.

Buoyed by my success in selling Alpha the no-interest package, I decided to approach Philby with a similar offer. My proposal was to bring my debt up to $100,000 with no further interest. I only owed Philby $55,000, but remember that he had been paid precious little to that date. By the time the next payment would be due just before Christmas, I would have had his money for over a year. The interest owed to Philby—$40,000 at 10 percent a month times twelve—would have been another $48,000. My offer was not really any more rash than the one I had made to Alpha. But for Philby, it was a sweet, clean deal, and he accepted.

Next stop, the Spinner. Astonishingly, Spinner was the easiest one to convince. I offered him the no-interest cutoff of $85,000. Maybe my regular light-in-the-pocket visits were as unpleasant for him as they were for me, because he bit, and I didn't get hit.

Be assured, patient reader, that the math gets easier, and the lessons less frequent from this point on. But bear this in mind as we go: my total debt by then was just over $600,000. My deals left me still weak, wounded, and hurting, but the bleeding had stopped.

The Chalet yielded again in December. We had a good crop of around twenty-four pounds. I put another $5,000 toward the mortgage and distributed the spoils amongst all the investors except King Ferd. We quickly replanted, and I was looking forward to a relaxing Christmas with the family, when the Beaver Lodge sent an early gift: yet another crisis.

The woman whose business was next door to the Beaver Lodge called the building owner. It was not odour-inspired. The issue was a little more difficult to explain. Excessive moisture is a fact of life within a grow operation. If you've ever been in a greenhouse or an indoor jungle exhibit at the zoo, you'll know that the humidity is remarkable. But those environments are also quite warm, as was our grow op. Our neighbour's office was less warm, and it was winter. In Canada. When the tenant opened her business one particular morning after a weekend, the combination of our moisture and her lowered thermostat had turned her office windows into an ice palace. She called the owner. The owner called us. What to do? We stalled, of course. We promised the owner that we would sort it out. The owner, in turn, assured our neighbour that we would address her problem.

We were three weeks from harvest. The key element of my stall strategy was to go in and water every three days at six in the morning to avoid detection. That way, the watering would be complete before nine am, when I assumed that my neighbour arrived at her office. That worked for two full weeks, but one morning, I was just locking our front door when she pulled up. My saving grace was our bogus front office. I explained to our neighbour that I only worked in the office and that the warehouse was a separate business run by two gentlemen who were down in Los Angeles until the New Year. I assured her that they were vacating at the end of the month and that the unit was going up for sale.

Even so, desperate for a sympathetic ear, she insisted that I come into her unit to show me why she was upset. In the spirit of a sympathetic third party, I agreed. The sight was remarkable. The ice on her office windows was about half an inch thick. There were frost crystals on parts of her outside walls. It was really quite lovely in a trippy sort of way, but I had the sense not to share that thought. I expressed mild concern, while assuring her that whatever had caused the problem could not be toxic and would certainly be investigated further. It was then that she told me that she'd had the health department in. I was starting to panic. But panic never made an interest payment, and I forced myself to exude calm and assurance.

Now, if the health department were called in to a similar situation these days, it would take them a microsecond to suspect the cause and just a little longer to have the cops at my door. But we were pioneers; back in 1993, nobody in the oblivious public or the more oblivious public service knew about grow houses. Surveying frost on a window in Canada in winter did not lead to the suspicion that fifteen hundred cannabis plants consuming six hundred gallons of water every seventy-two hours were basking in artificial light on the other side of your wall. Even so, I had to sell her on the idea that I would see the situation rectified. Somehow, I managed to do it.

So, the crop had to come down, and the place had to be empty before the Christmas break had passed—holiday and family notwithstanding. We rented a box van, and with a few trusted workers and the Kid as our immobile supervisor, I managed to get it all down on Boxing Day. We cut the plants and gently stuffed them into green garbage bags. Then we stacked the empty pots one on top of another and put everything we could—bags, pots, dirt, and all—into that twenty-foot truck. I drove it all to the Chalet.

On the drive, the thought occurred to me that, had that van been pulled over by the cops, the whole thing would have been over, there and then. But there was no choice. Thanks to our neighbour's affair with Jack Frost, we were certain that the authorities were only a brisk rap-on-the-door away. As of the load, we weren't completely inspection-ready at the Lodge, but the illegal stuff was gone, and besides, I knew that once the watering stopped, the ice problem next door would cease in kind. The good news is that we never heard from the neighbour again. The bad news was that, in spite of the time and money invested, the Beaver Lodge had to become history.

Once the Lodge harvest was trimmed, dried, and weighed, we had forty pounds. In my role as the budmeister, I was paid a thousand dollars a month for my effort. If that seems to you, considering the time, stress, and neighbour management, to be akin to robbery, it seemed that way to me as well. But I was, as I've said, a desperate man. The Kid knew it, and he took advantage by pressing me to a shit deal. He had a beautiful Palace Pier condo, overlooking Lake Ontario, and he drove home each night in a Porsche. I had over half a million dollars in debt.

I was bitter. It's funny how frustration manifests itself in unusual ways. As I attended to the messy drudgery of trimming and drying our crop at the Chalet, my thoughts drifted back to the honey wagon, the tanker truck that pumped out the septic systems in rural areas like my grandparents' farm. With that and my plight as my inspiration, I occupied myself with this little homegrown nursery rhyme:

> The Kid is in the penthouse, counting up his money,
> And Gerry's in the shithouse, sucking up the honey.

I was a songwriter at last. Happy New Year from the grow op genius.

The Young Turk: facial hair expertise a
precusor to later cultivation talents.

Brother Bernard: my first roommate after
exiting the parental abode.

The G man, a few years later. Someone call
Joe Jackson: we've located his shoes!

The Gang in the wild: Names withheld to protect the naked.

The mighty Kercules. Talented, handsome and gone. A great loss.

Bonnie Prince Plum. Young, wild and not forgotten.

The field Of dreams: Cinerama would have
captured it better. Odorama too.

Just Say No! Editorial content carved into the
vapour barrier by the local constabulary.

BUSTED

Police dig up $5M in potted plants

A 46-year-old Oshawa man has been charged after police cracked a $5 million indoor marijuana growing operation.

Durham Regional Police, armed with a search warrant, initially raided a residence at 724 Aruba Cres. in Oshawa on April 26. Police then searched business premises at 530 Westney Rd. S. in Ajax and on Shelter Valley Road in Cobourg, along with two locations in Scarborough and others in Brampton and Markham, finishing their raids on May 1.

Police seized more than 7,000 marijuana plants at the six business locations, including more than 2,000 in Cobourg and 450 at the Ajax premise.

All the business locations housed sophisticated indoor growing operations, police say. They were all similarly disguised as industrial units having a front office under a company name with the rear unit housing an enclosed ventilat-

POLICE from page A1

ed growing set-up.

Durham police were assisted by police drug units of Metro, Peel and York regions in the raids.

Gerald McCarthy has been charged with culti-

vation of marijuana, possession for the purpose of trafficking and possession of the proceeds of crime in Durham and faces similar charges in Metro, Peel and York.

Police say the investigation into further suspects continues.

My moment in ink. From Oshawa This Week and other Metroland Durham Regional Media Group papers.

CPIC Response

Ontario Provincial Police

Printed: 2004/07/10 12:56 by 9973

CRII FPS:530381A/REM:CLEE

Date sent: 2004/07/10 12:56   Status: Not read

Response:

```
Q CR LANG:E LVL: 2
REM: 9973 CLEE


*ROYAL CANADIAN MOUNTED POLICE - IDENTIFICATION SERVICES

*RESTRICTED - INFORMATION SUPPORTED BY FINGERPRINTS
SUBMITTED BY LAW.
*ENFORCEMENT AGENCIES - DISTRIBUTION TO AUTHORIZED AGENCIES
ONLY.

FPS: 530381A

MC CARTHY. GERALD JOSEPH


*CRIMINAL CONVICTIONS CONDITIONAL AND ABSOLUTE DISCHARGES
*AND RELATED INFORMATION

1978-09-08 POSS OF A NARCOTIC FOR 2 YRS LESS 1 DAY
KITCHENER ONT THE PURPOSE OF TRAFFICKING
SEC 4(2) NC ACT
(KITCHENER OPP     —
6-11-8-77)

1979-05-30 PAROLED

1995-11-14 POSS OF NARCOTIC $1500
TORONTO ONT SEC 3(1) NC ACT
(DOWNSVIEW OPP
95-0680)

1998-01-08 CULTIVATION OF NARCOTIC 18 MOS CONDITIONAL
SENTENCE
TORONTO ONT SEC 6(1)(2) NC ACT ORDER
(METRO TORONTO POLICE
```

My rap sheet, page one.

```
001780-72)

2000-08-22 PRODUCE A SCHEDULE II 105 DAYS amp
TORONTO ONT SUBSTANCE (TIME SERVED 35 DAYS)
SEC 7(2)(B) CDS ACT
(TORONTO PS
001780-72)

2001-02-19 POSS OF A SCHEDULE I $500
COBOURG ONT SUBSTANCE
SEC 4(3) CDS ACT
(COBOURG PS
172-00)


*END OF CONVICTIONS AND DISCHARGES


*SUMMARY OF POLICE INFORMATION - NOT INTENDED FOR SENTENCING
PURPOSES

1972-11-22 TORONTO ONT
POSS OF A NARCOTIC FOR THE
PURPOSE OF TRAFFICKING
ACQUITTED

1973-04-17 TORONTO ONT
POSS OF A NARCOTIC
WITHDRAWN

1973-12-03 TORONTO ONT
TRAFFICKING IN A NARCOTIC
DISMISSED

1974-03-14 TORONTO ONT
POSS OF A NARCOTIC
CONDITIONAL DISCHARGE amp
PROBATION FOR 1 YR

1976-11-17 NEWMARKET ONT
POSS OF A WEAPON
DISMISSED

1978-01-05 AJAX ONT
FALSE PRETENCES - WITHDRAWN

1989-12-12
DRIVING WITH MORE THAN
80 MGS OF ALCOHOL IN BLOOD
SEC 253(B) CC
```

Printed by: 9073   Date: 10/07/2004 12:56   Page 2

My rap sheet, continued: apparently one page is not enough...

```
-WITHDRAWN
(OPP TORONTO
13-89)

1995-11-14
POSS OF A NARCOTIC FOR
THE PURPOSE OF TRAFFICKING
SEC 4(2) NC ACT
-WITHDRAWN
(DOWNSVIEW OPP
95-0680)

1998-01-08
CULTIVATION OF NARCOTIC
SEC 6(1)(2) NC ACT
POSS OF A NARCOTIC FOR THE
PURPOSE OF TRAFFICKING
SEC 4(2)(3) NC ACT (2 CHGS)
-WITHDRAWN
(METRO TORONTO POLICE
001780-72)

2000-08-22
POSS OF A SCHEDULE II
SUBSTANCE FOR THE PURPOSE
OF TRAFFICKING
SEC 5(3)(A) CDS ACT
-WITHDRAWN
(TORONTO PS
001780-72)

*END OF POLICE INFORMATION
20040710125611200407101256 11
```

MARCH 1/2006

… and neither are two! My rap sheet, page three.

Patti and Gerry: wedding day bliss.

The Brothers and Sisters McCarthy. Back row: Paul, Bernard, Gerald, Don. Front row: Jennifer, Beth, Maureen

A lovely pair. Daughter Alex and Patti, a few years ago

Gerald and Patti, more recent times. That's
a field of corn behind us. I swear!

Chapter Twenty-One
Industrial Disease

The hasty collapse of the Beaver Lodge created another problem. The product, hastily bagged and trucked to the Chalet, ran a real risk of bud rot, a moisture-based problem that reduces the precious buds to mushy uselessness. The perilous circumstances with our neighbour had forced us to cut the crop prematurely and stuff it into watertight bags. Getting it to the Chalet was one thing, but then I had a lot of dope and a minimum of time to process it before it turned soft and worthless. I desperately needed workforce reinforcements.

I'm sure that you sense the problem here. There's a certain delicacy to recruiting for that kind of thing. You can't just place a newspaper ad.

> WANTED: Motivated young men and women with intermediate scissor proficiency for an exciting career in the alternative recreation industry. Master's degree in discretion a prerequisite. Relatives and friends of law enforcement personnel need not apply.

I've been told that 80 percent of all successful job candidates come with a personal recommendation. The pot business runs closer to 100 percent. I heard from trusted lips about a guy who was to become an essential part of the operation from that point on. He was a good-looking young man, who was over six feet tall with a sense of fun and a certain toughness that he carried well. He had a reputation of having astonishing good luck and of being one of those people whom fortune favours with a warm and constant light. For all of these reasons, we called him Golden Boy.

Golden Boy's job was not simply to grab the clippers and snip. I gave him the more challenging task of finding a trustworthy crew of two people he could rely on to execute the tasks at hand with speed and secrecy. That he did, hiring two helpers who were the first among a small battalion of young folks that came to be known as Gerry's Kids. Golden Boy and the helpers trimmed, bud rot was avoided, and the template was established for grander times to come.

Thanks to staffing up, we had a way to efficiently process the crop. But another problem was holding us back. You know how often we'd had to abandon locations, from the Riviera through the Beaver Lodge. It was obvious to me that the setup and reconfiguration of locations was an impediment, not only to better yields, but to control of overheads as well. I needed to find a good location that we could configure properly, amortizing the time and costs of doing so over multiple harvests.

Just after Dutchie's return from Amsterdam with the cursed brochure and the beloved magic beans, he and the Kid had set up an industrial location called the Shoot Shop. The shop has been named after its previous incarnation as a development lab for large scale photographic reproductions used for everything from store decor to theatrical sets. The sign was still above the door when Dutchie and the Kid fell out over the disappointing yield from the beans. It was still above the door when the Kid and I agreed to target the Shoot Shop as our long-term industrial base. I went to the landlord, in my guise as Mr. Moonlight, to negotiate a lease. Given our intended usage, those were always tricky encounters, but that one was made smoother when, in the process of the tour, the owner told me breezily that the former tenants had been, and I quote, "growing marijuana in here." He did not seem at all perturbed; the insinuation was clear. We had a sympathetic, hands-off landlord for as long as we paid on time. He saw cash in his future. I saw it in mine. We cut a deal. We fully intended for the Shoot Shop to be a long-term operation, and the landlord's nudge and wink made the prospect more viable. We set to work.

What we did at the Shoot Shop was to become a standard for subsequent industrial units. Our illicit activities were housed in a room within a room. Using Sir Gilley's team, we built a full drywalled room that took up most of the space available in the warehouse. The new structure was itself subdivided; one fifth of it was walled off as a nursery. We even installed a drywall roof inside the warehouse, a bit of paranoid overkill that was replaced by a black, plastic tarp in subsequent units. Our room would, we hoped, allow us to open the receiving doors and to endure the scrutiny of casual inspection by outsiders without interruption of our core activity.

Our theory was put to the test within the week. Because we were masquerading as a normal business, I had a policy of leaving the front door unlatched, reasoning that a constantly locked business would raise suspicion. I had set up a prop office, using the old desks from Moonlight Limousine, as well as phones, shelving, and some books and videos on the wall. I was comfortable that someone could walk in and, without seeing the warehouse, sense nothing amiss. What I had not anticipated was a weary bureaucrat whose job was to ascertain the nature of our business for more efficient taxation. He looked around the office, taking notes as he went and asked to see the warehouse. After an awkward moment and some iffy stalling, I excused myself to alert my crew, who were still putting the final touches on the grow room. All the clones were in the room, unplanted and certainly not up to receiving guests. I told my crew to close everything up fast and get inside the room we'd constructed and keep quiet.

I went back for the civil servant, ushering him into the warehouse, explaining that we were a photography reproduction studio that specialized in stage props and billboard manufacturing. I explained that our rather large room was one big darkroom designed for oversized materials and that letting him inside would compromise projects in progress. The latter part was actually true. He paused for a moment. I sweated for an equal period. Then he asked the dimensions of the room and whether it was carpeted. I answered succinctly. He nodded and told me to expect my tax assessment in the near future.

At the word *future*, it occurred to me how close I had just come to not having one. The bureaucrat went on his way. I went back to the warehouse and gave the crew the all clear. Work resumed on the structure that, from that point on, was referred to as the darkroom.

Dark it was not. It housed twenty lights and another four in the walled-off nursery. All of this was similar to previous setups, but the Shoot Shop was the birthplace of another innovation. It was there that I came up with the idea of putting the clones in four-inch pots and leaving them in the nursery under eighteen hours of light a day for thirty days. At that point, prior to transplanting them into seven-inch pots and transferring them to the grow room, we started to trim the bottom shoots and use them as our next generation of clones.

This had multiple benefits. It eliminated the need to keep mother plants to produce clones, and it eliminated the electricity needed for the mothers. It also meant shortening the entire cycle by rooting and developing the clones while the plants that they came from grew to harvest. That meant a new crop every sixty days. It also appeared that the plants grew more readily with the lower foliage removed. Heaven help us, we were embracing efficiency!

Another innovation that developed at the Shoot Shop was the practice of venting by splicing a squirrel cage fan into the exhaust vent already in place as part of the natural gas heating system. This was essential, because we needed to control the flow of air. These new drywall rooms were basically airtight. The drywall was strapped from ground to ceiling with a plastic vapour barrier. We forced air into the room with the fan and exhausted out the gas vent. In future installations, we managed to achieve total negative pressure in the rooms; that meant that no air went out of our rooms except through the vent on the roof. As we vented around the clock, there was virtually no odour build-up and no more trouble from the Skunk Patrol.

Even with all of that innovation, we had the Shoot Shop fully functional by February 1. Flush with newfound expertise and its anticipated efficiencies, I was ready for another location.

An old friend we called Noof (Canadians may remark on the sensitivity of this moniker) had approached me about setting up a location with him. Inspired by a small location set up by two other friends, Moonlight Promotions leased twelve hundred square feet in suburban Scarborough. I told the landlord that I intended to sublet a portion of the warehouse to a landscaping firm called GEM, another of my front companies. The landscaping front explained the presence of dirt, fertilizer, and the gardening accoutrements of our enterprise. Landscaping was actually Noof's day job, so our cover was a perfect fit with his truck, trailer, and equipment. The Scarborough location was intentional too, as it spread Moonlight's electrical bills into another township reducing the possibility of our high consumption coming to the attention of an attentive utilities clerk in any one jurisdiction.

So we had a location and a cover. But our funding was not solid at all. My partner, Noof, had enough for his share, but I was short of mine. The Kid had funded the Shoot Shop and had no interest in this operation. Remember, even without the interest, every cent I got was still going to my investors. After some internal brainstorming, I hatched my next inspiration. Inspired by other agricultural businesses, I hit upon the idea of selling futures. I had two crops about to come down: the Chalet in March and the Shoot Shop in April. The idea was to sell off upcoming crops at a reduced price to expedite access to funding.

I decided to take the proposal to the Spinner and the Fat Man. You'll remember that the Fat Man was the big fish that I had bought from Kiki in the importation days. He was still active as a dealer and was always looking to source product. I knew that my share from the Chalet would be at least ten pounds, so I sold futures on six: three to Spinner and three to the Fat Man. They paid two thousand dollars a pound, which was a saving of a grand per pound—lucrative but risky. If the crop didn't come in or if the police *did*, they would be out six thousand each. But those guys were accustomed to risk for gain. They were, after all, drug dealers.

So with their spec cash in hand and the contribution from Noof, we opened my next little industrial. We called it Dynamic. Now, before you think I had a Tony Robbins moment or was falling under the spell of pinheaded sales jargon, you need to know the name of the street where our operation was housed. The street was called Dynamic. It's a really goofy name for a street, and the simultaneous banality and perversity of our sense of humour mandated that we take our name from our new address.

And so the wheel rolled on. The Chalet yielded once again and went straight back up with most of my profits having been presold as futures. The Shoot Shop was nearing its first harvest. But just prior to that, I had an unlikely visitor. I received a social call from the amazing disappearing Dutchie.

The meeting was not very fractious. I took the opportunity to inform him that, because of his midnight dash with the Chalet plants and the hardware, I was assessing him a fine of twenty thousand dollars to be deducted from the money I owed to him and Buffalo Bill. He wasn't happy, but he had a motive to accept. He proposed that we open another industrial that he was prepared to finance. I would receive a salary of a thousand a month, and he would take the profit toward the money I still owed.

Remember that that was money toward the debt that had instigated this ever-expanding enterprise in the first place. Although I was to be a mere hired hand, I agreed to renew our business dealings for the debt reduction and, let's be honest, the grand a month in pocket money. However, mindful of the number of balls that I had in the air, I asked him to underwrite manpower at planting and at harvest.

Dutchie agreed to my terms, and I lined up Golden Boy and Gerry's Kids for the tasks. We chose yet another township for our location. That time, we went to Markham, a suburb just north of Toronto. We got our location, and within a week, we had the nursery up and were close to completion on the rest of the setup built based on the Shoot Shop template of twenty lights with a four-lamp nursery. In honour of my slave master, I called the place the Dutch Oven.

By that time, the Shoot Shop was ready to come down, so I transported Golden Boy into town from the Chalet, where we harvested a thousand plants. For that cull, we graduated from garbage bags to blue, seventy-six-litre tote boxes, the kind you can buy at housewares and hardware stores. The boxes turned out to be very practical; they had substantial capacity and were neatly stackable in the van. Some of my coworkers joked that the blue, tote boxes became my trademark. Over time, I bought literally hundreds of the things. To date, no thank-you note from Home Depot has been received.

We used the boxes for both the wheat and the chaff, as it were, packing fan leaf, stalk, and roots into one set of boxes and bud and calyx leaf into another. Typically, one box would hold about twelve pounds of rough, wet product, which was not too hard on the back. The dirt and detritus was less spine-friendly, but it had to be boxed and transported as well; the Chalet was our only safe dumping ground. The van would hold sixteen blue boxes at a time. But the wheat had priority; it went first, and subsequent trips transported the chaff. The van trip from the city to the Chalet was one I made hundreds of times, always at rush hour and always in a shirt and tie—just another semicomatose commuter wearing down his tires and his life simultaneously on the Trans-Canada Highway.

Before the Oven was fully constructed, two of our crew approached me with yet another partnership proposal. I had the skills down now, so I was hungry to apply them early and often. The new one was in Scarborough as well, but because Dynamic was so small, I reasoned that the electricity consumption would not be too much of a giveaway to the authorities. Besides, I planned to claim that I was only using the office there, anyway. The power drain came from the warehouse. We called the new twenty-lighter the Hen House in deference to the nickname of one of the coowners. It was a good, straightforward deal as long as you factor in that I had to sell futures again to fund it.

At that point, I had the Chalet, the Shoot Shop, the Dutch Oven, and Dynamic going as well as the Hen House. I wasn't making big money, because of the back-to-back startup costs and the discounting built into the futures. Even so, I was bringing a lot of smoke to market.

The key to any market economy is not only availability but also quality. At that point in the nineties, the pot business was sufficiently developed to produce a product rating system. No, I'm not kidding. Think of the Grade A or B system for meat or the VQA system for wines. VQA stands for "vintner quality assured." The cartel rating system was a kind of CQA or "cannabis quality assured." At the centre of the trade cooperative was a man who was sampler, judge, and jury over the street reputation of the goods at hand. His name was Kiki.

Yes, our old and eccentric pal, Kiki—he of the Birdhouse—was the pot business' Judge Judy. Over the years, he had continued to sell directly to consumers at a modest level and had developed a street reputation as a man with an inestimable palate for pot. He was no less eccentric, but that very eccentricity had moved him to develop a dope rating system.

At first, it was solely for the benefit, and no doubt amusement, of his clientele. But the accuracy of Kiki's assessments enhanced his credibility and broadened his reputation in the smoke community. Soon the cartels sought out his blessing in exchange for an honorarium of the very weed he was grading. They came to his door, seeking his blessing.

But Kiki took his job quite seriously. He hadn't stumbled upon his reputation; he had earned it, and his dottiness meant that he was too fruity to be bought. Each of his assessments was thoughtful and measured. I once saw him give some particularly spectacular Hawaiian a *9.5*, a rating as high as he has ever given before or since.

When I asked him about the rating, he explained that, "Actually, I thought it deserved a ten, but that would leave nothing to aspire to." Besides, he added, "I have a reputation to maintain."

As if to illustrate the very point, he then refused to rate the stuff that I had brought, afraid to risk his reputation by grading when he was still high from the Hawaiian. But I needed a judgement. I pressed him. Reluctantly, and based solely on our longstanding friendship, he agreed. He partook and pronounced my stash a 6.5. Then, and only then of course, I accused him of letting the Hawaiian cloud his judgement. But over the next few days, based on customer feedback, I realized that his rating, impaired or not, was right on the money.

I tried once to bribe Kiki into a better rating. The street value of his assessment was such that I called out our friendship and offered him a piece of hash to upgrade a 6.0 to a 7.0. He agreed to move from 6.0 to 6.5 but refused the bribe. When I looked more closely, I could see tears welling up in his eyes.

He did not take his calling lightly, but he often delivered his pronouncements with some wit. Once, in a nod to our beloved Hendrix, he rated one of my products as a 6.0 dressed up as a 9.0.

Every time I hear Jimi sing "If Six Was Nine," I think of Kiki, the man who, unlike Spinal Tap, could never go to eleven.

Back in my world of cinder block and artificial light, the first Shoot Shop crop was thirty-five pounds with a Kiki rating of 8.0. At last, the indoor machine was humming. It was time to step outdoors.

CHAPTER TWENTY-TWO
KING HARVEST HAS SURELY COME

It's not hard to understand the appeal of outdoor growing for someone in my position. Sure, I had a successful indoor in the Shoot Shoppe, but it was a perfect operation with an imperfect revenue flow.

The Shop's initial yield of thirty-five pounds would bring about $90,000 on the open market. But first, the Kid had to be reimbursed for his startup investment. That entailed the cost of twenty-four lights, the utilities to power them, the rent—including first and last months as per the lease—and the additional labour costs to get a crop of that size planted, trimmed, and replanted. The final bill for startup came to $65,000. Before I had any claim to it, overhead had reduced ninety thousand dollars of crop to $25,000. Under the deal I struck, even that had to be split with the Kid. So I had $12,500 to divide amongst investors who had been waiting impatiently for over three months. I got the Shop back up and running as quickly as I could, but even so, not enough revenue was sticking to me to keep my investors happy.

In contrast to my industrials, the enduring lure of a crop unencumbered by rent, utility, and hardware obligations beckoned from my own backyard. I was determined not to let another summer pass without a major crop in the acres that sheltered the Chalet. I longed to hear the heavenly music I had heard as I had gazed upon the wonder of that Napanee guerrilla outdoor. But this time, the music would not to be spoiled by the song of deep woods mosquitoes.

Around the first of April as soon as the snow had cleared, Shoolong and I went for a walking tour of the Chalet's gently sloping property. The whole northern side of the lot was a steep embankment with a fence along its ridge. Below the fence on the opposite side was an answering embankment that dropped quickly to the 401 Highway. A carpet of cultivated sod ran from the house to the southern fence at the boundary road, and to the east was scrub brush and sumac along the stream and around the pond. In front of the stream was a natural, visually impenetrable barrier of evergreen trees.

I often imagined slipping through the evergreen fortress using my druid spells for Open Portal and Close Portal. You may consider that playful. You may find it mildly insane. You may see it as evidence that I was doing more than trimming, harvesting, and selling the stuff that I grew. Reach your own conclusion. I have more than a passing familiarity with the act of being judged. But my own judgement was that the topography of our Chalet parcel was perfect for an outdoor pot patch.

The first thing that I needed was a young, enthusiastic worker whom I could trust to oversee day-to-day operations. Golden Boy fit the bill. I approached Golden Boy and offered him 10 percent of the yield if he would partner up with Shoolong and me on a crop of eight hundred plants. He took all of a microsecond to accept.

We resolved to dig holes in the last week of April. Golden Boy was, once again, in charge of personnel and recruitment. Gerry's Kid's got two new soldiers assigned to Shoolong. All of Gerry's Kids were paid twenty dollars an hour. We encouraged them to live at the Chalet—the less traffic in and out the better—and in addition to their wages they got, as the saying goes, "three hots and a cot." That looked like a pretty sweet deal to most, but they were to discover that the work was hard.

On our lordly tour of the estate, Shoolong and I had pondered the sumacs on the other side of the evergreen wall. We had some concerns about the Chalet property being on the flight path of the Trenton Air Force base nearby. Unlike American pilots, Canadian crews are trained to pay attention to what they're flying over. Though our concerns may have been civilian paranoia, our solution was to thin out the copse of sumacs and actually plant amongst and around them to simulate gradient vegetation in a way that we hoped would be less conspicuous from the air. I mention this to make the point that our planning was thoughtful and detailed. Some of that was management skill, but it was also evidence that I was really getting into the adventure. I even named our budding enterprise. You will not be surprised that we christened the new initiative the Field of Dreams.

In April, I requisitioned eight hundred four-inch plants. They were kept, pampered and moist, in the Chalet nursery and lavished with more attention than any plant in the building. I referred to them as my Ladies-in-Waiting. By the third week in May, the Ladies were radiant and ready to take part in what I prayed would be the salvation of he-who-was-both-master-and-knave. That would be me.

Outdoor growing differs from indoor cultivation in that the benefits—soil, sun, rain—are also the drawbacks. Too much sun or rain can be a disaster. One way to combat both is the depth at which the clones are planted in the earth. Conventional wisdom holds that the larger and deeper you dig the hole, the bigger the plant will get. I'm not arguing that, but when you're digging, planting, and refilling eight hundred holes, practical concerns justify some degree of compromise. We dug our holes about three feet apart at a foot deep and a foot across at the mouth.

Golden Boy had his crew do the muscle work, and Shoolong dictated where to dig as well as oversaw the modest culling of the sumacs. In the last week of April, the holes were carefully excavated, mostly amongst the thinned out sumacs but with a few rows meandering out from the main stand of trees. Each hole was supplemented with a soil formula that blended direct advice from a few outdoor vets as well as a few tricks that I had picked up on my own. Here's the recipe:

Mr. Mud's Magic Mélange

Into a 76-litre blue, tote box, mix:

A half bag of Supersoil
A half bag of Magic Soil
One cup of 100-day Nutra Coat
One cup of 70-day Nutra Coat
One cup of 40-day Nutra Coat
One cup of trace elements
One cup of vermiculite
One cup of perlite

Mix the ingredients evenly by hand and apply to the grow area. One 76-litre tote box is sufficient mélange for ten holes.

For those more at home in the world of salt, butter, and paprika, Nutra Coat is a time-release fertilizer imported from Japan. It consists of thousands of prills—nutrient capsules coated with forty coats (in the case of the forty-day) of shellac. The heat of the earth melts the shellac, releasing each prill's mix of nitrogen, phosphorous, and potash over the course of time.

We mixed up our mélange in the first week of May to be ready for the moment when the Ladies-in-Waiting were to be given their introduction to Mother Earth. The Ladies were, at that point, completely root bound, which is what you want. We would hollow out a hole in the substrate, pull on the roots, and then gently plant them in the hole. The entire Field of Dreams was planted in one day, and the Ladies looked ravishing. I helped with the dirty work—with eight hundred holes to fill, it's all hands on deck—and it was a much more spiritual experience than the guerrilla grow at Napanee. Dare I say that I felt at one with nature? No? Consider it unsaid, then.

My Johnny Appleseed moment over, I proceeded to the engineer of Rome segment. I set up a watering system from the conveniently uphill Chalet, running a hose down across the property and into the woods. Okay, it's not exactly an aqueduct, but it was a strategic process involving two hundred yards of hose that terminated in a plastic sixty-gallon reservoir at the northern edge of the field. The reservoir was to be used for mixing growth supplements into the water rather than applying nutrients plant by plant.

Next, I ran a series of extension cords down from the Chalet. The electricity powered a Blue Giant pump that I hooked up inside the reservoir. I attached a shorter hose to the pump. The idea was to enable the individual watering of plants to insure that each Lady got care and attention. This proved impractical in practice; the hose got tangled in the plants and could have done more damage than good. But the pump came in handy for filling the water containers we eventually used to the same end. Ten five-litre watering cans were purchased as an alternative to the local hose idea. It ended up making the process more time efficient, as it enabled multiple plants to be watered simultaneously.

The Kids would fill these green, plastic receptacles two at a time and proceed to the field to water. With the spouts aimed forward as they walked toward their target, they looked like a cross between gunslingers and door-to-door salesmen. Gerry's Kids relied on Shoolong and me to determine each plant's needs, whether it was nitrogen or phosphorus or just plain water. You can determine that, for example, by the tips of the leaves or the colour of the plant. Believe me, the Ladies got the very definition of tender, loving care. Over the summer the cannabis grew like, um, weeds. It was an exciting time, and I actually found myself fantasizing about getting out of the debt pit that had been my place of residence for far too long.

Back in the world of drywall and artificial light, Dynamic was due to come down in the first week in June. Just prior to that, though, I noticed that something was wrong. The plants, previously healthy and green, were turning brown and drying up. Looking more closely, I noticed that the thin bark on the stalks of the troubled plants had been stripped off. It took me a while to finger the culprit. As crime fiction will tell you, every criminal soul lives in peril of the damage done by the mouth of a rat.

My problem was a mouse—more than one mouse, to be precise. The mice had taken up residence in the pots themselves to facilitate feeding with the minimum commute. Now, I know that storybook mice and pet store mice are cute and possibly even desirable, but these little bastards were consuming my livelihood and they were doing so without any contribution to the overhead. And don't give me that circle of life stuff. Mouse crap is not a viable fertilizer.

I was at war. I went straight out and got a better mousetrap. They called the things glueboards, and they were sticky surfaces that little mice feet adhered to in the act of running to or from the damage that they inflicted. The devices were, frankly, disgusting. Glueboards don't kill mice, they merely detain them. When the pests got caught on the glueboards, which they did rather often, the devices were transformed into a kind of living, rodent collage. One Stuart Little on a board is appalling, but the sight of seventeen catches a day is stomach-turning. Then you have to kill the mice. We drowned them. Anyone picturing Mickey or Hunca Munca amongst the wreckage of the Titanic, get over it. A live mouse may be cute, but a dead mouse doesn't eat your cannabis. Or find its way back from the dumpster for that matter.

After the mice, I thought I had my pest lesson learned. I kept my eyes open for whisker prints at the other locations, including the Chalet. But at a small op like Dynamic, little critters are a giant disaster. Any level of decimation is a big problem in a small crop. My next problem, size-wise, made the mice look like Godzilla but was of equally disastrous import. One day at the facility, I noticed a few small white flies around the crop. The next visit, I noticed hundreds. I palmed a couple and took them to a professional to ask what they were. My professional told me that the white flies were a species called, well, Whitefly. But don't worry, he had more illuminating information as well. He told me that, left unchecked, the pests would suck the juice out of any plant they infested. Shit, that was my job! The upshot was that we had to spray the crop. No one complained of any lasting damage to the product, because after the mice and the flies, the harvest was negligible, as was the profit. The mice had eaten our cheese. The flies had sucked us dry. Undaunted, we set it up again.

The Dutch Oven came down and went back up around that time as well. But as per the deal with Dutchie, no profit troubled my pocket, just my monthly stipend for doing the work. The Hen House was harvested and went up again, but there, too, thanks to first crop overhead, I was treading water financially. I was doing only slightly better than the mice.

The forthcoming next indoor crops would be no better; it was summer, and the heat in the darkrooms was unbearable. We ran the lights from ten pm to ten am, but it was still brutal in the building. Ninety degree Fahrenheit readings were commonplace, but once I got a reading in the Shoot Shop of 140 degrees. Given that the plants won't grow when the mercury passes 85 degrees, the indoors that summer were exercises in futility.

Between the rodents, the insects, and the heat, the summer indoor operations were beset on a biblical scale. The torments that broke the Egyptians were being visited upon Gerry. But I managed to keep all five industrials going and hidden from legal scrutiny. I took what profits I could and set it all back up again. At the very least, I was keeping Gerry's Kids gainfully employed.

Take heart, for all was not dark. By mid-August, the Field of Dreams didn't look much like the curtain of corn in the movie; it looked more like stand of small Christmas trees. The plants were about three feet high, the buds were forming, and there were no dead ball players to cope with. The plants had about a foot to go, but that was the point when they started to take on the weight. The colas began to form, and the internodal growth tightened up. For the less botanically minded, picture this: If you were to grab the stalk of one of the bigger plants and shake it, about five or six plump buds would wave back and forth, like a dancing promise of the yield to come. From the downhill side of the field, you could look up and see the plants stretching up the hill as if they were making their own way to the Chalet for trimming. They were green and full, and they stunk to high heaven with no danger of tweaking the nostrils of neighbours. In short, it was beautiful. By October, it was ready to come down.

To facilitate harvesting, I brought a large log table and its benches from home. I had purchased the table at Woolco back in the days of the Mexican pot. It was quite large and heavy, so to facilitate transport from the Chalet all the way to the Field, I removed the table's legs and just rolled it down the hill to the edge of the sumacs. It must have been a bizarre sight. Imagine the RCAF guys reporting that to dispatch! My plan was to rough cut all the product right beside the field, then put it into tote boxes, and have another crew up in the Chalet do the fine cut and drying.

The harvest was a going to be a major project, so we had to increase the ranks of Gerry's Kids. To be sure that our enterprise was attractive to new recruits, I needed a good assessment of its worth. I decided to cut and dry the very first buds expressly for a trip to the Birdhouse. Kiki gave our sample a 7.0, but that was before I told him it was outdoor. He didn't change the grade, of course, but Kiki was astounded that it was outdoor product. He claimed it was the best commercial outdoor he had ever smoked. Bull's-eye! I had my Kiki quote, which was both a recruitment pitch and a little something to soothe the investors.

So we staffed up, and the harvest began. Many of the Kids slept over, and Golden Boy and Shoolong supervised their labours. It took the best part of October to process the crop. Both Shoolong and Golden Boy decided to hang on to some product as part of their share, but I did not. In fact, I could not. I was the sales guy, and what I had on my sticky little hands was a feeding frenzy.

Kiki's pronouncement was heard throughout the smoking community, and everyone smelled money—my beloved investors first among them. Individually, they each thought that they should be first in line. I never heard "Fuck the other guys" as often as I did from them. They expressed real sympathy for my financial situation and the predicament I found myself in. They offered counsel on the wisdom of cutting the other investors loose. They vehemently contended that the others were exploiting my predicament, never seeing that they were excising a parallel pound of flesh. Everyone saw the power of the product. It was great weed, and it was a great yield, but there wasn't enough to pay everyone off on the first date. And with outdoor, the next setup was at least six months away with twelve months to the yield.

So, I opened another indoor, but I swore that it would be my last. That one was just outside of Toronto in Ajax, and we called it … Ajax. It's telling, I think, that the industrial never found itself with a smirky code name. The will to mythologize and the capacity for personal amusement were draining fast. Perhaps it's like naming children. Coming from a large family, I was very familiar with an old joke. When the latest child is born, the parents are asked what they intend to call it. The mother's answer is, "Quits!" I intended Ajax to be my last-born child.

The Ajax location was closest to my home and in a brand new utilities jurisdiction, as far as our operations were concerned. My partner was Golden Boy, newly flush from the very harvest that nearly fed me to the sharks. Golden Boy financed Ajax, and it followed the template established at the Shoot Shop.

As another new year rolled around, I had five industrials and, of course, my interests at the Chalet. It was at that point that Shoolong walked. Well, actually, he ran. He never even announced his intentions; one day, he just never came back. Remember, thanks to the absence of debt and overhead commitments on his part, Shoolong, like Golden Boy, was way ahead and had the enviable luxury of leaving without investors to hunt him down.

I was stunned, but I had no such option. I owed Dutchie and Buffalo Bill $110,000, Alpha $140,000, Philby $70,000, Spinner $50,000, and good old King Ferd $17,000. That's $387,000 of debt, folks. Now, those of you following the math may have noticed that the number was coming down.

Unfortunately, so was I.

CHAPTER TWENTY-THREE
I'M A WILD ONE

Shoolong's departure was a shock. We had been co-conspirators for a long time. We had lived together with Buzzy down in the Beaches before a single seed was planted. I'll admit that I was hurt. I felt betrayed when he left without a word. I saw all of us in the operations as a family, and out of respect and concern for one another, I expected those I worked with to be honest and open. That wasn't just to facilitate the making of money. It was a way of protecting each other and staying out of jail.

To say that Shoolong was part of the family is a cliché, of course, but it brings me to a point that may have already occurred to more analytical readers. There is a family thread running through all of this. For someone who struggled with the realities of a large family early in my life, it's curious to me that I structured and viewed my business along family lines. After my days of apprenticeship as King Ferd's lieutenant, I aspired and eventually achieved a parental role in each of the business relationships I forged. Sometimes, I was the dominant partner, driving the van and calling the shots. At other times, I was the henpecked half of the equation, slaving away at the relentless daily grind, while others steered clear of the heat in the kitchen, content to consume the banquet.

Look, I know that those roles were assumed as part of a commercial enterprise. Much of my behaviour was driven by desperation and the dollar. But if I am honest, I was also motivated by the desire to draw the admiring gaze, to be the one looked to for the way forward. In short, I liked the idea of being the dad. In spite of my teenage reticence to assume leadership, as time went on, I aspired to being the head of the family. They weren't called Gerry's Kids for nothing.

There's another thread here. I actually had a real live family of my own. In nonmetaphorical terms, I was the dad in every sense. I had a wife and a child whom I dearly loved. Furthermore, I was convinced that my secret enterprise was being conducted for their future as well as my own. But it was not a traditional Ozzie-and-Harriet setup either. My wife was still working out of town, which was a challenge to our relationship though a blessing to me in maintaining five grow operations in addition to the Chalet. I struggled emotionally with the shortcomings of a weekend-only family, Still, that was the only way my subterfuge could have worked. I was still hiding my entire contraband life from my wife, and her absence through the week was crucial to that end. But make no mistake, I felt the tremendous weight of the well-intentioned dishonesty—a toxic cocktail of desperation and regret. An affair is never easy to camouflage, even when your mistress is a form of vegetation.

Back then, however, I had little time for the luxury of self-examination. My responsibilities to the business were time-consuming and fraught with potential pitfalls. The legal perils of my activities are obvious, We were also on the lookout for trouble from our own side of the law. As the business grew, so did the potential for our crops to be ripped off by those unwilling or unable to generate product with fertilizer and a hose. Pot pirates were beginning to be a real threat to the grow cartels. They were destructive, and they were violent. They didn't care what damage was done to your facility or those found inside it. And there was no recourse for the grower. Who do you call? The cops? I was concerned about my crop, of course, and the facilities that housed them and the people who tended them.

I had my investors to think about as well. God knows, they were thinking of me. I had partners in all of my enterprises. It still said Moonlight Promotions on the lease, making me the boss and the primary legal target, even in ops like Ajax, where I had on-site partners. But investors are different from partners. They shared less of the legal danger and, by virtue of the onerous interest rates, had made substantially more money from my labours than I had. There was no real danger of me forgetting my financial obligations, of course; my omnipresent investors often updated me on my status. Their encouragement had a veneer of brotherly concern, but the constant threat of violence was never far from the surface. Even though I saw those gentlemen as friends, it was serious business. I had serious debt and serious obligations that troubled me more profoundly than potential legal repercussions.

Fear, however, was a luxury that I could not afford. Fear of the police, fear of my investors, and the fear of bandits were all banished from the kingdom of my thoughts. I honestly think that, had I paused, even briefly, with a clear mind and an unclouded conscience to contemplate what I was doing, I would not have been able to continue.

Part of my solution was to take care in my dealings and my methods. Part of it was to do the opposite. There are two ways to obscure peripheral vision. One is to concentrate relentlessly on that which is directly before you. The other is to simulate a form of tunnel vision. There are very effective tools for that purpose. When they make them for horses, they're called blinders. When they make them for humans, they're called drugs. More and more, I was drinking and using other substances as part of my daily fortification. I rationalized that the substances were focusing me on the duties before me, banishing the demons lurking in the mists at the edge of the eye. I didn't yet realize that you often banish one demon by succumbing to another. I may have been an enthusiastic advocate of voluntary blindness, but it was unquestionably a pragmatic choice at the outset. I sought the balance that banished fear but retained the ability to execute daily obligations and necessities. That's what I tell myself. You may draw other conclusions.

As for daily obligations, plants need water no less than every three days. With six grow ops in operation I had to water two facilities every day except Sunday. The typical twenty-light operation took about three hours to water. If the nurseries had babies, it took longer, because the young plants had to be attended to daily. So with six operations and the geographical distance between them necessary to maintain separate utility providers, my days were full.

I tended to end each day with a visit to the Chalet. It was the center of operations and was continuously being used for growing, clipping, and drying. It was also the bunkhouse for Gerry's Kids. Age differences aside, I enjoyed their company and, it must be said, their recreations. For those ready to accuse me of going through a second childhood, I will argue that I had yet to leave the first. My days were as packed as the summer vacation of a kid with a friend, a tree house, and a river.

In spite of my crowded schedule, I still found time to lose money. Once the revenue from the Chalet had been harvested from our smoke-hungry consumers, I was handling some serious cash. We had finally reached the four ounces per plant from the legendary brochure. Substantial revenue was also flowing from my other six operations, counting the indoor part of the Chalet as the sixth. "That's great," you say. "Pay off those investors and get yourself free." True, that would have been the rational course, the wise thing to do. That's exactly why I didn't do it. I think that it's evidence of my repressed resentment toward the Usury Brigade that, potential physical harm aside, I was determined to keep a few squares from the brownie pan for myself. I wanted some uncounted part of the treasure as a personal talisman for all of my hard work. When I acknowledged being in my first childhood, I wasn't kidding. Like a kid, I rationalized that I had made a lot of people a lot of money, and that, in the shortsighted Gerry tradition, it was time to piss a bit of it away.

I'm being a bit hard on myself here. There was a reason for my actions other than petulance and recrimination. Having so much illegal lucre pass through my palms started me thinking about ways to legitimize myself and secure my financial future. Having no visible means of support in the eyes of straight society, I always felt the need, particularly with my parents, in-laws, and even my wife, to portray myself in some enhanced way, to smear some Vaseline on the lens, if you will, when the camera turned toward me. I needed to create a mirage that would account for the way I was living, including the long hours.

The truth is that I have always had a powerful drive to portray myself as a big shooter, as a high roller. When graced with an influx of cash, the astute thing would have been to pay down the debt, to spend lavishly only when the money was mine to squander. I know that some people are smart with money; I outsmart myself every time. So, with access to excess, I realize now that I looked around for a place to blow it.

I didn't have to look very far. In the days of Moonlight Limousine, I had worked with a couple of Toronto promoters who ran a club called the Spectrum. Somehow—and my ever-increasing drug consumption may have been a factor here—I decided that my salvation lay in turning that bar with a long-standing reputation as a disco into a blues club. Not content to risk money rebranding and promoting the venue, I was determined to back the bands and run the club as well. I was, as it transpired, successfully unsuccessful on all three counts.

My strategy was this: new menu, checkered tablecloths, rock bands, and a name change to Moonlight Blue. That's it; the disco was then a blues club. Very quickly, another necessity arose. We had to advertise. I spent thousands of dollars on advertising with a major Toronto rock station. I brought in name acts, both local heroes like Downchild and British bands like Spencer Davis Group. I even booked original Beatles drummer Pete Best. Steppenwolf, the last act I booked, had the advantage of being both an international name and a band of local heroes simultaneously. The venue had a capacity of two thousand people. Half of that capacity stayed away on a regular basis. The Steppenwolf show was not an exception. I like to dream indeed.

Sooner than later, the high-flying rock mogul was tapped out. I wasted a lot of money trying to build, or buy, an image as something other than what I was. My only recourse, in spite of the crimp it put in my take, was to sell marijuana futures again. The futures were for the outdoor crop to be planted in the spring. I only knew one person who was willing to gamble that far into the future, who had the wherewithal to accommodate a venture of that size. It was the Fat Man. I used his payment for the futures to compensate for the foolish investments of my past.

But by other measurements of illicit activities, I was a success. During the entire initiative, I had not had a single operation busted. But we'd had close calls in the past and continued to have others.

Around that time the Henster, my partner at the Hen House, left the doors to the enclosed room inside the facility open while doing a rough cut. He subsequently left without closing the inner doors. About an hour later, I arrived to pick up the blue boxes of rough-cut and transfer them to the Chalet. The place stunk of skunk. The scent was really powerful. I immediately closed the inner doors to give the exhaust fans a chance to do their job. But before I could leave, I heard a loud knock on the door. It was an agitated neighbour, determined to find the small, striped critter that had offended nostrils as far as several units away. He had been tracking the smell and knew that it got stronger the closer he got to us. By that time, though, the fans had done their work. Even though the neighbour actually walked into the warehouse and proceeded to the front office on his determined search, he found nothing and did not catch on. Once again, I had dodged a bullet. I said a grateful prayer for the odorous similarity between a black and white rodent and the green, green grass of home.

We had another close call at the Dutch Oven, when the pipes froze for the whole industrial complex that housed us. The shutoff valve for all of the units was—you guessed it—in our unit. With the maintenance people at the door, I shut off the lights, closed all the doors, and prayed. They came in and, in the course of attending to the valve, commented on the muskiness of the place. I assured them that it was the typical smell endured by those of us in the landscaping trade. They conveyed their sympathies and left.

We had many more near misses. But scary moments come with the job and besides, I assure you, with sufficient drink and drugs, their impact is curtailed.

But not everything bad fades so easily. Noof the landscaper, as you may remember, was my partner at Dynamic. I was very fond of Noof. He was energetic and entertaining. He used to wear a T-shirt that read "Gots to get me a moose, bye!" (For non-Canadian readers, grab the nearest Canuck-to-English dictionary for a translation.) The shirt was a gift, and he was immensely fond of it, but I had to tell him what it said. Noof could neither read nor write.

Just after the New Year of 1995, Noof was in a bar fight in Scarborough. The incident left him comatose, and he remained so for nearly nine months. When he awoke, he was not the same. The damage done had left him permanently incapacitated; he was sent home into the care of his family. Noof's tragedy shocked and saddened me. It also left me as the sole proprietor of Dynamic. Dynamic was the smallest of the operations, and I had mounted it primarily as a favour to Noof. I knew that I would need two thousand plants for the impending summer outdoor at the Chalet. So that spring, without Noof to benefit from the harvests, I decided to convert Dynamic from bud production into a big nursery with ten lights firing eighteen hours a day, to accommodate the Chalet's needs. I hired a full-time clone keeper and paid him a dollar a plant or two dollars for every one he was able to sell to other growers.

Noof's misfortune aside, some of my associates were making out pretty well. That trend continued. With Shoolong gone, I offered Golden Boy 25 percent of the upcoming Chalet outdoor for his continued supervision of Gerry's Kids and the operation in general. We also decided to offer his lieutenant J Bear 10 percent. That meant that they were employed full-time but would not be paid for their work until the harvest. We mapped out the next season's planting locations, fanning them out from the sumacs to cover the whole field, still staying on the far side of the concealing evergreen hedge. The team was instructed to go out in the last week of April and dig two thousand holes. I started to bring the necessary supplies to the Chalet with a planting session set for May's long weekend. In spite of the size of the crop, I wanted to make the area look as natural as possible to both the ground level and the overhead observer. To that end, we did not plant in rows. That cost us some layout efficiencies; we were only able to accommodate eighteen hundred holes by the time the digging was done in the first week of May.

Before putting the plants into the ground, I had the Kids whipper-snip the area with gas-powered trimmers. That was good strategy, but it was not without casualties. As the Kids, shirtless due to the fine weather, whipper-snipped the entire field, they spent precious little time on the nature of the weeds they whipped. There was little effort made to distinguish the trilliums from the poison ivy. There were, as it transpired, significantly more instances of the latter than there were of the former. Three of Gerry's Kids ended up at the local emergency ward, resembling nothing so much as alien reptiles from the realm of science fiction. We laughed, of course, but they looked awful and certainly suffered for their oblivious approach to fighting foliage. Of course, Golden Boy emerged tanned, rash-free, and unscathed.

By the third week in May the holes were dug, prepped, and ready for the arrival of the Ladies-in-Waiting, which were transported, somewhat ingloriously, in a cube van from Dynamic. I helped with the planting, then stood back in admiration, and threw up an obscure spell from my Dungeons and Dragons past to cast a protective mist over the Field of Dreams. It may seem eccentric, but I really needed that crop, and I was not about to dismiss any nonsense that might help.

I've detailed the hurdles of indoor in the past: leases, utilities, landlords, neighbours, and even frozen pipes. A well-situated summer outdoor has none of those challenges. Outdoor growing yields big, costs small, and God does much of the watering. The revenue potential of the Chalet fields afforded me the luxury of shutting down half the lights at the indoor operations during the punishing, overheated, and underproductive summer months. We were planted and running with a sunny summer ahead of us. Even the rain held promise.

It was right about then that I heard that Sir Gilly was dead.

Chapter Twenty-Four
A Knight in White Satin

Sir Gilly and I went way back, not all the way back like King Ferd and I, but far enough. I remember playing Dungeons and Dragons with Gilly at the place in the Beaches when my parents' house was not far behind me. His nickname, Sir Gilly, was born of those biweekly games. He and I spent many Sundays slaying imaginary foes in our D&D world. Back then, it had never occurred to us that the real world was comprised of real foes and real evil. Even now, I cannot understand how a friend as fine as Gilly could fall victim to both.

In the days that followed our obsession with Dungeons and Dragons, Gilly and I continued to be a part of each other's stories. It was his expertise, his crews, and even his hands that built the modifications to industrial units that kept both Dutchie and I from utter disaster in the early days of our indoor expansion.

As his expertise had broadened, Gilly had moved over to work more closely with Dutchie. He was Dutchie's right hand in much the same way that Golden Boy was mine. Gilley's last job was to run a clip joint in Dutchie's cartel. A clip joint is a home or a small industrial set up, the sole purpose of which is the clipping and drying of the harvested product. It is the clipping that, as Philby used to say, breaks the little perfume bottles in the plant. Once broken, the plant's unique aroma is at its most powerful, meaning that, at that stage, the marijuana is extremely vulnerable to detection. The strategy, therefore, entails transferring the product from your primary operation to a smaller, possibly more remote location where it can be clipped and dried with precision, speed, and reduced repercussion should it be discovered. If the clip joint alone is busted or robbed, your losses are reduced, and your main room is left to continue operation uninterrupted.

Because industrials typically cost about fifty thousand dollars in startup costs alone, there is real wisdom in protecting your investment by clipping off-site. Dutchie, never backward in improving his process, had entrusted Sir Gilly to run his clip joint. And make no mistake, the trust there is substantial; clipped and dried product is damned close to finished product. At that point, it's turning from green to gold. Only the parcelling remains. That is the most portable and most sellable form of pot in the process thus far, making a clip joint a perfect target for thieves. It is a sad reality of any business that the threat of theft is not only external but internal as well. For Dutchie to put Gilly in charge of the clip joint was the ultimate endorsement of Gilly's honesty, reliability, and efficiency.

Approaching the summer of 1995, Dutchie, too, had decided to go dark due to the summer heat's impact on working conditions and yield. He was in the process of taking down the final unit of the four he ran. The harvests from the first three had been successfully processed at Gilly's, and the locations were closed for the season. It was the first week of July, and that was to be the last clip until the units were lit up again in the fall. When Gilly's crew left the clip joint that last night, all of the pot had been hung on airplane wire strung across the rooms, ready for the final cut to begin at seven the next morning.

In a protocol similar to the one Golden Boy established with Gerry's Kids, Gilly's cutting crew met each morning at a rendezvous point down by the highway not far from the house. The intent there was to have a single arrival at the house, cutting down on the noticeable traffic in and out of a sensitive location. Just before seven am, with everyone accounted for, six cutters got in the van and headed for the clip joint. They arrived at the house at seven. One cutter went to rap on the door. The others busied themselves with unloading their gear, just like every other day in the cutting cycle. But that morning was different. When they rapped on Gilly's door, no one answered. After a couple of rounds of knocking and calling Gilly's name, the cutter reflexively tried the door. It was open.

Imagine this happening at a friend's house. You'd be concerned, but you'd reason that your friend had unlocked the door so that you could come in. Now imagine the same unlocked door on a house you know to be occupied by a seasoned pro and thousands of dollars of weed. Can you imagine the chill? The cutter felt it too. But he was not imagining. He was there. Reluctantly, he opened the door and entered.

The house was a shambles. And there were five garbage bags at the top of the stairs. As an experienced cutter, he didn't have to examine them very closely to realize that they were full of pot. At the top of the stairs, the cutter called Gilly's name again. There was no response. By now, the cutter's spine was ice. He bolted back to the front door. He told the other cutters that something was wrong. All six of them went back into the silent disarray of the clip joint, frightened but determined to find their boss.

As it turned out, Gilley was at home. He was in the basement, tied up, face down and lifeless. When the cutters discovered him, they turned and ran.

Once they were clear of the house, they immediately called Dutchie. At the other end of the line, Dutchie felt the chill, too, but he knew he had to go and check. On the drive to the house, he occupied himself with scenarios. *Maybe the cutters were mistaken. Maybe they were high. Maybe it was a practical joke. Maybe there was a mannequin or something on the floor and .... maybe. Maybe.* Maybe anything but the truth.

It took Dutchie almost an hour to get there and only seconds to see that the cutters were not mistaken. As if he knew what he was doing, Dutchie checked Gilly for vital signs. *Maybe. Maybe.* There was no maybe. Gilly was dead. At his feet was an open cash box. Haloing his head was a Rorschach blot of blood. It ran from the hole in the back of his skull and from a smaller wound at the corner of his eye. Careful not to touch a thing, Dutchie got out fast.

He knew he had to do something. But what he did was more of a problem than a solution. He drove to a nearby phone booth. He called the police and reported a robbery at the clip joint's address. Then he hung up. The police responded to the call, but seeing no signs of robbery and unable to get a response at the doors, they concluded that the anonymous phone booth call was a prank. The consequence of that was that Gilley's body lay in the house for three days until someone placed another anonymous call. That time, they reported a murder. The police responded in kind.

Part of me feels terrible that Gilly was not attended to immediately, particularly when I think of the grief and horror the circumstance must have brought to his family. Another part of me knows that what the cutters found in that house was no longer Gilly. The Gilly that matters to me was a charismatic and loyal friend. He was, at once, the awesome warrior and ferocious adversary of Dungeons and Dragons and also the kindest and gentlest of the human beings I have known. He was strong and true, cut down by cowardice and greed. We lost him to evil. I really fucking miss him.

Amongst his friends and family, Gilly's senseless demise left a lingering emptiness. But the legal waves that circled outward from his death were immediate and expansive. The police started investigating Gilly's universe, bringing in everyone they could find for questioning. It didn't take long before they got to the cutters. The cutters cooperated with the police in the interest of bringing Sir Gilly's killer or killers to justice. The police facilitated that by assuring those they interviewed that they were not interested in the pot business per se, just in Gilly's murder. They asked for the names of those in the marijuana operation, saying that they just wanted to talk to them. It's not my intent to trivialize Gilly's death, but I could not help but be reminded of the cop who had given the same assurance all those years ago to my friend who had stolen the pants. Gilly's murder was not the only thing on the interrogators' minds.

With the information derived from the investigation of Sir Gilly's murder, the police charged four people. Not for the murder, mind you, for the grow ops. One of those charged was a fellow I did not know. Amongst the other three was the guy from Bolton who used to offload the smuggled Mexican pot back in my import days. Remember him? The other two are likely easier for you to recognize. The cops busted Buffalo Bill and Dutchie.

How, you might ask, do the police get to Buffalo Bill and, particularly, Dutchie and pull up short without getting to me? After all, Dutchie was still my partner in the Dutch Oven. The answer is twofold. First, I had no business relationship with Gilly at the time. I ran a completely different cartel. Dutchie was just a money partner in the Oven, but the lease and the day-to-day details were mine. Second, and most importantly, I was not involved with Dutchie's proprietary business, the clip joint, or the events around Gilly's death. So when the cutters gave names to help the cops find the vermin that killed Gilly, it never occurred to them—thank God—to mention me.

Another near miss for Gerry. If only Sir Gilly had been as lucky.

CHAPTER TWENTY-FIVE
WAITING FOR THE BIG ONE

Sir Gilly's demise left me in a strange place. Not only was my friend gone, but the repercussions of his murder had put two of my ex-partners and a current one, Dutchie, in jail. I felt like the last pin in the alley, missed only because those around me took direct hits of varying intensities. I was upright, but I was alone and more than a bit wobbly. When you've been between the gutters long enough, staring back down that hardwood, it's hard to avoid the reality that there are more shooters coming. I wanted out, and I wanted out badly. But, in truth, I felt like I had no more options than a bowling pin. I had eighteen hundred plants in the ground, five industrial units in my name, and massive debts still to be paid. I could no more run away than a bowling pin can.

There's another factor in play here. I had Stockholm Syndrome, I think. I had been in the grips of my investors so long that I believed that their best interests were my own. I was the Patty Hearst of the grow op set, donning the beret and fatigues of those who held me hostage. I thought that they were the ones I had to please, and I put myself at risk for their cause.

So I felt the burden of that commitment even as the weight of my daily responsibilities was lightening. Sure, the Chalet was in full flight, but remember that I had virtually closed down the industrials for the summer. My daily routine of touring the units and watering and checking the crop was greatly reduced by this curtailing strategy for the hottest months. Ajax, the Hen House, and the Chalet indoor were shut; the Shoot Shop and Dutch Oven were running at half light; and Dynamic, then a nursery, had a full-time caretaker.

But my weekdays were still my own; my wife and daughter were not home until Friday afternoon. I started spending a lot of time at the Chalet with Gerry's Kids. First, that is where the business was still active. Second, I enjoyed the companionship of the only people with whom I could completely relax, people who respected me, people for whom I did not have to manufacture an existence other than the one I actually inhabited. But idle hands, as they say, are drawn to the devil's work. If you already believe that I was doing the devil's work, chances are that you haven't made it this far. But here's Reverend G's sermon anyway:

"Marijuana is *not* the devil's implement, brothers and sisters. Opiates and white powders *are*. Take the word of someone who has reached deep into Lucifer's toolbox."

I'm being cute here, but what I did that summer was most certainly not. I can argue the pressure of my predicament, the emptiness of my days, or the discolouration that Gilly's death brought to my soul. In the end, the excuses don't matter. I started using black tar opium; that's what mattered.

What also mattered was the fact that I did not just poison myself. I poisoned my crew as well. Gerry's Kids were not angels, but neither were they junkies. At least, not until I introduced them to black tar. I was Peter Pan, and they were the opiate equivalent of the Lost Boys. Where I flew, they followed.

One of the less attractive side effects of opiate use is an allergic reaction that manifests as a persistent itch. One by one, we all fell prey to the unconscious, hypnotic scratching of the frequent user. As we all came to the realization of the physical tic we had in common, we developed—or underdeveloped, if you will—a theme song, sung to the old children's tune "Head and Shoulders." Accompanied by the obvious hand movements, it went like this:

Assholes, armpits, nuts, and nose,

Nuts and nose, nuts and nose.

Assholes, armpits, nuts, and nose, all day long we go.

Assholes, armpits, nuts, and nose.

Nuts and nose, nuts and nose.

Assholes, armpits, nuts, and nose, all day long we go.

One more time …

Fortunately, I can stop there on paper, and you, dear reader, could, and may well have, stopped as soon as you caught the sense of our song and dance. But that summer at the Chalet, we could not stop. We were frozen, like insects in amber, performing the infantile chant and mindless movements of those who court addiction. The only thing that kept us from falling into the drug's clutches was access. Literally, we could not get enough. We would use and want more. But there was no more. We would wait and score eventually, consume what we scored, and wait before we could score again. The erratic supply cycle kept the hunger from becoming a habit. But the seeds were sown. The patterns would turn into deep trouble for many of us in the future when the supply was not so scarce.

Through the days of opiate nursery rhymes inside the Chalet, the general mood was lighthearted, and the Field of Dreams continued to flourish. Because most of my other locations were dark or truncated, I knew that the sloped ground outside the Chalet's windows held my sole hope. I had to keep my investors calm and my futures in play. To that end, I decided to do a little marketing. I did what every aspiring star does to engage his audience. I made a video.

With a camcorder rolling and my own dulcet tones for narration, I approached the Field of Dreams. Doing my best impression of the voiceover on the National Film Board nature documentaries we Canadians grew up on, I filmed the crop and waxed descriptive on the soundtrack. It went something like this:

"Now entering the Field of Dreams. Behold the beauty and future power of nature's greatest gift. This morning fog is the breath of the dragon that watches over the crop, bound by my spell to obscure its bounty from wanton eyes."

The video went on with verdant visuals and this Dungeons and Dragons stuff for about twenty minutes. It was amusing to make, certainly, but it had a serious purpose. I needed to instil confidence in my investors, to assure them that their trust, as well as their money, was in good hands, that a healthy and hearty crop was assured. And

I needed to make those points without the rash alternative of leading personal guided tours. Every trip in and out of the Chalet held the potential of attracting notice. It did occur to me that a video gone astray would have the exact same effect, so I personally supervised each and every screening. An Oscar was not forthcoming, I grant you. No lithe little gold man for me. But the Fat Man was mightily intrigued. He demanded futures, and he got them—eighty pounds worth—at the bargain price of about sixty thousand dollars.

With September's cooler weather, I decided to restart all the grow ops except Ajax. I was going for broke that time, pressing the yield so that I could get the hell out before I went down the road that had taken Dutchie or, worse, Gilly. Ajax, which was leased by Golden Boy and I, was reconfigured to be the trimming place of the outdoor crop from the Chalet. Ajax was the industrial closest to the Chalet location, and as Golden Boy was a partner at both places, it was the logical locale for a clip joint. We cleaned out Ajax's pots and stored them for future endeavours, dismantled the watering system, and raised the lights so that we could work the whole area under them. We built ten four-by-eight drying screens and spaced them around the room for maximum mobility and efficiency. We were ready. Bud rot was not going to take an ounce of the crop due to poor planning.

Elsewhere, Dynamic supplied the babies for the restart of the Dutch Oven and the Shoot Shop. The Hen House partners, close friends of Gilly's and original members of his construction crew, were skittish after being interrogated by the police following Gilly's death. They did not want to continue, nor did they feel the pressure of debt that drove me. So I set up the Hen House, and that time, it was 100 percent mine.

We left the Chalet indoor unlit, at least until the outdoor crop was harvested. Finally, I brought two more guys on as Gerry's Kids, bringing the total to eight, including Golden Boy. These would be the trusted souls that would travel between Ajax and the Chalet. No one else was allowed full access for reasons of security. I hired another six who would only work at Ajax. One of those gentlemen was none other than our old friend Kiki, yet another reminder of the small circumference of the circle of trust. Yet another was a Cobourg local, whose time inside the circle would prove to be my undoing. That guy was never invited to the Chalet. He worried the other Kids, but to my regret, I was not aware of their concerns until it was too late.

The plan was to have four of the Kids at the Chalet at all times, with either J Bear or myself as supervisor. They would rough cut the crop into the blue boxes in the field, putting approximately twelve pounds into each box. That translated into two pounds once dried. The field Kids' objective was sixteen boxes a day, exactly what I could fit in my van for transport to the clip joint in Ajax. They were also responsible for the weighing and bagging of the trimmed pot that I brought from Ajax on each return trip. The fine cut pot would then be placed on the drying screens in the Chalet's three bedrooms. We used dustpans to continuously turn the product on elevated screens, continuously blasting it with propane heaters to prevent mould and accelerate the drying process. We had additional screens in the Chalet for product suffering from bud rot. We would eventually have twenty-two pounds of defective rotted stuff, stored in the basement; that was a large number in and of itself but a small percentage of the final harvest. The intent was to salvage some of the investment by turning it into oil when the work cycle permitted.

I would arrive at the Chalet at about seven every weekday morning and load the sixteen boxes of rough cut plant into the van. I would leave for Ajax at about seven thirty in order to be shrouded in rush hour traffic. The commuting traffic was my cover; to travel when the roads were less crowded invited scrutiny. To be pulled over was a certain bust; the smell of the freshly cut hemp was dangerously pungent and a dead giveaway once the van was immobile. Once in Ajax, the clip joint crew would unload my cargo, and I would head into Toronto to water the industrials and to sell the dried pot that I had brought from the Chalet. I would time my stay in Toronto to coincide with rush hour on my way out. The idea was to hit Ajax at about two-thirty, so I could check progress with Golden Boy, who ran the show there. While we met, the crew would load the trimmed pot into the van for its journey back to the drying screens at the Chalet during peak traffic.

This would go on every day except on Saturday and Sunday. As befit the nature of my personal situation, everyone got to take the weekends off, so they could be with their families. Sometimes the

Kids would work through, but mainly the weekends were leisure time. Only the eight inner-circle Kids were allowed at the Chalet, but they were allowed to switch back and forth between Ajax just for a change of scenery. While in Ajax, they stayed in a modest hotel with all expenses paid. There were Kids at the hotel over the seven weeks it took to clip. The salary bill for clipping was an astounding $96,600, even without the food, accommodations, and recreational refreshments.

Even with a big time payroll, I could not get the goods clipped and dried fast enough to keep up with demand. I was committed to eighty pounds for the Fat Man, and the Spinner and Philby both wanted their shares in pot as well. Only Alpha wanted payment in cash. Oh, how he wanted it! I think that the enormity of the Field of Dreams operation made them all fear the worst—that I would get busted and they would get stiffed.

It was a shared dread as far as I was concerned. Gilly's death had spooked me, but the enormous exposure of the daily drives was weighing on me as well. I had as foolproof a routine as is possible, but every so often, circumstances dictated that the rules be broken. I broke my "never drive holding at night" rule just once. But once was enough. My ex, an original investor in the Chalet indoor as you may recall, had asked me for three pounds of pot, offering five thousand dollars. It was a bargain for her, but given her past financial support, I felt I should return the favour. I took along another pound promised to a friend in Oshawa with the intention of dropping it off on my way home. But I ended up staying with my ex for a few drinks more than I should have. I didn't leave Toronto until after eight at night, and even these days, eight pm ain't rush hour. As I was turning onto the highway to Oshawa, I was pulled over by the RIDE program. For those of you not from Ontario, RIDE stands for "Reduced Impaired Driving Everywhere." I'd had a few drinks, though I would not say that I was impaired, but R.I.D.E. is a random spot-check program, and I was on the spot. A female officer approached the van, caught a whiff, and called over a second, older, male officer. I'm not sure what the exact RIDE protocol is for officer/civilian communication, but in my case it was:

"Woo-ho-ho-ho-ho, what have we here? Now you know and I know that there's something illegal in this vehicle." Yes, I knew, and apparently, he did too. But Officer Number Two was not yet finished. "Now that you know that I know, are you going to get it for me?"

I said that I didn't know what he was talking about. Not even remotely clever, I grant you, but you get stopped with a pound of weed and $5,000 in the glove box and see what you can come up with.

It will not surprise you to hear that I was arrested for possession with intent to traffic and, thanks to the $5,000 in the dash, for possessing the proceeds of crime. I spent the night in jail and was released the next morning on a promise to appear. While being processed the night before, my arresting officer, Number Two as I like to call him, told me during the fingerprinting that the fateful pound that I no longer possessed was "goo-ood pot." I graciously thanked him for the compliment and slept that much better in my cell, knowing that I had impressed the Ontario Provincial Police. Another lifelong goal achieved.

The next morning I called my lawyer, the inestimable David Newman, but beyond David, it appeared that the word of my predicament was spreading on its own. My bust caused a shiver of concern throughout my investor community. But the most perturbed among them was Alpha. At that point, I owed Alpha $70,000. I had paid him $130,000 since the cutoff at $200,000. That was a significant amount on loans totalling only $70,000. It's worth acknowledging that Alpha had not had to accept the cutoff at $200,000; there are those who would not have. I considered myself lucky, and I never complained about the situation in which I found myself. Once again, I empathized with my captors.

A few days after the RIDE bust, I went to see Alpha to give him the details firsthand. I had not been up on a drug charge for seventeen years, and this was a small enough offence to have me released on my own recognizance. But I was in the middle of expediting delivery of a million-dollar crop. Everyone was anxious; I was the first, among many.

Well, perhaps not first. When I walked into the room where I was to meet Alpha, he was behind the bar, pouring himself a drink. As a gesture of peace, I asked him if he would like some pot, as it was nearly all gone. I meant that it was out of the field and virtually all spoken for, but I had set some aside for his personal use. I did not mean that the product had disappeared, nor did I mean that there was no money earned from what was committed to others.

As clear as that was to me, it was not clear to Alpha. He flew out from behind the bar and backed me up against the fridge. Then he punched me in the face. The fridge broke my fall; I slipped down the door like an otter down a well-worn riverbank. I'm told that I didn't hit the ground very hard, although it's hard for me to verify that. I was out cold before my head slid past the handle. Alpha tells me that his fury was not without control. He supports that by pointing out that he only hit me with a left. That left that knocked out four of my teeth, broken the bridgework that held them, and blackened both my eyes. So you will forgive me if I don't fall asleep at night admiring his self-discipline.

I wasn't out long. I stumbled to my feet with my rearranged face in my hands and made a hasty, if erratic, exit just ahead of a torrent of Alpha's verbal abuse. I was injured and humiliated. Fortunately, I was also high on opium. The incident did concern me enough to seek shelter at the house of a friend who was well equipped to assure my safety. Like most of my associates, he was outraged at what he saw as Alpha's overreaction. As he put it, "You were there to pay him money. He didn't have to drag you out of the Gasworks!" The Gasworks was a local rock club, for those who may not know or may have forgotten. I had been thrown out, to be sure, but I never had to be dragged out to honour my financial obligations. Other friends were equally outraged by the incident, and I understand that calls were placed to Alpha to assure that his violence toward me ended there.

And end there it did. My dentist and his assistant, in particular, were very upset with the damage done and insisted that I call the police. Of course, I did not. However, I did eventually dock Alpha's payback by $5,000 for my bills, pain, and suffering. By that time, Alpha was contrite and accepted the restitution as fitting judgement for his own lack of the same.

Not long after, it was my turn to be judged. But just before entering the courtroom to face my charges, I was paid a visit by

Alpha. I was wearing sunglasses to obscure my shiners, but Alpha was much less guarded. He was apologetic, and he wanted to continue working together. I could have been smirky and suggested that he had seventy thousand good reasons to be conciliatory, but when you've made as many mistakes as I have, you have to be prepared to tolerate them in others. We agreed to continue our relationship. But if I were to tell you that Alpha remained a payment priority, I would be less than honest.

Once inside the courtroom, on David Newman's sage counsel, I pleaded guilty and received a $1,700 fine. In an interesting twist, the $5,000 marked as proceeds of crime was split between David and the crown. David managed to convince the crown that the $5,000 was all the money I had in the world and that if David were not paid out of the $5,000, he would not be paid at all. The judge was sceptical, but the crown went for it. The proceeds of crime charge was dropped, the crown and Mr. Newman got $2,500 each, the trafficking charge was reduced to simple possession, and my legal fees were paid. I smiled broadly, displaying my brand new teeth.

Back at the Chalet, the last of the plants came down on the fifteenth of November. We brushed snow off the leaves some mornings when the colas bore a striking resemblance to ice cream cones, but we got there. Rotted materials aside, we weighed in at 483 pounds of prime outdoor pot when all was trimmed and scrimmed. The plants averaged over a quarter pound of yield each. One blessed overachiever clocked in at one pound and two ounces. I called that plant the Octopus due to its eight distinct colas that just about touched the ground before arching upward at their tips. The Octopus was only about four feet high, but its exquisite development had made it a regular attraction amongst the crew throughout that summer. The Octopus was my favourite. I almost hated to cut it down. But I did. After all, there would be other summers, wouldn't there?

Except for processing the oil from the rotted material, every aspect of the operation was complete by December 1.

I felt that a reward was due for one and all. I started to put together vacation plans for the inner circle. The destination was Hedonism in Jamaica. The idea was to take the inner circle of Gerry's Kids as well as my wife to that highly regarded, all-inclusive resort. Who would turn down a Caribbean vacation with a bunch of people half your age and an unlimited bar? My wife, that's who. To my absolute astonishment, my wife refused to go. I can see clearly now why she had no appetite for the lifestyle or the company. But it is a testament to how far adrift I was in the closing months of 1995 that I neither anticipated nor understood her rejection of my grand design. For the second time in a very few months, I felt like I had been knocked out cold. But I got up, I shook it off, and in a spectacular display of misaligned priorities, I went to Jamaica without her.

Merry Christmas, baby.

Chapter Twenty-Six
Wasted Days and Wasted Nights

The triumphant, celebratory vacation in Jamaica was something of a letdown, to be honest. There were saucy and perhaps juvenile hijinks galore amongst Gerry's kids, plentiful laughs, and even more plentiful drinks in the pool, in the Jacuzzi, and in the rooms. For all of my desire to be a player in the follies, I felt more like an audience member than an actor. I was there, and I was not there. Maybe it's because my companions were in their twenties, and I was on the far side of forty. More likely it was the realization that I would rather have been with my wife and daughter. That became crushingly clear when I moved from the resort to a friend's place for the last two nights of my stay. It was not quiet; it was peaceful. It was not a party; it was a family. I played cards, and I wrote, but mostly, I pined for my faraway wife and daughter.

The truth of my situation back home was never far from my mind. With the completion of the harvest, the felling of the last plant, and the packaging of the last of our produce, I felt both dizzying euphoria and gnawing anxiety. The last half of the year had added up to a remarkable achievement. In spite of a bust, two black eyes, and a handful of relocated teeth, the team had come through, and we had delivered a million-dollar crop. It was a massive undertaking in time, in planning, and in human resources. It was a massive yield as well. And with that yield came commensurate costs.

Ah, the costs. The reality of the almighty dollar was at the door. A quick trip to Jamaica only made its knock louder and more insistent. I knew it in the Caribbean, and I knew it in Oshawa. As remarkable an achievement as the crop had been, it was not enough. Nevertheless, it was time to meet the investors and settle up, and that's what I did.

The Fat Man was the first to get paid. It was a pleasure to watch that ample gentleman jump up in the air, dispensing high fives all around. He had prepaid for eighty pounds at less than $1,000 apiece. He was selling them on average for about $2,200 a piece. He had sufficient reason to dance like a demented Snoopy. Once he re-established his equilibrium, he expressed his pleasure in our transaction and assured me as I left that his wallet would always be open.

I paid the Spinner a visit next. He took his payment in product. That made him easier to accommodate, but it also gave him grounds for renegotiation. He pressed me on price and we settled for credit toward my debt of $1,800 a pound. And guess what? That payment was the end of my debt to Spinner. He was one of the big three lenders, and then he was not a lender at all. I prefer him in his capacity as a friend.

Next stop, Alpha. Not first, not second, but third. Can you guess why? The payment to Alpha brought my debt to him to $60,000, below the principal of his original loan for the first time. As a pleasant change, he greeted me with an outstretched hand. It quickly became an upturned hand, I grant you. But an upturned hand is genuine progress from the fist of our previous encounter. When I left Alpha, I was many dollars lighter but still in the possession of all of my bridgework.

After my payment visit to Philby, the last of the major investors, my obligation there was down from the $100,000 cutoff to a more reasonable $30,000. I heard much moaning about what he could have done if he'd had the funds in hand earlier, but I don't buy it. I didn't see evidence of any other gravy trains in Philby's station. I held my head high and walked on.

Dutchie, who was out on bail and hence my very silent partner in the Dutch Oven, got $50,000 to reduce my debt to him and Buffalo Bill. That was my core debt, the one that had started me down this road in the first place. I had once owed them $225,000, as you may recall. I certainly recall it. That debt had been reduced to $40,000. Both Dutchie and Buffalo Bill acknowledged that I had neither slid nor forgotten the long-standing obligation.

Then came Ferd. Ferd had maintained his position beyond the borders of my operation for some time, but he was always near to my heart. At that point, I brought him near to my wallet. I owed Ferd a mere $10,000, the exact amount that I had originally borrowed. To be honest, I wanted to pay him more. But I could not. I was broke.

I was so broke after the payouts, that Big Ben, my real estate partner, paid for my ticket to Jamaica. We had become good friends in the course of our joint ownership of the Chalet. Amusingly, Ben had not visited the Chalet since he had assumed the mortgage three years before. I had not encouraged him to visit—you might even say that I had dissuaded him—for obvious reasons.

So the grow op mogul with the million-dollar outdoor and six industrials was, as the British say, "skint." I did not have any earnings left. But what I did have was the capacity to earn. It was time to run the cycle one more time, and this time, the math was irrefutable: I would come out ahead.

When I returned from Jamaica in the first week of January 1996, I immediately began bringing all of the operations to their capacity. In the case of Ajax, we decided not to go with a mother room any longer, because of the availability of clones from Dynamic. That left us with two lights and the mothers to spare. Golden Boy and I decided to give those to one of Golden Boy's workers as a wedding gift. We thought of it as the gift that keeps on giving. If only we had been wrong.

It was right around the time that Golden Boy started his own operation. One of his initial transactions in that capacity was to purchase twenty thousand dollars worth of hash from a new supplier in Kingston, Ontario. Because it was his first deal with Mr. Kingston, Golden Boy decided that it would be prudent to take some backup muscle. He offered the job to the beneficiary of our light and plant generosity, the Bridegroom. Before leaving for the rendezvous with his new connection, Golden Boy divided the payment between himself and the Bridegroom. They both had two bundles of five thousand dollars that they would combine and give to Mr. Kingston when the deal was completed. The transaction itself went well, but a few hours later, Mr. Kingston phoned Golden Boy and said that he was short five thousand dollars. Cars were checked, and everybody went over the minutiae of the deal, but the money was never found. The next week, the Bridegroom bought a new car. He managed to haggle the price to just under five thousand dollars. He was able to do it because he paid in cash.

When a couple of Gerry's Kids heard that, they told me the story about the Bridegroom that had spawned their distrust. It seems that, at a previous legit job, he had befriended his employer to the degree that the poor guy had offered to take the Bridegroom to Las Vegas the next time he went. The Bridegroom had accepted. They had fun in Vegas, but the Bridegroom had showed his appreciation by stealing five thousand dollars from the employer shortly thereafter. The employer had confronted him. The Bridegroom had denied it. In a move that would never have happened in our business, the employer had taken the Bridegroom to court. The Bridegroom had testified that his employer had spent the money on the hookers and cocaine while in Vegas. He had said it under oath in a packed courtroom in the presence of the employer's wife. Gerry's Kids, to their credit, never fully trusted him again and kept him out of the loop, regarding the location of the Chalet. To their discredit, they never conveyed his past treachery to me.

But the operations were going full tilt again in January, notably Dynamic, which was given the task of growing babies for the summer 1996 Chalet outdoor. I was back to my regular life with six days of watering and a weekend-only family. In spite of my overall anxiety, I felt strangely confident that this was my year. I was broke but sufficiently optimistic that I sold my perfectly good van to one of Gerry's Kids for a mere thousand bucks, forcing me to turn right around and lease a new one, a suitably anodyne family hauler, perfect for the anonymous commute with sixteen boxes of pot. I even got involved in the music promotion game again, investing, albeit modestly, in the road show of a tribute concert/dinner show called Rock and Roll Heaven. Once again, I had a money-laundering outlet, and no money to launder. What to do? Back to the futures, of course. The Fat Man was waiting with his promised open wallet. Fool that I am, I even went back to the Spinner.

It was not largesse on either's part. I had successfully delivered a million-dollar harvest to market the previous growing season. I was bankable, baby. So, I had money in my pocket. With money in my pocket came, I cringe to say, heroin up my nose. I began to dabble in the white arts. And I began to lose it. That did not help matters on a day-to-day basis, and it certainly did not help me with what came next.

The Bridegroom got busted.

Chapter Twenty-Seven
But If You've Got a Warrant ...

It's hard for me to face the fact that the sunlight of my financial deliverance could be so easily eclipsed by someone like the Bridegroom. All of those hours, all of that toil, all of that fear and loathing—pinched out by a simple manipulation of his hand. I still find myself sickened by the fact that he snuffed out my operation and the efforts of those around me like dampened fingers on a single wick.

When Golden Boy and I gave the plants to the Bridegroom, we had assumed that he was going to go into business for himself. He did. He used the plants and the two lights to set up an operation in the basement of his matrimonial home. I do not know all the details of his business, but I do know that he intended to sell clones. I know that, because we taught him how to do it and actually planned to have him supply us. However, after his underhanded dealing in Golden Boy's hash venture, we wanted nothing more to do with him. The Bridegroom pressed on and, in a blinding example of poor judgement, sold plants to a teenager with even less sense than the Bridegroom himself. In short order, the hapless kid got busted when he flipped the plants to two undercover RCMP officers.

It didn't take long for the kid to roll over on the Bridegroom. He was not a career dealer. He was a kid, for heaven's sake. He was facing a trafficking in a controlled substance charge, and they had him dead to rights. Of course, he rolled. Soon after, the cops came knocking on the Bridegroom's door. As timing would have it, he was home, as was his pregnant wife and the lion's share of their relatives. The police strode into the Bridegroom's house, drug dogs and all, in the midst of a baby shower. They arrested the Bridegroom. They arrested his wife. Assorted aunts, uncles, nephews, and neighbours went free. There is no record of the fate of the shower gifts.

I know the preceding to be true. What follows is conjecture. I believe that the Bridegroom rolled over on me. I was not alone in that belief. For being insubstantial and for his lack of balls, he was known thereafter by the street name of Sara Lee. Sexist, I grant you, but a reminder that I was not always as highly evolved as I am today.

I say conjecture, but let's examine the evidence. Within days of Sara Lee's bust, a marked police car took up residence just outside of the Ajax operation's front door. It was a surveillance vehicle. I know that now from court documents, but at the time, we were not so certain. Most times when we looked, the vehicle contained two uniformed officers having coffee. That might not seem that odd to have cops sipping java in an industrial parking lot, but it had never happened there before, and we'd been in the Ajax building for over a year.

We were pretty disturbed by that turn of events. We knew that the Bridegroom had been busted. We thought, as a career criminal, that he might take his medicine and hold the line. On the other hand, given his betrayal of his former employer and his theft of Golden Boy's hash payment, it seemed possible, even likely, that he would turn. And if he did, we knew that Ajax was what he was most likely to give up. It was the only one of my operations where Sara Lee had worked. He knew of the other operations anecdotally, but he had never physically been to any of them. He had certainly not been to the Chalet, because, as I said before, Gerry's Kids had not trusted him from the outset.

So, with the appearance of our coffee cops, we made some concessions to caution at the Ajax location. We had always gone in and out by the back door, but then we did so in as clandestine a manner as possible. One of my righthand guys took to wearing a wig for the journey to and from the car. Now, I suspect some are saying,

"Why didn't you get the hell out of there?" Indeed, Golden Boy, who was still a partner at Ajax, argued for the same strategy. But I felt trapped by my financial obligations, by the enormity of the overall operation, and by the name of my company on the lease. If those cops were just caffeine addicts in an empty parking lot, there was no sense in risking it all, when my deliverance outdoor was only weeks from its start. Or, if it was a bust, I was going down no matter how many plants we hustled out the back door in the dead of night. There was no wig big enough to cover my head on that one.

So I carried on. For three fucking weeks those cops sat in that car enjoying the best of what Tim Horton's had to offer. Maybe it was a new beat. Maybe our parking lot was a convenient hub from which to access their territory. Maybe Sara Lee was not the weasel we believed him to be. Maybe, maybe, maybe …

There was no maybe about how I pressed on. I went about my business as if the cops in the parking lot were the steam from their paper cups. I had the two newest members of Gerry's Kids dig the holes at the Chalet. I had the caretaker at Dynamic put up 1,700 pots for the clones to fill those holes. With little in the way of options, the quest for solvency went on.

One night, after leaving the Chalet, I paid a visit to my old friend Gordon, with whom I had worked on the Sunny Days festivals years before. We had recently set aside our differences, particularly the one where I had married the mother of his child. As part of our reconciliation, I had comped him a dinner performance of Rock and Roll Heaven, which he had enjoyed immensely. He was still active in the music scene, and I was hoping that we could collaborate on some new shows. We met up at a hotel in Cobourg, had a few drinks, and did a couple of lines of heroin to celebrate our friendship. I got home very tired, very late, and very wasted. As I stumbled up the stairs of my place, I remember thinking that the next day was Friday and that Patti would be home for the weekend. Alas, as it transpired, she would be home, but I would not.

It felt like I had just fallen asleep when there was a loud knocking on the door downstairs. As I tried to shake the junk out of my head, my first thought was that it might be a collection agency looking for money still owed on the limousines. The limo business had been gone for years, but, strangely, that's what came into my head. I did not spend long on that thought.

The knocking on the door was louder—sufficiently loud to suggest knocking *down* the door instead. I jumped out of bed, naked as it turned out, and went to the top of the stairs just in time to see the edge of my front door fly toward me in shards. The door flew back and apart, and half a dozen long-haired males came charging up the stairs. *Jesus, it's a home invasion*, I thought, *bikers have come for me.* What I thought next was more focused on the nine-millimetre Glock pressed uncomfortably at my temple and the man applying the pressure.

"Do you have dogs," he barked. "Are there any booby traps?" I answered in the negative to both. I must have been convincing, because his next order was to tell the other ten or so officers—some in civvies, others in uniform, all more substantially dressed than I was—to stand down. He then turned back to me and told me to put on some clothes. That was my introduction to Detective Tom Andrews of the Durham Drug Squad.

As soon as I was dressed, the questions began. Detective Tom wanted to know about a marijuana operation in Ajax, Ontario. The rest of his team wanted to know about drugs or money from drugs on the premises. I was told that they knew the address of an industrial unit leased by Moonlight Promotions, and in the interest of the health and well-being of yet another door, they asked me for the key.

My keys were in my briefcase. The briefcase also held $1,700 and an ounce of hash. But I was less concerned about those items than I was about the key they had requested. That key was amongst five other sets of keys for enterprises that Detective Tom had yet to, um, detect. Each key set was on a lovely pewter fob to facilitate identification by your often-addled narrator. There was the elephant, the hummingbird, the goose, the fish, and so on. They had only asked for the keys to Ajax. However, the combination of that morning's battering ram and the previous night's opiates kept me, at that moment, from remembering which little animal was which. Not only that, but I was somewhat reluctant to display so dense a population of pewter creatures to my companion. After all, they don't call those guys detectives for nothing. But I pulled myself together and gave the cop the key, praying that I had chosen correctly. I hoped that he had not noticed all of the similar sets, but it was a foolish, wasted wish. He did notice the hash and the cash, and they came upon three pounds of weed in the garage, so I knew in my heart that the end was at hand.

With that thought in mind, I was head-ducked into a cruiser, and we set out for the Ajax location. We toured the rooms of the unit briefly, and I was chauffeured to the Durham OPP station and booked for cultivation and possession with intent to traffic. As part of the process, I was apprised that the benefit of cooperating was that my case would not be "splashed all over the papers." I was more concerned with the splash my body would make if I turned anyone in. I told them that and related the story of my errant teeth and my travels down the front of a refrigerator. The detective seemed genuinely sympathetic. He asked me if I was involved with the mob or the bikers. Attempting to dance around any specifics, I said that my partners existed in a kind of "grey area." Then he asked me if it was the Grey Gang that I was involved in. I was stunned. I had never heard of any such organization, and I strongly suspected that no such gang existed. Things were getting surreal. I tried to get back on track by clarifying that I was referring to the grey area of criminality—loans sharks and ticket scalpers, for instance.

Without another word, I was escorted to a holding cell. Less than an hour later, the detective returned, jangling the remaining keys. When asked what they were for, I replied that they were old keys that I had kept because I liked the fobs. He left, returning about an hour later to tell me that they had found Dynamic. Once again, he asked for cooperation. Once again, I kept what I knew to myself.

Now let's think about this for a minute. Sara Lee gets busted. The only place that he had worked is busted in turn. When I refuse to divulge the locations that match the keys, the cops figure out the first one, also the one closest to Ajax, in less than an hour. Are we seeing a pattern here? Someone is talking and it's not me. I'm just sitting quietly in a holding cell and letting the nice policeman do his job. Miraculously, the routine goes on. The whole rest of the day, the native habitat of my little pewter animals becomes known, until there is only one left: the hummingbird, a lovely creature and also the key identifier for the Chalet.

There could be several reasons for that. It could be because the Chalet was not in the name of Moonlight Promotions. Officially, my friend Big Ben owned the mortgage on the property. The cops could also have been held at bay by the obscuring spell that I had cast on the location and its surroundings. Maybe Dungeons and Dragons sorcery was keeping drug squad fingers from the Chalet's latch! Or maybe the cops were impeded by the fact that Sara Lee knew little or nothing about the Chalet other than its existence, forcing the cops to wade through my bank records to follow the trail. You decide. I vote for the spell, myself.

So, with five sets of keys identified, I was taken in front of a judge at about four o'clock on the afternoon of the bust. I pleaded not guilty and was remanded until Monday. I was then whisked to the Whitby *bucket*, as us hardened criminal types refer to a short-term incarceration facility, for the weekend. I got my phone call, of course.

I called Patti, which was possibly the hardest part of the ordeal so far. She was distressed, to say the least. But nurses have a way of acting with agility and economy under pressure, and Patti had that gift to a greater degree than most. She had already called my lawyer David Newman and arranged for him to come out. He wasn't coming until Monday, of course; there was little he could do over the weekend. She also arranged for someone to fix our door. The friend who did that is not to be undervalued. It's one thing to help out when work has to be done and done quickly. It's quite another to do so knowing that your act of kindness and support could make you the target of police surveillance. My good friend Biggie came to Patti's aid, prepared to deal with both. I've never forgotten that.

David Newman had not forgotten me. He arrived Monday, armed with an update on the bust-go-round. The Durham cops had hooked up with their brethren in the other jurisdictions in which we had operated, and they had raided all of the industrials. Amazingly, I still held out hope that my Chalet operation would be spared. I asked about the Chalet, and David said that they knew of its existence but had yet to find it.

That is why the bust had not yet hit the papers. The cops were holding off, hoping that they could catch the occupants of the Chalet by surprise. They also suspected that the Chalet would be the jewel in the crown, and they wanted full impact when they paraded their prey in front of the media. As it turned out, they were being naïve on both accounts.

David also assured me that he and Patti were working on bail. The hearing was to be Wednesday, and the star witness was the lovely Patti.

When I shuffled into that courtroom on Wednesday, shackled and handcuffed, Patti looked more than lovely. She looked like an angel. That's because an angel is exactly what she was. I can only imagine how foreign and frightening the courtroom and my physical state must have been to her, to say nothing of the sledgehammer realization of how I had passed my time outside of her company.

Ironically, my dishonestly about my activities served us well in that instance. Patti did not have to lie. The judge sensed that Patti's part in it was nonexistent and held her testimony in the esteem it deserved. That was more crucial than ever, because, just before the hearing, David had taken me aside and told me that the cops had found the Chalet at last. I have never needed an angel more.

On the stand, Patti was a marvel. She came across just as she was, as a small-town nurse in a big-time mess. She had served the public for twenty-five years and had never had trouble with the police in her life. Our female judge was empathetic and gently guided my angel through the proceedings in spite of the crown attorney's ham-handed attempts to trip her up. At one point, he asked her sceptically if it was really true that she had never traversed the law. She looked straight at the crown attorney and said, "Well, there was that parking ticket … "

David said later that, if he had a hundred witnesses like Patti, he would never lose a case. As for bail, she had to put up our house as collateral and sign, saying that she would be responsible for my behaviour. Grateful beyond words, I was released into her custody. But not for long.

Leaving the Durham Region courthouse, I was collared by the York Region Drug Squad and escorted to the Markham police station to be charged with cultivation and possession with the intent to traffic. That charge pertained to the Dutch Oven. I spent the night in another police station cell and, after seeing a judge in the morning, was transferred to Toronto East Detention Center. My bail hearing was set for Monday, so I spent a second weekend behind bars. That time though, I had a visit from Patti. It did not escape my attention that, during her brief stay, we sat on the very stools that I had made in wood shop during my incarceration in Guelph seventeen years before. The odd coincidence is not a marker that suggests progress, I admit.

On Monday morning I was in the Markham courthouse in the latest of my shackles and cuffs, looking once again for bail. The crown refused to accept our house as collateral for a second charge. When we heard that, Patti offered her mother's house as collateral instead. The judge was not as sympathetic as the first. Even though Patti had power of attorney on her mother's affairs, the crown would not accept her signature on the bail papers. I spent another night in jail while Patti returned to Cobourg to get my mother-in-law's signature. If ever you want evidence that your life has gone awry, try being over forty and still needing a written note from your mother.

So the next day I was once again released into Patti's custody, but with barely a thank-you kiss between us, the Peel Police met us at the courthouse door, and I was arrested for the Shoot Shop operation. I spent *that* night in the Peel police station and, after seeing a judge and having a bail hearing set for Thursday, I was escorted to Maplehurst Correctional Institute in Milton. Are you sensing a pattern here as well? Perhaps if I had been writing an encyclopaedia of southern Ontario prisons, this would have been useful, but as it was, it did not have a bright side.

To make matters worse, I was still in Maplehurst when the bust, or should I say busts, hit the newspaper. I was touted as the Five Million-Dollar Man, and my operation was said to have stretched from Brighton to Brampton. (Non-Ontario residents are invited to go directly to Google Maps to decipher that. For those without computer access, all are in a hundred-mile radius of Toronto.) I quickly became a jailhouse celebrity, the pot prince of the pokey. Everyone inside had a million questions about growing weed, which is a testament to how rare an operation like mine was at that time. I was suddenly the master of a unique art form, and everyone wanted my counsel.

But that was on the inside. Beyond the walls of the jail, the cops must have been mightily disappointed. Their showcase bust, incorporating multiple jurisdictions and millions in contraband, generated a lackadaisical trickle of media attention. It was big enough in the Oshawa paper, which termed it a "five million-dollar bust," but the Toronto press barely even bothered. And Ontario news ignored in Toronto is rarely seen in other papers across the country. The cops were hoping for a giant gold star, but what they got was barely a checkmark.

Here's the weird thing. I was, on some level, as disappointed as they were. Deep down, I was so hungry for recognition that I was hoping to achieve celebrity while ignoring the question "Celebrated for *what*?" To my frustration at the time, the question never came up. I was busted, I was broke, and I was in jail. To top it off, the world did not know my name.

But enough of that. Back in court, Judge Number Three had no problem with Patti's power of attorney and no problem with the fact that her mother's house was already surety for another charge. Bail was granted, and as we exited the courthouse, guess what? There was nobody there. In what I can only assume was a communication breakdown between the jurisdictional police forces, no one from Scarborough, where I was wanted for Dynamic and the Hen House, nor anyone from Northumberland County, home of the Chalet, was waiting for me at the Peel Regional Courthouse.

Sensing an opportunity for a sliver of freedom, Newman instructed me to get out of there. He then called the rather sheepish cops in Scarborough and told them that I was offering to turn myself in—on the following Monday. Amazingly, they accepted David's offer, and I was able, with my wife and family, to take my first steps through my brand new door.

I spent that weekend in the nurturing company of my wife and daughter. They took the edge off of the uncomfortable task of dealing with the shock, concern, and disappointment of my parents and in-laws. I knew I was screwed, but it was still great to be home. Now that I was out, I was determined to do everything in my power to stay out of the facilities that had consumed so much of my preceding two weeks.

So with a Monday date at Forty-First Division to hear the Scarborough charges, Newman was able to arrange a bail hearing for the same day. My brother Bernard came with us to court and offered the deed to his house in exchange for bail. As for the cops, David and I had decided that the most prudent course from there on in was to plead guilty and give the police some insight into the circumstances that had gotten me there. I would not be naming names, of course, although it did occur to me to finger the Grey Gang. The nonspecific openness served me well in that the police essentially corroborated the desperate nature of my situation when the cases came to trial. But on the day at hand, the judge accepted my brother's house as surety, and one more jurisdiction had been addressed.

As we left the courthouse, I turned to shake my brother's hand in thanks. But before I could press flesh, a cop had my elbow. I was escorted back to Scarborough Forty-First Division for pickup by the Cobourg OPP. The officer who had come to get me knew my wife, and as a result, we chatted amiably all the way to the Cobourg jail. You have not experienced surreal until a police officer asks you how your daughter is enjoying kindergarten as he's taking your fingerprints. I spent two nights in the Northumberland lockup, because the judges in Cobourg don't sit every day. Not enough moonshiners to warrant it, I suppose.

At one point during my two-day stay in Cobourg, I met with the head detective of the Kawartha Drug Squad, an Officer Katz out of Peterborough. Katz and Special Detective Jake Berga, the Cobourg detective assigned to my case, took me into a room that doubled as a prayer hall on Sundays. They introduced me to two plainclothes detectives from Caledon, just northwest of Toronto. Those two detectives wanted to know what I knew about the murder of Sir Gilly. Now, that was a police investigation I wanted to help. I cooperated with them fully, even naming Dutchie, although I knew he had already come clean. I was confident that Dutchie felt as I did, that nothing should impede progress in finding Gilly's murderer(s). I doubt that I was much help, but they thanked me for my candour and promised to put in a good word in for me with Katz about my bail intentions. They left.

Then it was Katz and Berga's turn. They told me that they knew that I thought that information from a certain gentleman, recently married, had led to my arrest. They were not prepared to confirm or deny my suspicion. But they wanted to underline that one thing I had going for me with regard to my bail was that I had no violence on my record. They offered yet another good word if I promised to behave myself when I was released. I understood their intent. They were trying to protect their informant. Rather flippantly, as I was still seething about my predicament, I told them that I was not a violent man but that if I saw that gentleman swinging from a bridge, I would not cut him down. A tad too gangsta, I grant you, but I enjoyed my little movie moment. The lift lasted only for the instant as the quip crossed my lips. It was, of course, the wrong thing to say. The demeanour of both men changed instantly. They started growling.

"We don't want to hear any of that fucking bullshit from you. If you want our help, then just smarten the fuck up and cut the crap."

I was taken aback, not only because of the rapid turn of the conversation, but also because I realized that they had tipped their hand. They did not say that Sara Lee was not the informant, nor did they say that there was no informant at all. When violence entered the conversation, even as a throwaway wisecrack, they never denied Sara Lee's involvement. They knew that I knew, and that's that. To say that I heeded their advice would be a joke. I'm not a violent person, and I'd already seen the result of pretending, even in a thoughtless moment, that I was.

But those two cops were not done with me. Detective Berga started bragging about how he had been the one to figure out where the Chalet was. I should mention that, in my briefcase at home, along with the $1,700 and the ounce of hash, had been my homemade promotional tape for the Chalet's Field of Dreams. I know, I *know*— another staggeringly imprudent, opiated move on my part. But that's where the tape was, and the cops had it now. Berga informed me that the guys at headquarters were left howling at some of the stuff in the promo, particularly my mystical voiceover. I believed it.

What was harder to believe was Berga's contention that the tape had assured the demise of the Chalet by giving him the clues he had needed to find it. He claimed that he had deduced the Chalet's location, because I had shown the Highway 401 and Lake Ontario as the northern and southern borders of the Chalet acreage.

I still doubt that. I remember saying, "But Jake, the 401 and Lake Ontario run in close parallel from Kingston to Toronto. That's four hundred miles!"

To that, he sheepishly replied, "Well, we had some general information a few weeks ago."

Yeah! I bet you did. I bet you did, I thought.

When I did finally have my day in Northumberland court, my brother Paul accompanied me, house deed in hand. Charges were noted; bail was granted. I had a slew of charges and half a million dollars of my family's homes on my shoulders, but that time, when I walked out of that courthouse, there was nothing awaiting me but a soft Ontario breeze.

Chapter Twenty-Eight
I Fight the Law, Part Three

It didn't take long for the sweet breeze of freedom to raise some goose bumps. I was broke. I was highly dependent on drugs and alcohol. And I was almost certainly going to jail.

I was looking, not very affectionately I might add, at two years of federal time. Bear in mind that I had already done the maximum provincial time with my two years less a day sentence in Guelph. As I awaited my trial, I began to take stock. I was broke, but the bust had pretty much wiped out my illicit financial obligations. It was an accepted part of the dealers' code that if one is busted, all outstanding illegal debt is on hold, until you restore your illegitimate money stream or win the lottery. I decided not to buy a ticket.

I also decided to make some resolutions. First and foremost among them was to clean up my bad habits while incarcerated. I saw jail as an opportunity to leave the nasty baggage of my stress, pressure, and enforced secrecy behind. In a perverse way, I looked forward to having some assistance in stopping my consumption of the heroin, opium, and alcohol that had been my emotional Kevlar during the whole debt-and-threat ordeal.

I was also entertaining ideas of writing. In the past, I had written a play based on the life of my beloved Jimi Hendrix. But this time, I had a less beloved protagonist in mind: me. The parallels are there of course: the era we lived through, the temptations to which we were subjected, and the pressures to be what our people wanted us to be. You could even argue that I was a groundbreaker as well. Where Jimi had used a guitar; I had used a shovel. He was celestial; I was, quite literally, earthy. But the template is there. Surely, you can see it. Think of me as Jimi Hendrix if he were unsuccessful, white, and alive.

I'm joking about this, of course, but the truth was that, while sitting on my own sidelines, awaiting my fate, the remarkable nature of my journey began to dawn on me. I saw that, unlike the much-examined tragedy of Hendrix, my perspective on my story was unique. No one knew its twists and turns better than me. I may have been naïve about the amount of work involved, but the idea buoyed my spirits.

I remember telling my lawyer David Newman my jailhouse Hemingway idea. He seemed to like the concept, but he reminded me that he was doing his very best to keep me out of jail. I didn't see how it was possible, but I had come to understand that David could work legal wonders. I was glad that I had given him a ten thousand-dollar retainer in the days when I was flush, because at this point, I was well and truly broke. Cut off from my illicit source of revenue, I didn't have an income of any kind. I had never actually had any personal claim to most of the money that had flowed through my hands, though I had redirected as much as I could toward my pocket. Still at this point, there was no flow to redirect.

What I did have on my hands was time. In the wait for the trial, I decided to meet with my landlords and see what could be done. The idea of honouring the leases was not even a consideration, but I did hope to get a last access to the properties. I was looking for anything the police had left behind that was saleable. I'm not talking pot, you understand; all the plants went as evidence. The cops seized the lights as well, but with whatever was left, I was planning a rather unique yard sale. For instance, those buildings contained over four thousand plant receptacles, and even at fifty cents each, that was big money. In a matter of a few weeks, I had gone from selling pot to selling pots.

I had another motivation there. In a move that can only be seen as very Canadian, I felt an obligation to clean those locations up. When you grow up in a house of nine, you learn pretty early that not cleaning as you go is the road to chaos. Many of these landlords could have been a much greater impediment to our activities than they were. So I felt obliged. My mother taught me well. I decided to visit my landlords and explore the possibility of making mutually beneficial amends.

My first meeting was with the landlord at the Shoot Shop, and it was there that the precedent was set. He was appreciative that my cooperation with the police—those fateful keys—had kept his property from unnecessary damage during the raid. I offered him help in returning the location to a state fit for occupation. I proposed to rent a large disposal bin and empty the place of everything that I couldn't use. Drywall was the main ingredient there, but the other was dirt. As it made no sense to pay to haul fertile soil to the landfill, my landlord proposed that we spread the earth in the flowerbeds and around the bushes outside the complex. It was a great idea—a good deed and a short haul simultaneously. We used it as the template for the subsequent locations.

With the dirt and the drywall sorted out, I rented a storage unit to house the pots, desks, air conditioners, and anything else I could sell. J Bear volunteered to help me out, and between the two of us, we spent the next two weeks going around to all the industrials, renting bins and salvaging what ever we could. I admit to regretting that the police had confiscated the lights; we had over fifty thousand dollars worth. But we all know that those lights would not likely have gone to a florist, so I saw their position.

We received an interesting insight into the law enforcement sense of humour when we arrived at the Dutch Oven. Just inside the door, one of the York Region officers had cut a message into the vapour barrier in about twelve-inch block letters. The sign read "Just say no." It was rather well executed and must have taken some time. It had probably served as a respite from the thankless job of hauling sticky, smelly plants into the evidence wagon.

Three weeks into my short-term freedom, I met again with David Newman. He had decided to get the Provincial Crown Attorney to have all matters addressed in one jurisdiction. That was feasible, because all the charges were the same—cultivation and possession with the intent to traffic. The idea was to have a judge at Old City

Hall in Toronto address all of the charges with sentencing to follow. The Provincial Crown agreed to the plan. In theory, it expedited the matter and saved the prosecution of five different trials in five different jurisdictions. It facilitated the Crown in the address of six sets of charges in one fell swoop.

That's the theory, mind you. The practice was somewhat different. For my part, it was still a five-piece puzzle. I had been granted bail in five jurisdictions, so I was obligated to attend court in each of the regions to set trial date or get a remand. David and I developed a system that saved his time and my money. He gave me a letter that I carried to each court appearance. The letter outlined all of his available court dates and eliminated the need for him to attend every date. When the dates were in Toronto proper, we would meet and discuss strategy.

One bit of strategy on which David and I disagreed was my intent to give Detective Tom Andrews a video statement. David was concerned that I would further incriminate myself, but I was determined to cooperate in any way, short of naming names. In the video statement, I told the police much what you already know and some things that you know to be false. I admitted to having assistance in building the rooms but claimed that I did all of the handling of the marijuana myself. That is ridiculous, of course, but I was determined to be everything my detested informant was not. I was not giving names, and in a massive assault on common sense, I was adamant in suggesting that there were no names to give.

A lot of the detective's questions during the taping revolved around the money that they hadn't found. They thought they hadn't found it, because of how well it was hidden. I knew they wouldn't find it, because it was gone, snatched like a pensioner's purse by my relentless investors. Over the course of the process, I believe that the nature of my financial predicament began to dawn on those who had arrested me. They may have busted a kingpin, but there was no pin money to be found.

Yet the process was not without benefit to the police. I do remember discussing the grow op process at length. Bear in mind that the whole idea of local marijuana cultivation was very new to those guys. Marijuana came from Mexico or South America or the

Caribbean. Police wisdom at that time was that "Drugs are grown elsewhere." I was the first insight that *elsewhere* could be suburbia, Ontario, Canada.

I'll admit that I kind of enjoyed schooling the constabulary. I went on at length about indoor versus outdoor yields and how you toss most of the plant after harvest—a lot of stuff that you, dear reader, know by now. But the cops didn't know it then, and as long as they weren't asking for names, I was glad to prattle on. I remember that the videotape ran out before I thought I was finished! The detective seemed pretty relaxed about the matter; he knew that I was going to plead guilty, regardless.

Just before Christmas of 1996, David Newman died. I was devastated beyond imagining. Aside from the functional part of our relationship, David had been a pillar to me. He had never let me down; he had always been a source of vision and savvy. He had not judged; he had left that to others. And he had always told it the way he saw it.

In that way, he was like John McDonough, my philosophy teacher from Centennial College. I had lost regular contact with John over the years, but his wisdom and counsel had always stayed with me. I thought often about his gentle distain for the flashy trappings that had seduced my youthful eye. I thought about him more poignantly then. John, too, was dead. He had died just a few days before my bust. I had cut his obituary out of the newspaper. It had been in the briefcase with the hash, the money, and the pewter-fobbed keys.

When John McDonough died, I remember my cousin remarking that I had lost my guardian angel. With David Newman's passing, I had lost another. But if you've read this far, you've figured out that my life is not without remarkable angels. My newest one was named Adam, and he was David Newman's son. I had known that David had a son who was just finishing up his bar exams, so I looked him up and signed on with the firm where he was articling. The firm with which Adam Newman was associated was Robbins, Bernstein, and I had the good fortune of having both of those partners work on the case. This whole turn of events, of course, required a completely new set of remands, as the new team needed time to review the case. All of the judges were very sympathetic, and I could tell there was a deep respect for David Newman amongst them.

With my new legal team in place, the strategy was much the same as David had envisioned. I was to plead guilty but ask for the courts consideration of my cooperation and of the physically perilous debt spiral in which I had been trapped. To reinforce my physical peril, we were ready to call my dentist as a witness.

To my absolute astonishment, Anthony Robbins was still pressing for a conditional sentence. This was something new in the system at the time and was designed to keep nonviolent criminals out of jail. One was still convicted and maintained a criminal record, but the conditions set out by the judge could include house arrest, along with a variety of other restrictions. The key was that there would be no incarceration.

I was sceptical. I had resigned myself to a period behind bars; I had even laid out some resolutions for the passage of the sentence. But I also remembered that David Newman had seen a chance, as did Anthony Robbins, so I made room in my plan for a glint of hope. I waited and hoped, but mostly waited. Anthony was overseeing my case with Steve Bernstein and Adam Newman assisting. I felt rather pampered and was grateful that the Newmans were family friends, due my relationship with David over the previous twenty-five years.

The trial was set for November 10, 1997. It was my sincerest hope that the trial would come before Christmas. For those who have discerned the important part the holidays play in my life, that may come as a surprise. But I knew that the magical properties that I had once attributed to the season were not going to forestall my fate. I did not want to go into a new year without a direction and a quantifiable future. I had spent a staggering amount of time in court over the last year and a half. I had probably had fifty court appearances on the set of charges. I had to appear in person at all five jurisdictions for every remand. To cap it all, my financial situation was dismal. I had been working part-time here and there and spending what little money I made on drugs and booze. I was spent. I was so tired of purgatory that I had accepted the inevitability of hell. I wanted to serve my time and change my life.

By the time the tenth of November rolled around, I had said my goodbyes. I got into my vehicle, and my stepson followed me to the leasing company where I turned in my van. I was ready. But when we arrived in court, the Crown was not. They had not received the transcripts and disclosures from all of the various jurisdictions, so they could not proceed. Anthony jumped all over that, immediately citing the Askov case. That was a Supreme Court of Canada precedent citing the Charter of Rights assertion that a defendant has the right "to be tried within a reasonable time." Anthony contended that sufficient time had passed for the Crown to have their case assembled. The judge listened and then asked me to stand. He personally apologized on behalf of the Crown, promised that I would be tried at the next hearing, and confirmed that he would be presiding and that he would take my inconvenience into account in his judgement. In short, he asked me if I could give them some more time. I was tempted to ask for a rental car as well, but I decided not to push my luck. I was not going to jail that day. I asked for a date before Christmas, but nothing was available until the New Year. We settled on February 4, 1998, and before he dismissed us all, the judge gave the Crown a stern warning that they had better have the case together for February.

It was a sad Christmas for our little family. It was the first we spent that was not in our home in Oshawa. We had lost our house. I was out of work, and we just couldn't carry it on Patti's salary alone. We had moved to Cobourg into a modest rental near Lake Ontario. That result of my activities really weighed on me, but I took solace in the fact that our new place was closer to Patti's work and family, particularly in light of my upcoming incarceration.

On February 2, at around seven in the evening, I got a call from Anthony. We were two days from court and he had been talking to the Crown. He asked if I would take a deal for eighteen months.

At that point, the way the system worked would have meant that an eighteen-month sentence would have to be served in provincial jail. There was a huge downside to that for me. Provincial facilities are not as progressive as federal ones. There are no programs and no training to speak of. It is also much harder to get parole. In the federal system, you are eligible for parole after just six months. In addition, provincial jail does not allow such things as your own computer, which I was counting on to write my story. I was torn and unsure how to answer, and I told him so. It was at that point that Anthony told me that there would be no incarceration. I did a double take and asked him to repeat what he'd said, exclaiming that I could not have heard him right. This was real life, and I reacted like I was in a sitcom.

Remember the judge's warning that the Crown had better have their house in order? They didn't. The challenge of getting all the transcripts and all of the disclosure from all the jurisdictions had escaped them. For all intents and purposes, the system had eaten their homework. They didn't dare go to court and ask for an extension after the way the judge had berated them the last time. This time, were Anthony to cite Askov, it was more likely to work. There was a high probability that the judge would throw out the case. And the Crown was not prepared to play the odds. They offered to cooperate in a joint submission, where Crown and defence agreed to terms and asked the judge to do the same.

Anthony asked me what I wanted to do. I said … what do you think I said? I took the deal. It's not like we could have gambled and gone to court, expecting outright dismissal. The Crown was not completely without options. They had all of the necessary paperwork from Scarborough, home of the Hen House and Dynamic. Those were small operations, a sliver of the pie if you will, but they were still jailable offences.

So we went to court with the joint submission, based on the Scarborough charges. Yes, that's right—no Shoot Shop, no Ajax, no Dutch Oven, and no Chalet. The judge was shocked by what they were dismissing. I remember it vividly.

He said, "I realize that this is a joint submission, but just the sheer magnitude of this has me somewhat overwhelmed."

The Crown countered that the arresting officers from Scarborough had noted my cooperation and recognized the veracity of my loan shark pressures. She also pointed out that I was a married man with a young family. The judge called a twenty-minute recess to consider the information that he had been given.

Ever heard the cliché "the longest twenty minutes of my life"? Well, you've heard it now, and I lived it then. After about twelve hundred crawling seconds, the judge reseated himself behind the bench. He agreed to the joint submission. But here is the wild part: he gave me no house arrest, no curfew, no postsentence probation, and very little in the way of conditions. I was ordered to report once a month for the duration of my sentence and was not to leave the province without permission. I was not to own hydroponics equipment, and I was required to do one hundred hours of community service. But the minute I was rearrested, my sentence would no longer be conditional. I would go straight to jail for eighteen months. The judge did this on faith, prepared to take heat if his confidence was misplaced, and believe me, I did not want to be facing him again, having broken that trust.

I was flabbergasted. I felt like I'd won an Oscar. I thanked the judge profusely on behalf of myself and on behalf of my family. I pulled up just short of tears and thanking the Academy. At this point, Anthony leaned in and suggested that I wait until after the judge had left to slobber appreciation over the Crown. I heeded the advice, but at the moment that the back hem of the judge's robe slid through the doorframe, I ran through the whole, genuine speech of thanks again to the Crown. She showed her respect for Anthony by replying that my lawyer was a sharp cookie. *God among men* was more what I had in mind at that moment. We exited the courtroom with me showering my mantra of gratitude over Anthony and the work of Steve and Adam.

I pretty much ran out of conversation along that line. After a brief silence, I remarked to Anthony that, in the absence of incarceration, I would never write my book. He helpfully offered to call the judge back from his chambers. I declined the offer and made my way down the steps of Old City Hall as fast as I could without falling on my face.

That's it. It was over. I was free. All I had to do was plan and execute a brand new life.

Chapter Twenty-Nine
When the Music's Over,
Turn Out the Lights

"Life is what happens to you while you're busy making other plans."

Okay, I didn't write that. I remember hearing it in the voiceover to a Warren Miller skiing movie, of all places. Without doubt, Warren lifted it from John Lennon's "Beautiful Boy." Where John lifted it from, I have no idea. Maybe directly from the Almighty Song God, for all I understand of the way genius works.

I can't say much for certain. But pondering my freshly minted freedom and my unforced future back in 1998, I applied the well-travelled lyrical gem to the beautiful mess that I'd made, thus far, of my existence. I felt like a thundercloud. Every illegal scheme I'd ever hatched had fallen from the heavens, pissed unceremoniously onto a random rooftop, slid dazed into the eaves trough, and ended up lost in the rain barrel below. The trip was exciting, and the destination unanticipated, but the future was not without promise. The potential of a single raindrop is one of nature's wonders. But anyone who wants to further ponder the sense of anticipation, or for that matter the sentience, of a raindrop has spent far too much time in my Field of Dreams.

In 1998, I was free and broke. It's true. But I was alive. It's hard to look back on your journey without reflecting on those who did not make it to the point where you stand. I've talked about David Newman and John McDonough, of course. As much as their passing saddens me, those are not the kinds of losses that I mean. I mean senseless losses like Kerc, like Plum, like Gilly. Those are futures that, because of the path we chose, will never bear fruit. I loved those guys, and I think of them often, sometimes with a dark musing that invites me to wonder if I could have prevented their demises.

But I know that I could not. I found myself in similar danger more than once through thoughtless indulgence, through those shadowy confrontations with the end in a strange room with someone else's needle stuck in my arm. In each of those cases, I could not save *me*. All that kept me alive in perils parallel to those that took my friends was the flippant grace of happenstance. I had come to understand that, in order to survive from that point on, I could not give happenstance the controlling hand.

So I concentrated on the mission before me. I resolved to love and nurture my family instead of a bunch of smelly plants. I resolved to apply my work ethic to work that was ethical. I resolved to write about my past unblinkingly and, in doing so, rob it of its seductive power. I didn't get famous. I didn't get rich. All I nearly got was alone and dead.

Can I keep my resolutions? I don't know. Have I changed? In some ways, maybe, but not in others. My judgement is better, perhaps, but I still have dreams. I'm still the same guy who successfully harnessed those dreams to buy his first guitar, get a college diploma, and marry the love of his life. Granted, other, less lofty endeavours were unfulfilled and less successful.

So at the very moment of my reflection on these matters in 1998, let me tell you what I was doing. I was on my knees with my hands submerged in earth. Praying? Well, that too. But primarily, I was applying a sliver of my pirate skills—digging holes and planting nature's botanical marvels around Cobourg's City Hall and Botanical Gardens. I was doing one hundred hours of the government's bidding, tending to beautiful tulips from Holland, the birthplace, as it happens, of the magic beans.

What, you don't believe me? Hey, there's a brass plaque on a post at the entrance to the botanical gardens listing the names of those who helped to build them. One of the names engraved thereon is Gerald McCarthy. I challenge the doubters among you to gather your tourist dollars, take the scenic drive to Cobourg, Ontario, and see for yourself. It was in that way that I fulfilled my community service—dirty and content, planting Holland's finest, or second finest, export in the well-planned garden of a public park.

POSTSCRIPT

I'M A CORK ON THE OCEAN,
FLOATING OVER A RAGING SEA

In January of 2004, many years after police redesigned the entrance of Gerry McCarthy's home with a battering ram, the cops finally got what they wanted. They busted a massive grow op, and that time, they got the publicity that they had hoped for when they had successfully shut down Gerry's five million-dollar operation years before.

If you're Canadian, you might remember the story; it was national news for almost a week. The police busted a giant, indoor marijuana plantation in a staggering location—the old Molson Brewery just south of Barrie, Ontario, about fifty miles north of Toronto. The decommissioned brewery is a massive building on the east side of one of the most heavily travelled of Ontario's highways.

For those unfamiliar with the six-lane monster Ontarians call the 400, it's a freeway regularly cursed and detested by north-south commuters and weekenders alike for its choking traffic and perilous seasonal conditions. The old Molson building is so close to the eastern shoulder of the 400's northbound lanes that it seems like you could throw a bottle cap from your sunroof and hit the block-long, three-storey structure. Why the bottle cap would be inside your car in the first place is a matter best left to the authorities.

When those same authorities burst through the doors of the brewery building, they crossed the threshold of a former Canadian institution, the wellspring of a brewski-lover's fantasy. There's a good reason that the Bob and Doug Mackenzie movie *Strange Brew* imagines exotic goings-on in a brewery. The huge kettles and gleaming pipes are exotic and magical to the suds-sucking public—a Willy Wonka's for adults.

Of course, the beloved brewers had vacated the building quite some time before the grow op took up residence. But the headlines played on the cross-pollination of the public's top recreational indulgences—beer and bong, together at last in the national headlines.

But that kind of whimsy is misleading. The sinister side of the brewery grow op is the sophistication of the criminal enterprise behind it. This was not Gerry's daisy-chained, water-your-own-crop enterprise. Sure, a quick look at the photos the police released from the brewery bust offers a visual that is much the same: rows of plants under rows of lights between plastic vapour barrier walls. It's the same technology that Gerry assembled, step-by-step and mistake by mistake. But Gerry's operation was spread over a half-dozen modest, anonymous locations. The Barrie brewery grow op was under the enormous roof of a southern Ontario landmark. And the denizens of the former brewery were not the old crowd either. No one Gerry knew from all of his years in the weed business was involved. And as productive as Gerry's enterprise may have been in its time, the brewery grow op was the twenty-first century model—huge, well funded, and until the bust, no doubt highly profitable. To some law enforcement observers, all of that had the markings of organized crime, which is hardly the hippie fantasy at the core of Gerry's story.

This reminds us of why the general public may have heard of the brewery bust but not know of this book's pot pioneer. The newsroom knows a good hook when it sees one, and with the Molson building bust, it was handed the whole tackle box. The lure of the Molson name, its brands—Canadian and Export—and the link to society's other choice in recreational consumption in the same news item and possibly the same sentence was irresistible. For the media, it was less of a lead item and more of a gift from the gods.

They arrested ten people in connection with the brewery bust. Clearly, there was a well-staffed and -stratified operation at work. Gerry McCarthy was arrested alone, not to mention naked—not very *Goodfellas* to anyone's way of thinking.

This is not to minimize the serious repercussions of the grow op business that Gerry helped develop. Not long ago, the courts convicted a man for the murder of two people who had allegedly stolen marijuana from him. That happened long after the final events of our story, but we need only consider the terrible fate of Gerry's friend Sir Gilly to know that the dark thread has always been there. Even so, what was world-shattering and unprecedented when Gerry was active is disturbingly commonplace now. It's clear from the Molson operation and the recent murder-for-robbery scenario that the present-day "business" is a long way downstream from the wide-eyed naïveté of G's original enterprise.

The aforementioned pot murder conviction was covered locally, but it wasn't national news like the Molson bust. Free of the darkness of the murder-among-thieves angle, the story of a brewery turned grow op was a better fit with the ephemeral sensationalism of the contemporary media. By 2004, the media judged its public to be ready for a front-page grow op story in a way that it had not been at the time of Gerry's arrest. Statistics suggest that the brewery bust headlines were not much of a gamble. According to government data, the incidence of marijuana use by the Canadian public jumped by 50 percent between 2002 and 2004. The trending is obvious. And the public—users and abstainers alike—was becoming increasingly aware that the weed in its streets and TV rooms was not its father's reefer. This weed was stronger; it was fresher; and it was more accessible, because it was local.

That's why Gerry's story begged to be told. In those nascent days of the early-to-mid-nineties, people walked right through Gerry's buildings, mumbling about skunks without a blessed clue about what he was doing. That would never happen now or even would have happened when the raid on the old Molson building took place. But it happened to Gerry. And it's worth remembering—for better or worse—how we got to where we are.

Now you know. And Gerry knows, too, because Gerry McCarthy was there when it all began.

CPSIA information can be obtained at www.ICGtesting.com

231161LV00004B/1/P